PRAISE FOR *THE BRONX ZOOM*

"2020 was a baseball season like never before. *The Bronx Zoom* brings you inside all the challenges, highs, lows, and everything in between."

—Aaron Boone, New York Yankees manager

"*The Bronx Zoom* provides tremendous insight into how wild and challenging the 2020 season was for all parties involved. Bryan Hoch takes fans inside the Yankees clubhouse, uncovering never-before-told stories from a year that the players will never forget."

—Meredith Marakovits, YES Network clubhouse reporter

"Bryan Hoch goes inside baseball to tell the story of the most outside-the-box season anyone has ever seen. *The Bronx Zoom* takes you inside the Yankees clubhouse and behind the Zoom cameras to deliver fascinating details from a colorful cast of characters. It's another home run for Hoch."

—Mark Feinsand, MLB.com executive reporter and MLB Network insider

"Bryan Hoch has long been embedded in the Yankees universe, but 2020 was unlike anything he—or anyone—had ever seen. The countless challenges of a pandemic season are brought into much clearer focus than any Zoom picture. Hoch brings you behind the computer screen and pierces the digital force field. *The Bronx Zoom* is a must-read for any baseball fan curious about a Yankees season like no other."

—Michael Kay, YES Network play-by-play broadcaster

"The key to storytelling is the attention to detail. That's what good reporters do— they find nuggets in every nook and cranny, or in Bryan Hoch's case, every corner of the Yankees clubhouse. *The Bronx Zoom* doesn't just relive the most unique season in the Bombers' history, it pops the hood of this storied franchise. Page after page, readers will be amazed by how much they didn't know about the summer of 2020 until now."

—Bob Klapisch, MLB columnist, *The Newark Star-Ledger*,
co-author of *The New York Times* best seller, *Inside the Empire:
The True Power Behind the New York Yankees*

"This is the book Yankees fans need to truly understand the inner dynamics of the team's 2020 season. Bryan Hoch chronicles in fascinating detail what it was like for the players, staff, and front office to go through a shortened season and expanded postseason in the middle of a pandemic with no fans in attendance. *The Bronx Zoom* delivers what actual Zooms cannot—an up-close and personal look at a season unprecedented in major league history."

—Ken Rosenthal, MLB on FOX reporter/MLB Network insider

"*The Bronx Zoom* is a stunningly personal account of the strangest year the Yankees could have imagined. Bryan Hoch takes you through it all: from the players' realization and acceptance of life in a pandemic, the strain and toll that social unrest and responsibility can take on a team, and how this group came together to put a winning product on the field. You'll hear from players, the manager, coaches, front office, broadcasters, and writers. It's a roller coaster of emotions, which I promise you will not put down!"

—Suzyn Waldman, New York Yankees radio color commentator

"To know the Yankees better than Bryan Hoch, you'd have to be on the roster. In *The Bronx Zoom*, Hoch gives an illuminating look at life behind the pinstriped curtain in a season like no other. With rich details and fresh insights, Hoch humanizes a group of Yankees just as uncertain as the rest of us, revealing the bonds they forged and the lessons they learned. What a treat for fans to get such an up-close view of a year defined by distance."

—Tyler Kepner, national baseball columnist for *The New York Times* and author of the best selling *K: A History of Baseball in Ten Pitches*

"The shortest, strangest baseball season there ever was deserves another look, this time from an insider on the Yankees beat. Bryan Hoch delivers the goods. Yankees fans will enjoy the behind-the-scenes anecdotes and insights."

—Tom Verducci, *Sports Illustrated* writer/FOX and MLB Network studio analyst

"*The Bronx Zoom* captures the nuances of the most challenging baseball season of all time."

—Zack Britton, New York Yankees pitcher

The Bronx Zoom

INSIDE THE NEW YORK YANKEES' MOST BIZARRE SEASON

Bryan Hoch

TRIUMPH
BOOKS

Library of Congress Cataloging-in-Publication Data

Names: Hoch, Bryan, author.
Title: The Bronx zoom: inside the New York Yankees' most bizarre season / Bryan Hoch.
Description: Chicago, Illinois: Triumph Books, [2021] | Summary: "This book chronicles the Yankees' 2020 season"—Provided by publisher.
Identifiers: LCCN 2021003481 | ISBN 9781629378923 (hardcover)
Subjects: LCSH: New York Yankees (Baseball team)—History—21st century. | COVID-19 (Disease)—Social aspects. | Baseball players—United States—Social conditions—21st century.
Classification: LCC GV875.N4 H624 2021 | DDC 796.357/64097471—dc23
LC record available at https://lccn.loc.gov/2021003481

This book is available in quantity at special discounts for your group or organization. For further information, contact:
Triumph Books LLC
814 North Franklin Street
Chicago, Illinois 60610
(312) 337-0747
www.triumphbooks.com

Printed in U.S.A.
ISBN: 978-1-62937-892-3
Design by Patricia Frey
Photos courtesy of AP Images unless otherwise indicated

For Connie, Penny, and Maddie
My All-Star quaran-team. I've loved every minute in your bubble.

CONTENTS

FOREWORD

"Yankee Fan Today Tomorrow Forever."

Those were the words on the sign that I held during the 2001 World Series, a picture you've almost certainly seen by now. I was 11 years old, and the Yankees were already a huge part of my life. When I started to get into baseball, there wasn't a better team to watch. Even though I lived in Southern California, the Yankees were inspiring. You watched them and knew that the organization would stand for excellence, for competitiveness. It gave you something to shoot for and showed you where the bar was.

That was special to my heart, and I kept the sign hanging on my bedroom wall for many years. The blue letters faded to tan, and I brought it to Yankee Stadium for the press conference that day just to tell you that I'm here and I've always been here. That was a tremendously emotional day, filled with a lot of excitement about the future. For me, it was the beginning of fulfilling a dream.

I tried not to have expectations for my first year as a Yankee, but I certainly don't think anybody could have imagined a pandemic—since one hadn't happened in a century. This season wasn't easy, and I was proud of being able to get out on the field to compete, to be able to push ourselves and fight for something. We poured it all out there. Hopefully, we provided some joy and entertainment. What a wild ride!

When I look back, the highlights for me were all about checking off some of the firsts. Getting the start on Opening Day for my first game as a Yankee was a thrill, and pitching in the pinstripes at Yankee Stadium was incredible. On a personal level, I'll always remember the day that my son Caden was born. I didn't leave that hospital room for two days. That undisturbed family time was quite magical. Amy and I had a lot of happiness, a lot of adrenaline. It was awesome.

On the field, there was nothing more fun than making it to the playoffs, pitching in some of those games. I have to say: we missed the energy that the fans bring. Part of why we chose New York was the atmosphere and the environment. I'm still as hungry as ever, so I look forward to seeing you in person again, lacing them up, and going to win a World Series. We'll do it together.

Yankee fan today, tomorrow, forever.

Gerrit Cole

OPENING DELAY

The fastball hissed toward home plate, missing the outside corner and thudding into the padded leather of Kyle Higashioka's glove. *Ball one*, the catcher thought. Scanning the pitches available to call for Jonathan Loaisiga, a young right-hander with four electric offerings and erratic command, Higashioka peered at the playing field through the iron bars of his midnight blue mask.

It was a postcard-perfect afternoon on Florida's Treasure Coast. The rust of a long winter was beginning to knock off for the New York Yankees, who were visiting the defending World Series champion Washington Nationals. Their 21st exhibition of the spring brought an opportunity to trot onto the diamond of a sparkling new facility in West Palm Beach. The calendar read March 12, and there should have been two more weeks to finalize bids for roster spots before the team would head north for Opening Day.

Higashioka set his target low and inside, crouching near the right foot of Trea Turner, Washington's talented shortstop and leadoff hitter. He flashed two fingers to summon a curveball that Turner chopped to shortstop Thairo Estrada, who whipped the ball sidearm toward first base for the out. The seemingly routine play generated a smattering of applause from the grandstands. It was a scene that was about to become a relic of better days. "Oh yeah," home-plate umpire Angel Hernandez said. "They're about to shut this whole thing down."

The 30-year-old Higashioka rolled his eyes. A few feet from where the catcher and umpire squatted, nearly every seat was sold, strangers in tinted sunglasses sitting shoulder to shoulder as they gulped beers or sodas. Home or road, the Yankees always drew a crowd, and the paid attendance on this day was 8,049. Vendors in neon yellow roamed under rustling palm trees to hawk hot dogs and cotton candy. The scent of spray-on sunscreen wafted toward the infield.

"I was like, 'No way. No chance that's possible,'" Higashioka said. "I kind of thought everything would continue as normal. I don't think anybody realized the severity of the situation."

One night before, players and coaches had watched with disbelief as the NBA halted its season, wiping all games from the schedule after Utah Jazz center Rudy Gobert tested positive for the novel coronavirus. The events of March 11 indelibly altered the American landscape, as the World Health Organization declared COVID-19 to be a global pandemic. Major League Baseball permitted its afternoon games to begin on March 12, and general manager Brian Cashman mingled in the field-level seats. A few hours earlier, Cashman received notification that baseball was about to go dark, following examples already set by the NBA, the NHL, and MLS. There was no argument: it was happening. A backpack slung over his right shoulder, Cashman relayed the information to manager Aaron Boone, then acted as though everything was normal—even posing for photographs with fans.

Boone resolved that he would remove some of his position players an inning or two early while permitting hurlers like Loaisiga to reach their intended pitch counts before shipping them off to the clubhouse. With the season about to be turned upside down, there was no sense in wasting their bullets. The resulting box score provided a last vestige of the Before Times, though no one bothered to tell the men on the field, who blissfully played through to conclusion.

The clock read 3:55 PM when a flyout sealed the Yankees' 6–3 victory, 48 minutes after the league sent emails announcing that it was delaying the beginning of the regular season "by at least two weeks." Boone rocked on the heels of his navy Nike sneakers as he stood outside the visiting clubhouse, circled by a cluster of the team's beat reporters. Ever the optimist, Boone wondered if they'd be reunited for an Opening Day to take place on April 9. "Up to that point, it was: 'Wash your hands; it's not that big a deal,'" Boone said. "I didn't really understand enough yet. I didn't think the season was going to be cancelled, just paused. I guess I didn't know the magnitude of what was going on."

Boone's on-scene assessment was rosier than one offered by the home-plate umpire Hernandez, who had jogged past the group a few minutes earlier, announcing to no one in particular: "See you in June!" The words hung heavily in the air, echoing against the concrete walls. To that, George King—the *New York Post*'s beat writer since 1997 and no stranger to Hernandez's unpredictable strike zone—quipped: "Another bad call by Angel."

King and his colleagues were tangentially aware of what had transpired since the first human cases of COVID-19 were identified in Wuhan, China, three months earlier. News occasionally wandered into the daily lunchroom chatter during the early weeks of the spring, when someone would casually remark about the stunning scenes of vacant streets and highways being broadcast from China and Italy. Those comments were inevitably followed by a review of the chicken cordon bleu or an inquiry as to what time the clubhouse would re-open to media after batting practice.

As the Yankees stripped their road gray uniform pants and hoisted their travel duffels on that March afternoon, there were more than 1,200 reported cases of COVID-19 across 42 states and the District of Columbia. At least 38 people had died. The situation did not seem to be "totally under control," as president Donald Trump assured the public weeks earlier, when he claimed that it was "just one person coming in from China." But in those days, it seemed inconceivable that the gears of a billion-dollar professional sports league could grind to a halt because of a virus that measures one-10,000th the size of the period that ends this sentence. "We saw that it was ravaging Europe, so anybody with common sense knew that it was coming our way," Cashman said. "There was concern and fear about what it was going to do to our society in the U.S.—let alone our sport. We knew it was something we were going to be dealing with. We just didn't know when."

A pair of chartered buses idled on the asphalt lot beyond the outfield walls, their drivers hired to steer the team to George M. Steinbrenner Field in

Tampa. The conversation was sparse over those 204 miles of Florida highway; everyone was carrying the usual fatigue of another nine innings in the books, plus a three-hour bus ride on deck. Yet there was also the nervous electricity of uncertainty that powered their text messages to wives, girlfriends, and parents. Would they play their next game in an empty stadium? Would there be a next game at all? Everyone wanted answers, and no one had them. "I got the alert on my phone that they were suspending the league. I turned on ESPN right away, checking in on what they had to say," said outfielder Aaron Judge. "Talking about playing without fans in stadiums and stuff like that, it's tough. As a competitor, you feed off that energy and excitement."

The Yankees gathered in their home clubhouse the next morning, where club brass briefed players on their options. Hal Steinbrenner, the team's managing general partner, exited his fourth-floor office for a rare locker-room visit, assuring his players that he would keep the Tampa facility open for anyone who wanted to continue using it. Steinbrenner believed that the stadium was exponentially safer and cleaner than any facility or gym accessible to the general public. Perhaps, as Judge suggested, continuing their hitting and throwing routines would provide an advantage once play resumed. They voted to remain together. "I thought, *We've got a chance to play 100, 120 games*," said Zack Britton, a relief pitcher who also doubled as the team's union player representative. "I was just telling the guys to hang tight, that they'll get this thing under control in a few weeks. I think everybody was really unsure about what was going on."

That plan was shredded within two days, when two of the team's minor leaguers tested positive for COVID-19, the first known cases to impact professional baseball. Upon advice from the local department of health, the team quarantined hundreds of minor leaguers, coaches, and staff members in area hotels and apartments, while the big leaguers were advised to go where they would feel most comfortable for the next four to six weeks. Many accepted the hint to fill their gasoline tanks, returning to their respective homes. "It was," first baseman Luke Voit recalled later, "kind of a shitshow down there."

The year of 2020 began with the Yankees toasting the richest contract ever bestowed upon a starting pitcher, installing Gerrit Cole at the head of their rotation and speaking optimistically about a deal that would produce multiple championships. Backing their newly-acquired right-handed ace with one of the league's most fearsome lineups, they were poised to even old scores, still smoldering after a winter in which details of the Houston Astros' sign-stealing scandal came to light.

Injuries figured to be the stumbling block to the goal of a 28th World Series championship, coming off a 2019 campaign in which they set records with 30 players serving 39 stints on the injured list. Strained hamstrings and sprained ankles were assumed occupational hazards. No one foresaw global pandemic marked on their bingo cards—let alone a season played amidst historic protests against racial inequality and a bitterly contested U.S. presidential election.

The resulting 60-game slate would bear little resemblance to any played before it, a bizarre gauntlet of headaches and obstacles the likes of which long-gone greats like Joe DiMaggio, Mickey Mantle, and Yogi Berra could never have imagined. On this, the 2020 Yankees would agree: they were fortunate to get through it. They pray that there will never be a season like it again.

• CHAPTER 1 •

THE WHITE WHALE

Three miles from a scenic pier where the Pacific Ocean surf crashed into the sand of Newport Beach, Brian Cashman walked past the palm trees standing sentry over the posh Fashion Island hotel, scanning the gray morning skies for a peek of California sunshine. It was December 3, 2019, and for the New York Yankees general manager, the next five hours would arguably be his most important of the decade.

Cashman had logged nearly two decades overseeing the trades and signings that augmented one of baseball's most valuable rosters, an unthinkable run in a seat that had once experienced about as much turnover as your local McDonald's drive-through. Over that span, he had brokered dozens of multi-million dollar deals like the one he hoped would result from this cross-country excursion. Eleven years prior, Cashman boarded a flight to the Bay Area and performed what he'd refer to as his "best John Calipari impression," wielding $161 million of the Steinbrenner family fortune in CC Sabathia's sunken living room.

Successfully selling the game's most prized free agent of that winter as though he were a college basketball recruit, the resulting seven-year deal set a record. History judged the contract well, as Sabathia helped to inaugurate the new Yankee Stadium with a World Series championship in his first year wearing pinstripes, then continued on a path that could eventually merit Hall of Fame induction. The figures that Cashman pitched to Sabathia in December 2008 were staggering at the time, coinciding with a recession triggered by the collapse of the subprime mortgage market. They seemed downright quaint when compared to what Cashman and his executives

17

believed Gerrit Cole deserved. "I've been in that position so many times, sometimes with successful closures and other times not," Cashman said. "I don't consider it: 'I've got to get this guy.' I make sure we put our best foot forward and provide all the accurate information possible. I don't want to mislead or trick anybody to come into this environment. I just want to make sure I present the New York Yankees in the most accurate light possible. It's a very proud light that we can project."

Several floors above the boutiques and hip restaurants, Gerrit Cole waited in a swanky suite, accompanied by his wife Amy and making small talk with super-agent Scott Boras. A coastal city with a population of about 85,000, Newport Beach represented familiar ground for Cole. He had been born within the city limits, taking his first steps toward stardom at nearby Orange Lutheran High School, where he'd been asked to autograph boxes of baseballs in the boys' locker room—requests that came from students and teachers alike.

This was a home game for Boras as well; his team serviced a clientele of about 175 big league stars from a $20 million, two-story glass-and-steel hub a mile away on Corporate Plaza Drive. The location allowed Boras to clock daytime office hours, then zip away for regular visits to his choice box seats behind home plate at Angel Stadium and Dodger Stadium. As Boras prepared his stack of questions for the Yankees hierarchy, he saw a proud franchise on the cusp of glory. They needed a big arm who could get them there.

It had been 45 days since Jose Altuve's home run cleared the left-field wall at Minute Maid Park in Houston, ending the American League Championship Series and forcing the Yankees to make a slow trudge into the visiting clubhouse. Within those walls, power-hitting outfielder Aaron Judge had been among those venting anger and frustration, advising his teammates to use the pain in their hearts as workout fuel for the winter months.

As those words spilled from Judge's mouth, Cole was a few hundred yards away, gleefully bathing in bubbly and Budweiser as the Houston Astros celebrated their advance to the World Series. The Fall Classic did not go as Cole might have imagined. During the regular season, he was dominant, leading the American League with a 2.50 ERA while pacing all major leaguers with 326 strikeouts. Unbeaten from May 27 on, he'd finish second to teammate Justin Verlander in a tight battle for the Cy Young Award.

Battered by the Washington Nationals for five runs over seven innings in Game 1, Cole accepted the loss in Houston's 5–4 defeat, snapping a run of 19 consecutive winning decisions. It wasn't Cole's sharpest outing, prompting the hurler to say that he didn't like the snap of his curveball and had left too many meaty fastballs over the plate. Though Cole rebounded with seven stellar innings in a Game 5 victory, he watched from the bullpen as the Nationals scored six runs over the final three innings of Game 7 to finish the Astros' season.

As Washington celebrated, Cole seemed to be counting the minutes until he could file for free agency. He glumly cleared his belongings from a Minute Maid Park locker, initially refusing to speak with the waiting media. "I'm not employed by the team," Cole told Gene Dias, the Astros' director of media relations. After some cajoling, Cole acquiesced, tugging on a silver ballcap bearing the Boras Corp. logo and telling Dias: "All right, as an affiliate of myself."

"It's uncharacteristic of how I try to handle my business, but I was angry," Cole later said. "I came eight hours away from getting a ring. I felt like I could see the light underneath the door, and then it was slammed shut in our face."

Arguably the most consistent knock against the Yankees' title hopes was their lack of a bonafide ace, the unquestioned Game 1 starter that Cole represented. Each member of the club's projected 2020 rotation carried significant question marks: manager Aaron Boone believed that Masahiro Tanaka, J.A. Happ, James Paxton, and Domingo Germán would be in his starting five, though the club expected Germán, still serving a suspension under the league's policy against domestic violence, to miss 63 games of the regular season.

Pitching had not been the Yanks' most significant issue during the 2019 postseason; instead, it was a lack of situational offense that sent the Bombers home, part of the danger in matching boom-or-bust power hitters against elite arms. The prospect of adding Cole while prying him from Houston made for an appealing double whammy, which was why Boone's cell phone buzzed with a text message while his flight idled on the runway. It was Sabathia: "We need to get this dude."

As Boone retrieved his carry-on luggage from the overhead bin, he was more outwardly optimistic than Cashman, whom the manager jokingly described as "Debbie Downer," Rachel Dratch's famed *Saturday Night Live* killjoy. Yet Cashman and Boone hadn't flown this far to be shut out. Joined by assistant general manager Michael Fishman and newly-hired pitching coach Matt Blake, the gang from the Bronx also had a secret weapon joining the party.

At the suggestions of Boone and Sabathia, the Yankees booked a flight for Andy Pettitte to travel from his Texas home. The five-time World Series champion was a fan favorite; Cole had once plastered his California bedroom walls with images of Pettitte, Derek Jeter, and the rest of the dynasty-era Yankees. Cole was 29, an age by which Pettitte had experienced the dizzying highs of big city stardom and savored four World Series parades through Manhattan's Canyon of Heroes.

In his folksy mashup of Louisiana drawl and Texas twang, the lanky left-hander would attest to the joys of winning in New York. That testimony would be valuable, mostly since he had made the reverse move that Cole was entertaining. Pettitte left the Yankees after the 2003 season, spending three years with the Astros in large part so he could spend more nights at his home in the Houston suburb of Deer Park. The uniform switch had produced one of Pettitte's finest seasons, a 2005 campaign that saw a career-best 2.39 ERA while the Astros reached their first World Series.

It also resulted in endless ribbing from Jeter, Jorge Posada, and Mariano Rivera, Pettitte's forever teammates in what came to be known as the "Core Four." When the group reunited to fête Pettitte and Rivera's dual retirements toward the end of the 2013 season, Jeter delighted in teasing Pettitte that he hadn't been a wire-to-wire Yankee like the other three and Bernie Williams. Perhaps not, but only Pettitte could properly provide Cole with the perspective of sporting poly-knit pinstripes for the long walk from the first-base dugout to the Yankee Stadium bullpen. There was nothing, Pettitte said, like the pulsing energy of a postseason game in the Bronx.

Cashman couldn't speak as well to that; his playing career as a scrappy middle infielder and leadoff hitter stalled at the Catholic University of America. His trade tools resided more in the realm of a tucked-in polo shirt and a perpetually drained cell phone. Yet Cashman knew that he would drive the meeting, carrying Hal Steinbrenner's blessing to ensure Cole would wear pinstripes for years to come. "We have an amazing ownership family," Cashman said. "We have a tremendous facility, and our fans are second to none. If you care about competing and winning and playing on the biggest stage in the world, this is the place. If you'd rather just make a lot of money and you really don't care about winning or dealing with the pressure that comes with that, this isn't the place for you."

Though Steinbrenner had little interest in social media, even eschewing so much as a Facebook account, he felt the heat from the online masses. His team passed one offseason prior on a loaded free-agent market that included left-hander Patrick Corbin, outfielder Bryce Harper, and infielder Manny Machado. Their imaginations teased by digitally altered headshots on the large center-field scoreboard, Corbin and Machado received Yankee Stadium tours. Yet, the club limited its spending on the duo to the moment when Cashman slapped his credit card down to claim the dinner check. Corbin went to the Nationals, Harper to the Philadelphia Phillies, and Machado to the San Diego Padres.

The Yankees' big winter signing was infielder DJ LeMahieu. He would prove to be the club's most valuable player over the next two years, though no such expectations accompanied his arrival. This time, Steinbrenner was ready to write the big check. "Unlike other top free agents in years past, I really felt that Cole would be a game-changer for us," Steinbrenner said. "Starting pitching, obviously you can't have enough of it. He's unbelievably talented skill-wise, great makeup, very tough, very intelligent. He has an unbeliev-able work ethic and he's 29 years old. You put all those together, and that's an opportunity I would pursue any given year. This just wasn't a guy that I wanted to pass on."

Several days after their season ended, Cashman summoned the club's analysts, talent evaluators, and other decision-makers into a war room on Yankee Stadium's suite level, beginning their preparation for the offseason ahead. Scouting reports on prospective free agents littered a large table, and the annual process of ranking them in order of preference seemed to be elementary. They dabbled with backup plans—even preparing a presentation for right-hander Stephen Strasburg, late of the defending world champions—but there wasn't much energy wasted in steering the conversation away from Cole.

It was an old story in that room, filled by baseball men intimately familiar with the play-by-play of how Cole had twice slipped through their fingers. Any radar-gun-toting Southern California scout worth his salt had seen the prospect by 2008, when he was pitching to a sensational 0.46 ERA in his third year on Orange Lutheran's varsity. Each start in the Lancers' red, white, and gold uniforms provided Cole with an opportunity to make hitters look silly, scarcely needing more than his fastball to gas the local kids, most of whom went on to careers in professions that did not require baseball spikes. Cole struck out 121 batters in 75 innings, permitting only 30 hits. "A ridiculous competitor," recalled David Keith, a Yankees area scout who attended several of Cole's high school games. "With Gerrit on the mound, his aura, his velocity, ability to spin the breaking ball, it was so fun to watch—even just as a baseball fan. He had that tempo and knew what he was dealing with. His attitude was: let's go to work."

It was no secret that Cole had received a baseball scholarship to UCLA, but the Yankees believed that his affinity for their franchise might tip the decision. Cole's father, Mark, was born in Syracuse, New York, and adored the "Bronx Zoo" Yankees of the late 1970s, counting no-nonsense infielder Willie Randolph and speedy outfielder Mickey Rivers among his favorites. Though Mark Cole moved to Michigan, he retained that fandom, passing it down a generation. Gerrit Cole remembers racing home from school to his family's back patio so he could catch the first pitch of games from New

York, which came on the air at 4:00 PM local time. "It was hard not to fall in love with the Yankees," Cole said. "Every young kid wants to be like their dad, right? That bond just inspired me. The Yankees aligned with a lot of the things that my dad was trying to raise us on. You can draw parallels from sports to life, and certainly as a kid, watching those teams permeated not only my professional career, but how my dad raised me."

In November of 2001, with the Yankees facing the Arizona Diamondbacks in the World Series, an 11-year-old Cole had begged his parents to travel to Phoenix. They scored tickets to Game 6 of an emotional Fall Classic that had been delayed by the September 11 attacks, marked by a pair of incredible Yankees comebacks in Games 4 and 5. When Tino Martinez, Jeter, and Scott Brosius indelibly attached their names to embattled D-backs closer Byung-Hyun Kim on successive nights, their homers prompted cheers from cops and firefighters nine miles south, digging through the smoldering hellscape of what used to be the World Trade Center. "The 2001 World Series," Cole said, "was probably the only time the entire nation was rooting for the Yankees."

The Coles stayed at the Ritz-Carlton in Phoenix, where they were delighted to learn that principal owner George M. Steinbrenner and his team were sleeping under the same roof. The Yankees jetted west after Brosius and Alfonso Soriano delivered big hits in Game 5, touching down in the desert while savoring a 3–2 lead in the World Series. Cole wandered into the hotel's concierge lounge and discovered an arts-and-crafts project created by another guest, a pinstriped piece of poster board with large blue letters that read: "YANKEE FAN TODAY TOMORROW FOREVER." "I actually didn't make it," Cole said. "There was another family that was there. We were staying on the same floor. They didn't have tickets, so they left the sign with me since we were kind of all hanging out at the park."

Cole wore a replica pinstriped jersey and a Yankees cap as he carried the sign into Bank One Ballpark, where he draped his slight frame over a wall down the first-base line, seeking autographs from his heroes. Jeter trotted by, flipping a batting practice baseball to Cole. William Perlman, a photographer for the *Newark Star-Ledger*, was also in the vicinity. He spotted the sign and snapped a picture. Dutifully asking the youngster for his name, age, and hometown, Perlman transmitted the image to the newsroom and forgot about it, moving on to shoot a game that the Yankees wanted to delete from their memory card.

With a chance to end the World Series, Pettitte had no answers for a D-backs lineup stacked with right-handed hitters, later realizing that he had tipped his pitches by the way he held his glove. Pettitte recorded only six outs, absorbing a six-run shellacking in a 15–2 loss. As reliever Jay Witasick bore the brunt of Arizona's eight-run third inning, rowdy fans pelted the young Cole with peanut shells. The Coles weren't in the ballpark when Luis Gonzalez's ninth-inning flare off Mariano Rivera decided the Fall Classic one night later, and it would be seven years until anyone had reason to rediscover the digital image buried in *The Star-Ledger*'s archives.

In the weeks ahead of the June 2008 draft, the Yankees weighed the risk of steering Cole away from his college commitment, eventually agreeing that a seven-figure signing bonus would seal the deal. Four years earlier, they'd used a similar playbook to talk another Southern California high schooler out of college, using the 23rd overall selection on right-hander Phil Hughes. Years later, Hughes recalled that Cole—then an eighth grader seeking inspiration to refine his own game—had attended his starts at Foothill High School in Santa Ana. "I taught him everything he knows," quipped Hughes, who pitched to a 4.52 ERA in 290 games over a dozen years with the Yankees, Minnesota Twins, and Padres before retiring after the 2018 season. Set for life financially, Hughes now fills his free time opening packs of sports cards on a popular YouTube channel, which he described as "all things cards from a guy who used to be on a few worthless ones."

Dazzled by his live arm and maturity, the Yankees forecast an even brighter future for Cole. During that senior season, Cole touched 96 mph during a showcase for top high school talent, commanding the attention of nearly 50 scouts during the first game of the year. As Damon Oppenheimer shuffled pre-draft reports in a Tampa, Florida, office, the Yanks' director of amateur scouting identified Cole as the top high school pitcher in the country—and it wasn't even close. "He was a man amongst boys," Cashman said. "It wasn't just the physicality; he was a fierce competitor. That jumped off the page: how he reacted toward his opponents and the umpires. He was a very young, strong-willed, fierce competitor—and he was backing it up."

Cole would pitch professionally; there was no question about that. It was a matter of when. Keith, the Yankees scout, was in contact with the Coles weeks ahead of the draft on that topic. Access to Cole came via a Tustin, California, batting cage, where father and son cycled through meetings with clubs in 30-minute sessions. Keith spoke frankly to Mark Cole, saying that the Yankees would need more time. The Coles nodded, scheduling the veteran scout last and engaging in a wide-ranging chat that neared the two-hour mark. Keith's resulting reports to the home office in New York and Tampa identified Cole as a first-round pick. "Sometimes you find out things about the player that isn't what your eyes are viewing," Keith said. "With Gerrit, it was: he's got it. He's on his own. He's not afraid. He can let his dad talk; he won't interrupt him. He was strong; he was under control. You could see how much passion he had for the game, the way he spoke. That was the first time I was like, 'I'm in, let's go.'"

Quarterbacking the draft, Oppenheimer figured that Cole might be bluffing about college; if he was so dead-set upon UCLA, why had his family retained Boras? Oppenheimer took a deep breath and gambled, making Cole the 28th overall selection in the nation. "That talent level," Oppenheimer recalled years later, "was just too good to pass up."

With all players, including Cole, the Yankees generally view signability as the final calculation. You identify the best players on the board, hope they are still there when it's your turn, and make the numbers work later. They were confident in their chances a few days after the draft when Cole participated in a conference call with the New York media. Over a speakerphone, Cole animatedly told the story behind the "TODAY TOMORROW FOREVER" sign, recalling how he had run into Jeter and Paul O'Neill in the lobby during that World Series.

As Cole spoke, Suzyn Waldman scowled. Monitoring the call before her on-air duties in the radio booth, the veteran analyst tartly muttered to Oppenheimer: "He's not signing here. He's going to school." A quizzical Oppenheimer assured her that they would strike a deal. Waldman did not budge. "He talked about being a fan and he loved the Yankees," Waldman said later. "He was so good. But he never said the one thing that they all say: that they can't wait to put the uniform on."

The Yankees were prepared to write a check for $4 million, but Cole and his family opted not to receive the offer. Three years earlier, Mark Cole had formulated a Microsoft Excel spreadsheet that served as a road map for his son's career, calculating the odds of career-ending injuries and the financial implications of a college education. Cole recalled that one column contrasted high school first-round picks against college draftees, showing the difference in their average career gross. With his father's help, Cole bet that his talent would create more lucrative opportunities in the future. The Yankees would have to wait. "There was internal frustration," Cashman said. "You wondered where we went wrong and how we missed the signability. But how can you be upset with a family that's making life choices? You can't make someone do something they're not willing to do. We weren't mad at the Cole family. We were more mad at ourselves for messing up the pick because we never had a shot. He didn't want to hear any offers. He wanted to go to UCLA."

UCLA head coach John Savage had wooed Cole over a series of dinners, selling the hurler on college life. As a freshman, Cole was named the Bruins' Friday night starter, and during his sophomore year, he teamed with future big leaguer Trevor Bauer to pitch UCLA to a 52–17 record—the best in school history. Following Cole's junior year, the Pittsburgh Pirates made him the No. 1 overall pick in the nation, delivering an $8 million signing bonus— twice what the Yankees would have offered in 2008. Mark Cole's spreadsheets were money. "His dad's an investor, a very smart businessman," Keith said. "Gerrit was a big leaguer; there was no doubt. It was not a question of if—just how long. That one really hurt because Gerrit could have done a lot for the Yankees. That one stuck with me for a long time."

Making his major league debut in 2013, Cole posted a 59–42 record and 3.37 ERA in 127 games over five seasons with Pittsburgh. Recognizing that he would soon eclipse their shoestring budget, the Pirates dangled Cole in trade talks before the 2018 season. Cashman tried to find a deal, balking when Pittsburgh insisted on including third baseman Miguel Andújar and outfielder Clint Frazier. The Yankees would part with Frazier, but not Andújar. Pittsburgh instead opted for a four-player package from the Astros that included right-hander Joe Musgrove and infielder Colin Moran.

The Houston pitching laboratory raised Cole's game to a new level, as he enjoyed improvements to the spin and velocity on his fastball, slider, and curveball. Healthier and stronger, Cole benefited from the input of Astros pitching coach Brent Strom, who pushed him to be more of a north/south pitcher instead of east/west. Strom mentioned that many Hall of Fame pitchers emphasized using four-seam fastballs up in the strike zone, using Nolan Ryan as an example. It made sense to Cole, who scrapped his two-seamer in favor of challenging hitters with the high, hard stuff. Hey, who didn't want to be like Nolan Ryan?

Cole had come a long way from the confident high schooler who burned the Yankees more than a decade prior. Their shared history was jangling through Cashman's mind as they exchanged pleasantries. Pacific Coast sunshine poured through a floor-to-ceiling window that allowed a gentle breeze to enter from Newport's Back Bay. Cashman nodded in the hurler's direction and remarked, "You're my white whale."

Cole laughed, recognizing the allusion to *Moby Dick*. Like the Captain Ahab character in Herman Melville's 1851 novel, Cashman's Yankees had indeed exhibited a monomaniacal pursuit of Cole. Left unsaid was how Ahab's obsession resolved; in the book's final act, the sailor harpoons the whale—only to drown in the sea when the line tangles around his neck. "It just came to me," Cashman said. "We drafted him in the first round, and he chose to go to college. We tried to trade for him, and they chose to trade him to Houston instead. As an organization, he was our white whale. We were hoping the third time was the charm."

Betting on Cole's affinity for high-tech gizmos, the Yankees unveiled a 30-pound, 12-inch-tall golden box in the shape of home plate, which opened to reveal pinstriped embroidery and a miniature version of Yankee Stadium. A pre-loaded iPad featured crash courses on the franchise's storied history, development programs, New York City's neighborhoods and places to live outside the five boroughs, and personal messages from several players. "I was impressed," Cole said. "The contraption was really sweet. I guess I'm a millennial, right? We're all suckers for tablets."

The club included bags of T-shirts and other swag, including a field model Yankees cap for Cole to try on. As Boras scribbled notes furiously, Cashman asked the Coles about their goals. The GM nodded when they agreed upon their shared desire to win a championship, promising, "We are a franchise that is going to give you that opportunity every year."

Satisfied, they next appealed to Cole's oenophilia. Boone grinned as he presented the couple with bottles of 2004 and 2005 Masseto, rated as one of the world's finest red wines. A full-bodied merlot that *Wine Spectator* described as carrying scents of "chocolate mousse with crushed raspberry and hints of flowers," they were the same vintages that the Coles had enjoyed during a recent candlelit anniversary dinner in Florence, Italy. "I was a little bit on my heels," Cole said. "I remember trying to stay focused through the meeting and not think about booze the entire time."

Boone saw the gears churning inside Cole's mind, describing the hurler as "perplexed." The wine tip came from Lou Cucuzza, the team's longtime visiting clubhouse manager, who had shared conversations with Cole about their shared Italian heritage during Houston's visits to the Bronx. Cucuzza relayed that factoid to traveling secretary Ben Tuliebitz, who passed it along to Cashman in a $1,600 game of telephone. "I'd always come into Lou's office when I've got nothing to do and kick my feet up on the table. We just talk about stuff," Cole said. "I was showing him some pictures of a meal that we ate in a cellar in Florence, and there's a picture of a bottle of Masseto on the table. It's definitely my favorite bottle. I did Ancestry[.com] and I'm like 35, 37 percent Italian, so a top-notch bottle of Masseto is close to my heart."

More first date than sales pitch, the meeting stretched past the four-hour mark. Cole listened intently as Boone described his personality and game-management style. He nodded when Cashman and Fishman spoke to the amenities that would create a championship-caliber environment. Cole volleyed a few viewpoints when Blake outlined his plan to transition the pitching staff into a more analytically-driven workplace. Boone used the opportunity to quiz Cole on his thought process during Game 3 of that year's ALCS, when he pitched around five walks in seven scoreless innings, leading the Astros to a 4–1 victory at Yankee Stadium. "It was a lot of fun to talk to him about how he looked at it, the reverence he had for our lineup, and how he had to navigate that game," Boone said.

As business plodded along, Cole's inner child banged on the door. He briefly paused the meeting to ask Boone about his pennant-winning home run, a blast off knuckleballer Tim Wakefield that toppled the Boston Red Sox in the 2003 ALCS. It hit the sweet spot of fandom for Cole, a 13 year old at the time of the memorable dinger. Boone's homer raised his Q rating; had he not entered that game as an eighth-inning pinch-runner for the lumbering Ruben Sierra, would the Yankees have granted him a managerial interview? Would ESPN have selected him to go in front of the *Baseball Tonight* cameras? It certainly hadn't hurt his resume in either case.

Having Pettitte on the travel squad proved to be an inspired choice. Though the hurlers threw with opposite hands and alternating styles, they clicked instantly, bonding over their intense competitive streaks. Pettitte had the floor for about 20 uninterrupted minutes. He assured the Coles that they would love New York, describing areas where they could seek respite from the bustling metropolis. Pettitte and his wife, Laura, had spent their summers in New York's suburbs before relocating their full-time residence to Texas. Pettitte described how in the latter years of his career he'd jet to Houston on off days to steal extra hours at home with the kids. Cole nodded. "Andy Pettitte threw a nine-inning shutout in that meeting," Boras said. "The dialogue between them—you almost wish you had it filmed. Gerrit clearly understood from a player's perspective what it's like to be in New York and grow a career there. His cutter was working, for sure."

Pettitte said that he left with a sense of Cole's meticulous nature, recognizing that the pitcher seemed to understand what he wanted to do and how his mind operated. Cole played it cool, but he'd later gush to friends about Pettitte: "His number is in my cell phone!"

As the Yanks' contingent returned to their respective hotel rooms, Cole settled into bed, replaying the day's events. The bottle of Masseto was still on his mind. He leaned over and looked into Amy's eyes, wondering aloud, "How the heck did they pull that off?" Amy offered a shrug, and as Cole's head rested upon the pillow, he closed his eyes. He pictured himself atop the Yankee Stadium mound, a capacity crowd on hand for Opening Day—no, make that a crisp October evening, a World Series game in the Bronx. He imagined the voice of a public address announcer intoning: "*Pitching for the Yankees, No. 45, Gerrit Cole. No. 45.*"

The clock read 11:30 PM as Cole's eyes opened wide, and his head jerked toward the ceiling, the mystery solved. He yelped: "Lou! It was Lou!"

Cole's situation remained unresolved six days later as the baseball world filled the lobbies of San Diego's Manchester Grand Hyatt. It was time for the Winter Meetings, a four-day December extravaganza that pours thousands of executives, agents, sportswriters, and job seekers into the same crowded arena. The Yankees were viewed as front-runners in the Cole sweepstakes, but some opined that Cole might prefer a West Coast team like the Los Angeles Angels of Anaheim or the Los Angeles Dodgers. The Yanks team hedged their bets during that first California visit by engaging with Strasburg, a sturdy 31-year-old right-handed free agent coming off an 18-win season with the Nationals.

Weeks removed from twice outdueling Verlander in the World Series, Strasburg impressed Cashman during the meeting. They'd never need to pursue the backup plan. Cole had departed the Newport Beach meeting with a clear favorite. The same guy who placed his trust in his father's spreadsheets was now listening as Mark Cole advised his son to "choose his dream," which they both knew was spending the rest of his career in a Yankees uniform. "What better way to extend an example for my future kids and family than to follow through on that?" Cole later said. "It's an unbelievable opportunity. It's my dream."

Strasburg stole the headlines on the second day of the meetings, re-signing with the Nationals for seven years and $245 million, a deal that represented the richest ever issued to a pitcher. The Yankees had planned to make a formal offer to Cole before the Strasburg announcement, but Boras advised Cashman to hold off, hinting that there would be "new information" to review. Cashman thought Boras was teasing that another team had entered the Cole sweepstakes. Indeed, Boras suggested that two "mystery teams" were now in pursuit—believed to be the Astros and the San Francisco Giants. It was a red herring. When the terms of Strasburg's deal leaked, Steinbrenner chuckled from the Tampa compound and pinged Cashman with a cross-country text message: "Now we know the new information that he's referring to."

"Gerrit was interested in organizations that were going to give him an opportunity to win," Boras said. "I knew that Hal was very comfortable in his role as an owner now, and it was clear to him that Gerrit was the guy. He had great trust and confidence that he would be a very diligent employee and execute the contract."

The Yankees' initial proposal to Boras was an eight-year pact, prompting conversation but no agreement. With fewer than 36 hours left in the meetings, Cashman wanted to sweeten the offer and force a decision. Steinbrenner approved increasing the proposal to nine years and $324 million, which would shatter Strasburg's day-old record and make Cole just the fifth player in history to sign a contract worth more than $300 million. Steinbrenner calculated that other clubs would eventually increase their offers to a ninth year, so it was better to be the first to dive off the deep end. Cashman thanked Steinbrenner and tapped out a text message detailing the new terms to Boras. The white whale was out there; this was the final harpoon. "If it wasn't going to be good enough, it wasn't going to be good enough," Cashman said. "There weren't going to be any more negotiations after that."

Boras eyed the numbers and smiled. The coiffed 67-year-old carried the title of "Most Powerful Sports Agent in the World," an honor that had been bestowed upon him by *Forbes* magazine each year beginning in 2013, and his bank accounts reflected the superstar commission fees to back that boast. Having just finished Strasburg's monster deal, Boras was deep in talks to relocate third baseman Anthony Rendon to the Angels, closing in on a seven-year, $245 million pact. In February of 2019, Boras brokered a 13-year, $330 million deal between Harper and the Phillies. It had been an amazing year, and now Cole's contract would join Harper's in the greatest hits catalog. He dialed Cole with the news, then listened as the chatty pitcher turned silent for several seconds. "G, are you there?" Boras said, wondering if his phone had dropped the call. "You're supposed to be fucking screaming."

Cole stammered, replying that he had been taken aback by the reality of the offer. On some level, Cole knew that the numbers would be magnificent, but he had tried to approach the negotiations without expectations. As Boras waited, Cole described feeling light-headed as he searched for words and then uttered the only one that mattered: "Yes!"

Evening fell upon San Diego's marina district as Cashman and several Yanks front-office executives huddled in a corner booth at the Seasons 52 restaurant, about a 490-foot walk from the Hyatt's bell desk. It was roughly the distance from home plate to the center-field fence in the old Yankee Stadium before the 1974–75 disco renovation of The House That Ruth Built.

Cell phones buzzed throughout the restaurant at 8:56 PM local time, illuminating dishes of wood-grilled boneless rainbow trout and caramel-ized grilled sea scallops. Twitter pulsed with reports that Cole had chosen the Yankees. Cashman strode toward the exit. Angels manager Joe Maddon intercepted him with a handshake. Twins general manager Thad Levine also rose from his chair, congratulating his counterpart. Melville's epic was due for a rewrite; this time, Ahab gets the whale and lives happily ever after.

Cole pulled out the New Era 59/50 field model cap that had been gifted during the club's visit, bending the brim and tugging it over his curly locks. Much to Amy's delight, he cried, then laughed as he danced around the living room. His parents dug the crinkled "TODAY TOMORROW FOREVER" poster board out of storage. The navy blue letters had faded to tan. "You're kidding me. You still have it?" Boras said. "We are bringing that sign to the press conference. We're going to present it to the Steinbrenner family and to the fans about your destiny and how you had a desire to be a Yankee ever since you were 11 years old."

The Yankees set the coronation for December 18, announcing a morning news conference in Yankee Stadium's Legends Club. Such events were once commonplace, but some employees needed a refresher in organizing show-cases of that magnitude. The Yanks hadn't issued a nine-figure contract to a free agent since 2014, when they welcomed right-hander Masahiro Tanaka to the majors with a seven-year, $155 million pact.

In a suite at the Mandarin Oriental hotel high above Columbus Circle, Cole shook hands with barber Davey Castillo and conformed to his new employer's grooming policy. The militaristic orders that George Steinbrenner once scribbled on a scrap of paper back on Opening Day 1973 remained in place: no hair touching the collar, no beards, well-kempt mustaches accept-able. Like big-ticket free agents Johnny Damon, Jason Giambi, and Randy Johnson in the years before his arrival, Cole watched his lustrous locks fall per The Boss' wishes. Cole joked that he hadn't felt razor burn since college. "So be it. That's the way it is," Cole said. "If you're a Yankee, you shave. That's what's up."

Then the Coles were off to do some big-ticket shopping, eyeing a $5.6 million home in the leafy suburb of Greenwich, Connecticut. Boras treated the couple to dinner at Estiatorio Milos, touted as one of the world's finest Mediterranean seafood restaurants, on West 55th Street. It was a long way from their days at UCLA, where Cole frequently walked to Trader Joe's on Weyburn Avenue, forking over $14 to fill a grocery bag with chicken and roasted vegetables. That freed the rest of his cash for beers with the boys. Mark Cole's son knew how to budget.

It was a Wednesday morning as members of the print, television, radio, and Internet media entered the large area behind Yankee Stadium's home plate. White cloth tables were pushed aside in favor of hundreds of high-backed chairs. They all pointed toward a 100-foot podium at the room's center. There were plates of complimentary chocolate cupcakes bearing white baseball icing and a blue No. 45, the uniform number that Cole once selected in silent homage to great hurlers of yesteryear like Hall of Famers Bob Gibson and Pedro Martinez.

It was a number that first baseman Luke Voit had worn for the Yanks during the 2018–19 seasons, and Cole made Voit an offer he couldn't refuse. The players swore to keep their transaction private as Voit agreed to switch to No. 59. Voit said that it would serve as a tribute to his younger brother John, who wore the number for Army football as a three-year starting defensive end and senior captain.

Cashman and Boone were at the microphone first, an appetizer for the main course. Next came Cole, who beamed while buttoning a pinstriped Yankees jersey for the photographers. Flanked by his wife, Boras, and Steinbrenner, Cole spoke about realizing his childhood dream, then reached underneath the podium and revealed the crinkled "YANKEE FAN TODAY TOMORROW FOREVER" poster that had been in his possession for nearly two decades.

"I just want to say that I'm here," Cole said. "I've always been here."

It was a dramatic moment that would have delighted George Steinbrenner, a man who once seduced Reggie Jackson in the winter of 1976 by sweetening a $3.5 million contract with a Rolls-Royce Corniche, sealing their deal on the back of a cocktail napkin at the Chicago O'Hare Hyatt. Accounting for inflation, Cole could now purchase a thousand of Mr. October's convertibles. Cole had no use for a fleet of beautiful rides; he only cared about bringing the World Series back to New York. The Boss, who famously said that he considered winning second only to breathing, would have also liked that. "I was thinking about how wonderful a commitment it was," Cole said. "I was sold on an organization that puts its best foot forward year in and year out. I don't think that's comparable to any other team in the league. There's a sense of peace as a player that comes with that. And from a certainty standpoint, now I knew where I'd be for a good long time, as opposed to picking up and putting things down several times in my career."

A self-proclaimed "finance geek," Hal Steinbrenner preferred to yield the spotlight to his employees, especially the ones who could hit and throw, and he offered a pursed, nervous smile for the cameras. Perhaps Steinbrenner was calculating that, given a typical track record of 34 starts in a season, his family would effectively write a check for $1,058,823 each time Cole walked to the mound. Joking that he should have been more balanced with his Christmas shopping, Steinbrenner indicated no gift receipt would be necessary on this purchase. "He's an unbelievable player and an unbelievable human being. He's going to be an unbelievable Yankee," Steinbrenner said in a clipped staccato. "He checks all the boxes. He's great with his teammates, great in the clubhouse. We need to win some world championships, and I believe we're going to do that sooner rather than later. I believe we're going to do that—plural."

The bar was set high. Cole did not flinch. During his five years in Pittsburgh, Cole's teams had twice been eliminated in the first round of the postseason, missing the playoffs altogether two other times. Pittsburgh's focus was on waves of player development, cost-cutting, and rebuilding. Cole loved the suggestion that every season would matter. The objective was to win it all. Nothing less was acceptable. "I was a Yankee fan, man," Cole said. "Every year, you have that expectation that they're going to be competing. It doesn't scare me. It's what I dreamed of."

Cole checked the calendar and counted. Pitchers and catchers would report to spring training in 56 days. He could not wait to see what 2020 had in store.

CHAPTER 2

SUN DAZE

A gaggle of gawkers peered through a chain-link fence at one of the New York Yankees' practice fields in Tampa, Florida, hoping to catch a glimpse of spring on a Wednesday morning in early February. Some 200 miles to the southeast, cleanup continued following the Super Bowl LIV showdown between the Kansas City Chiefs and San Francisco 49ers. More than 62,000 fans had packed Miami's Hard Rock Stadium, including a 6'7" former high school football star who happened to play right field for the Yankees.

Aaron Judge sported a throwback Jerry Rice 49ers jersey for the occasion. Wearing No. 80 on his chest and back and accompanied by girlfriend Samantha Bracksiek, Linden, California's favorite son watched his Niners squander a 10-point lead in the fourth quarter. Judge muttered expletives as Kansas City scored 21 unanswered points to claim the championship. A few days later, Judge was recounting his trip at the Himes Avenue player development complex, a four-diamond jewel bordered by a Burger King and a 7-Eleven. At least the parties had been fun, where they'd mingled with the likes of Jay-Z, Dennis Rodman, and Emmitt Smith.

Manager Aaron Boone teased his star slugger, telling him that he'd accurately predicted the exact final score of 31–20. Boone's pregame social media posts, gleefully retweeted by the team, confirmed his claim. It was yet another stroke of good fortune for a man who'd already launched a pennant-winning home run that forever endeared him to a generation of fans.

The Super Bowl's final whistle signifies an unofficial handoff to baseball, but the season had never stopped in Judge's mind. Three months removed from the abrupt end of the American League Championship Series, Judge knew about the emotional swing that the 49ers had experienced in the moments after they shed their shoulder pads. Judge's response to the Houston Astros' victory had been to keep pushing, bypassing his usual weeks of rest and recovery while November bled into December. He wanted to use that anger and frustration to fuel his offseason workouts. Back in the batter's box again, Judge hacked at a lobbed fastball and winced. A thunderbolt of pain coursed through his right shoulder.

That damned shoulder. It had been an issue since September, when Judge attempted a diving catch on a sinking liner from Los Angeles Angels slugger Albert Pujols. Judge's 282-pound frame thumped hard into Yankee Stadium's right-field turf, and he rose to his feet in discomfort. As he tamped the grass with his cleats to replace a divot, Judge stared toward the outfield wall, not wanting Boone or the television cameras to log his reaction. Judge completed that game but was absent from the lineup the next two nights, quietly reporting to New York-Presbyterian Hospital for the first of several pain-killing injections that allowed him to play in the postseason. "I felt a crack. I felt a pop," Judge would later say. "But you've got adrenaline flowing, you've got the postseason coming up. That's the main concern. I wanted to be out there on the field."

Minutes after Jose Altuve's Game 6 homer cleared the left-field wall and sent the Yankees into winter mode, Judge had turned his attention to 2020. In a normal offseason, Judge typically allowed himself several weeks to rest before picking up a bat. The allotted span for R&R was measured this time in days. He'd felt soreness in the shoulder at times, believing it was not a concern. He could warm up and work through it, Judge told himself. As he staggered around the cage on that February morning, tossing aside his 33-ounce black Chandler bat, Judge regretted not allowing himself more time to recuperate.

Judge's size has never afforded him the luxury of blending in. As a rookie in 2017, he once stood at his Yankee Stadium locker and marveled that pedestrians on the streets of New York were now asking for his autograph or cell-phone photos; they'd stopped him before that, but usually to ask something along the lines of, "You're pretty tall. What sport do you play?" Three years later, he was on billboards and television commercials, offering his stamp of approval to companies like Adidas, Oakley, and Pepsi. It was impossible to miss the big guy with No. 99 on his back. As such, the reporters covering the team swiftly picked up the scent when Judge was absent from the first batting practice drills at George M. Steinbrenner Field. The team's most recognizable player appeared in the outfield only to shag fly balls, making underhanded tosses into a bucket that rested near second base.

Boone claimed it was nothing out of the ordinary, initially describing Judge's shoulder issue as "crankiness," but there was more concern than the manager indicated. The team ordered what general manager Brian Cashman described as a "car wash" of tests to investigate Judge's malady. Many were inconclusive, swelling Judge's frustration level. It took at least 10 examinations before doctors agreed: Judge was attempting to play through a fracture to his first right rib and a punctured lung, all of which likely stemmed from the September dive. "If I'd have known it was a broken rib, maybe I would have done things a little bit differently," Judge said. "If somebody breaks their leg, they're in a cast and they're immobilized. You give the bone a chance to heal. But I was pissed about how the season ended, so I went right back to it. That cost me."

It felt like a new chapter in the same old story. The 2019 "Next Man Up" Yankees reveled in their ability to overcome absence, setting league records by having 30 players serve 39 stints on the injured list. That necessitated what Cashman described as a "*CSI: The Bronx*" investigation into the practices of the organization's strength and conditioning staff, which received a top-to-bottom overhaul. They had hired Eric Cressey, a prominent voice in the sports performance world who boasted a client roster of more than 100 professional athletes at facilities in Massachusetts and Florida. Still, the Yanks were ringing in the new year fighting their hangover.

Right-hander Luis Severino reported to spring training expecting to serve an apprenticeship under Gerrit Cole, forming what would be a dynamic one-two punch at the top of the rotation. That never materialized. Severino experienced discomfort in his right forearm following his earliest bullpen sessions, a five-alarm warning sign for any pitcher. A baffled Severino said that his fastball velocity seemed normal and he could snap curveballs without issue, but it hurt to throw his change-up. That prompted enough concern to board Severino onto a commercial jet back to New York, where an MRI revealed a partially torn ulnar collateral ligament. With Tommy John surgery recommended, Severino's season was over.

The ranks around Cole thinned further when left-hander James Paxton traveled to Dallas, seeking an expert opinion on his ailing lower back. It had affected Paxton in his final start of the regular season against the Texas Rangers, forcing his exit after only one inning. The team described Paxton's issue at the time as nerve irritation in the left-hander's buttocks, challenging the beat reporters to delicately dance around asking a grown man about the pain in his ass. As with Judge, pain-killing injections kept Paxton on the mound through October, and he turned in one of the club's best postseason starts, a nine-strikeout gem to beat the Astros in Game 5 of the ALCS. When Paxton's discomfort lingered into January, surgery was recommended. In medicalese, that meant a microscopic lumbar discectomy with the removal of a peridiscal cyst. What had projected as a top-tier rotation of Cole, Severino, and Paxton now featured Cole, Masahiro Tanaka, and J.A. Happ in the top spots. It was solid but a significant downgrade for a team that believed it had addressed its most glaring weakness—starting pitching.

Fortunately, the Yankees welcomed back most of the same thunderous lineup that led the majors with 943 runs scored during the previous season. Boone constructed his ideal batting orders regularly, sometimes even sketching ideas on the backs of napkins. Now in his third year on the job, Boone remained blessed with an embarrassment of riches to fill spots one through nine. The Yanks were so deep that Boone hardly fretted when Giancarlo Stanton limped off the field in late February with a right calf strain, putting his availability for Opening Day in question.

The 2017 National League MVP, Stanton tallied 305 home runs through his first nine seasons, but the hulking He-Man played in only 18 games during an injury-marred 2019. For better or worse, the Yanks were growing accustomed to his availability being a bonus. Without Judge and Stanton, they boasted plenty of thump between Gleyber Torres, Gary Sánchez, Brett Gardner, DJ LeMahieu, Luke Voit, and Gio Urshela, all of whom had slugged 20 or more homers a year prior.

That powerhouse offense helped Boone become the first manager ever to win 100 or more games in each of his first two seasons. Having moved from ESPN's *Baseball Tonight* studios in Bristol, Connecticut, to Yankee Stadium's home dugout, Boone boasted rich baseball bloodlines—his grandfather Ray, father Bob, and brother Bret all played in the big leagues, as did he, yet he hadn't coached or managed so much as a beer league softball game before 2018. Boone understood his good fortune; he'd been something of a courtesy interview following Joe Girardi's dismissal, then wound up lapping the six-man field.

After Boone completed a grueling eight-hour interview with the Yankees' decision-makers, the front office universally agreed that his affable personality and media savvy edged runner-up Hensley "Bam Bam" Meulens, a one-time Yanks infielder/outfielder with more than a decade of professional coaching experience. In effect, the Steinbrenners handed Boone the keys to a Lamborghini, a team that had come nine innings from advancing to the World Series. Blessed with that incredible horsepower, he'd steered between the white lines and continued sending the club back into October. "He's honored who he is every step of the way," Cashman said. "He's an approachable person that connects well with his players, connects well with his coworkers. He's very patient and open-minded, very intelligent. He's willing to put the work in to decipher the right next move and then live with the results. Aaron Boone is everything that I thought and felt from that interview process."

In the infield, Boone planned upon a double-play combination of LeMahieu at second base and Torres at shortstop. Boone considered LeMahieu to have been the team's most valuable player in 2019, when he led the club in batting average (.327), runs (109), hits (197), and total bases (312), earning the nickname "The Machine" for his robotic success in driving runners home from scoring position. Boone remarked of LeMahieu, "When he does speak, it's like E.F. Hutton. Everybody listens."

Torres emerged as one of the game's bright young talents at age 23, returning to his natural position following Didi Gregorius' departure in free agency. Torres' defense presented questions, but the team expected his potent bat would compensate for any shortcomings in the field. Gregorius and Torres spoke briefly during the winter, during which time Gregorius advised Torres to be ready to take over as the shortstop. Torres had chuckled, but Gregorius wasn't joking. "You'll see," he told his soon-to-be-former teammate.

Gregorius' take proved prescient. He had excelled in the face of an unenviable task, replacing Derek Jeter at shortstop following a ballyhooed retirement tour in 2014, but Gregorius had hurried back from Tommy John surgery in 2019 to bat .238 in an underwhelming half-season. The Yankees made only one courtesy call to Gregorius during his free-agency period, essentially telling him that the club was stuffing its available funds into the pursuit of Cole and wishing Gregorius well with his next team. That turned out to be with the Philadelphia Phillies, where Gregorius reunited with Girardi.

At the infield corners, Boone intended to station Voit at first base and Urshela at third base. Both were shining examples of the organization's success in plucking undervalued talents from other organizations. A brawny right-handed hitting first baseman who once taped posters of Mark McGwire to the walls of his childhood bedroom, Voit won quick points with St. Louis Cardinals fans, announcing upon his first big league call-up that he was coming to Busch Stadium to mash "doubles and bombs." A middle linebacker in baseball spikes, Voit dreamed of wearing pads for the St. Louis Rams before a pair of shoulder surgeries redirected his efforts to the ballpark.

The hometown-boy-makes-good story line was tastier than the saucy rib racks at St. Louis' revered Pappy's Smokehouse, but it contained one fatal flaw: a lack of playing time. With Matt Carpenter, Jose Martinez, and Jedd Gyorko already in the lineup, the Cardinals had no room for Voit, who grew salty as he compiled Triple A at-bats with the Pacific Coast League's Memphis Redbirds. It was a city that had once helped to start the careers of iconic musicians like Elvis Presley, Johnny Cash, and B.B. King, all of whom recorded albums at the iconic Sun Studios decades earlier. Yet to Voit, Memphis felt like a dead end.

Voit received the opportunity he needed in July 2018, when the Cardinals shipped him to the Yankees in exchange for relievers Giovanny Gallegos and Chasen Shreve. At the moment the trade went down, Voit had been in Las Vegas, spending a few bleary-eyed hours blowing off steam between games against the New York Mets' top farm club. Voit returned to his room with a lighter wallet, but the Yankees hit the jackpot. Voit proved to be one of the most impactful players obtained by any club during that year, batting .333 with 14 homers in 39 games. Senior director of player development Kevin Reese (then the team's scouting director), assistant general manager Michael Fishman, director of quantitative analysis David Grabiner, and director of baseball operations Matt Ferry all lobbied for Voit's acquisition. "It was more numbers than scouting," Cashman said. "They had been pounding the table that, 'Hey, this is a dude,' as Aaron Boone would say. And they were right."

Voit's Yankees career started slowly. Three hits in his first 16 at-bats earned him a return ticket to Triple A. Back in the minors, Voit recognized that he'd adopted a flawed all-or-nothing approach, "trying to prove that I could hit 50 homers." He showed better plate discipline upon return nine days later. Cashman relished in pointing out that Voit's resulting production exceeded what superstar infielder Manny Machado—traded the same week by the Baltimore Orioles—provided in his new uniform for the Los Angeles Dodgers. Voit's 2019 production remained high until June, when he sustained an injury while running the bases during a two-game trip to play the Boston Red Sox in London, Major League Baseball's first games on European soil.

Though Voit gamely grinded, his power was sapped for the rest of the season, leaving him as a spectator for the playoff run. When Voit finally submitted to surgery in November, Philadelphia-based specialist Dr. William Meyers reattached three ligaments to each side of Voit's groin. When Voit awoke in the recovery room, he remembers the doctor telling him, "Dude, you tore everything down there."

"I didn't realize it was that bad," Voit said. "There were times when I felt like I was back, but then the next day, I'd get out of bed and be like, 'Ack, it's not supposed to feel like that.'"

As for Urshela, even the Yankees could not have predicted his breakout. Known as a slick defender with a light bat during his previous stops with the Cleveland Indians and Toronto Blue Jays, the Yankees acquired Urshela in August 2018 in exchange for $25,000. They imagined him as minor league depth behind hot-hitting rookie third baseman Miguel Andújar, who was on his way to finishing second in the American League Rookie of the Year race behind the Angels' fascinating hitter/pitcher Shohei Ohtani. An awkward dive into third base during the first homestand of 2019 ruined Andújar's season, pressing Urshela into service. Only then did Cashman and the Yanks' analytics crew realize their good fortune: for the list price of a Hyundai Santa Fe, the Yankees acquired a player who batted .314/.355/.534 with 34 doubles, 21 homers, and 74 RBIs in 132 games, compiling 3.9 wins above replacement (WAR). Baseball people will tell you that each WAR is worth about $8 million in free agency. No midsize sport utility vehicle gets mileage like that.

Though Andújar's right shoulder injury had healed, Cashman viewed third base as Urshela's job to lose, indicating that the club did not believe Urshela's excellent 2019 had been a fluke. During a January visit to the club's complex in the Dominican Republic, Boone confirmed as much to Andújar, suggesting that he try playing the outfield to increase his chances of making the roster. To Boone's surprise, Andújar presented an outfielder's glove, telling the manager that he was ready to shag fly balls for the first time since childhood.

Without Judge and Stanton, Boone planned on an outfield that would feature the longest-tenured Yankee in center field. When pitcher CC Sabathia retired after 2019, Brett Gardner became the only remaining link to the club's most recent championship in 2009. Beginning with his days as a freshman walk-on at the College of Charleston, the South Carolina-born Gardner fought long odds to cement a role with the sport's most decorated franchise. A third-round draft selection in 2005, Gardner arrived in the big leagues three years later, serving in a part-time role as the "Core Four" of Derek Jeter, Mariano Rivera, Jorge Posada, and Andy Pettitte savored their final World Series. Gardner recalled being the quiet rookie in the room then, having tailed veteran Johnny Damon like an eager puppy to observe how big leaguers conducted themselves.

As he approached his 37th birthday, Gardner had transitioned into a leadership role. His preferred style was to keep the mood light and snarky, frequently playing practical jokes on teammates and coaches. Gardner used food as his preferred method of torture. Clint Frazier's chili might be accented by an entire salt shaker, or a coach might bite into a turkey sandwich to find it had been loaded with chewy Mike & Ike candies. When the team prepared protein shakes for younger players during the 2019 season, Gardner surreptitiously jammed globs of mustard into each straw, measuring the perfect amount that could go undetected before the first sip.

In one of Gardner's most elaborate pranks, he used the downtime after batting practice to pry open a teammate's car key fob. A day or two later, the bewildered player brought his vehicle in for service, where the technician discovered the issue—a tiny photo of a grinning Gardner was jammed where the battery should have been. "I'm not going to spray paint your car in the parking lot or anything like that," Gardner said. "But I've definitely got it coming to me at some point."

The outfield corners projected to feature Frazier and Mike Tauchman, at least in the early going. The centerpiece of a July 2016 trade that sent left-handed reliever Andrew Miller to the Indians, Frazier was entering his fourth full year in the organization. Miller's professed flexibility out of the bullpen was a harbinger of things to come in terms of league-wide bullpen management, helping Cleveland reach the World Series that autumn. Yet the Yankees celebrated the acquisition of a talent that Cashman lauded as having "legendary" bat speed. From the very beginning, Frazier's brash, unapologetic love-me-or-hate-me personality made for a volatile mix in a clubhouse that leaned toward corporate calm.

When Frazier reported to spring training in 2017, he sported long locks of red hair peeking out from his ballcap. Girardi professed to have no issue, acknowledging that Frazier did not violate the club's grooming code, but others seemed irked. Sabathia walked to the mound for an exhibition start sporting a beard. That was interpreted as a clear message: if the rookie didn't have to conform, then a former Cy Young Award winner wouldn't either. Ultimately, Girardi told Frazier that, while he hadn't done anything wrong, the team would appreciate it if he got a trim. Not wanting to make more waves, Frazier unhappily acquiesced, grumbling as he eyed the buzz in a Clearwater, Florida, clubhouse restroom. "It seems like it's gotten a little more lenient," Frazier said years later. "Some guys might test the boundaries a little bit, but everyone's trying to be respectful of it. I think that they've given us more of a leash because we know the limit. Once we reach that limit, we take care of it ourselves. I wish that we could have a little bit of facial hair, I'm not going to lie."

Controversy would continue to follow the former first-round pick. Frazier's bat had been his calling card at every level of the minor league chain, and though he didn't expect to contend for Gold Gloves, he was an adequate defender. Traced to a concussion sustained by crashing into a chain-link fence the previous spring in Bradenton, Florida, that skill declined in 2019.

For months, Frazier quietly battled sensitivity to light and a loss of equilibrium, saying he felt like a fish out of water in the outfield. The low point came when a national television audience witnessed Frazier misplay three balls in an 8–5 loss to the Red Sox on a Sunday night in June. A crowd of reporters and camera operators circled Frazier's locker following the final out, but vice president of communications Jason Zillo found the rookie outfielder in the players' lounge. Frazier refused to emerge, prompting Zillo to inform the waiting media members that Frazier was was declining to speak. Gardner made his displeasure clear as he prepared to exit the clubhouse, loudly announcing: "Anyone need to talk to me?"

The Yankees departed to open a series against the Blue Jays in Toronto. Boone and Zillo counseled Frazier for more than an hour in the visiting clubhouse at Rogers Centre, informing him that he was responsible for being available after games. Because he dodged the questions, others like Gardner and Aaron Hicks had stepped in to answer for their teammate's misplays. Frazier nodded, then went off script for nine raw minutes in front of the microphones.

"I am confident 24/7, which is why I think people feel the need to knock me down," Frazier said. "I know I don't fit the mold of what some of the past and current Yankees are like, and that may be why it's a little bit harder for me to navigate every day. I am trying to be myself in here. Sometimes it feels like people have an issue with me just being myself."

As Frazier spoke, his teammates scattered, and some of their eyes were wide in disbelief. By the fifth minute of Frazier's address, only Masahiro Tanaka remained seated nearby, and the pitcher's face displayed a befuddled expression. In uniform that day as a special advisor, Reggie Jackson shook his head with frustration as Frazier continued: "I didn't feel like I needed to stand in front of everyone and explain myself. The plays were what they were. I sucked." Mr. October had fought his share of battles with the media decades earlier; he knew a losing argument when he heard one.

Though he would not produce the same volume of newspaper copy or Internet clicks, Tauchman enjoyed his lower profile. When the Yankees acquired Tauchman toward the end of spring training of 2019, the reporters simultaneously whipped out their smartphones to Google his unfamiliar name. There were shrugs as they discovered that the newest Yankee owned a .153 batting average in 52 career games for the Colorado Rockies, who played their home games in the offense-inflating altitude of Denver's Coors Field.

Once again, as with Urshela and Voit, the Yanks' analytics department had spotted an undervalued asset. A wallflower during two early-season stints with the Yanks in 2019, Tauchman was promoted after Stanton injured his knee making a June dive into third base and emerged as a contributor in the "Next Man Up" storyline. Boone favored Tauchman's mild temperament and his capability in any of the outfield spots. In 87 games, Tauchman compiled an excellent .277/.361/.504 slash line with 13 homers and 47 RBIs. It was an impressive season that ended three weeks too early; Tauchman's left calf popped in pursuit of a ball at Fenway Park in early September.

The most polarizing Yankee resided behind the plate. Gary Sánchez's boosters pointed to a powerful throwing arm and the 27-year-old's status as the fastest player in American League history to reach 100 home runs in terms of games played, offering the brand of muscle that teams generally do not receive from catchers. Sánchez's detractors decried his defensive shortcomings. The Yankees catcher led the major leagues with 34 passed balls during the 2017–18 campaigns. That issue was addressed during the '19 season, thanks to Sánchez's increased emphasis on ball blocking, but it came at a price. Advanced metrics suggested that Sánchez became so focused on ensuring that balls didn't skip to the backstop, he neglected his framing—the art of making borderline pitches look like strikes. In response, the Yankees hired catching coach Tanner Swanson away from the Minnesota Twins, hoping that Sánchez could replicate the improvements that Minnesota saw with Mitch Garver, another big-bodied catcher with a similar offensive profile.

The report date for pitchers and catchers was set for February 12, a date that commemorated the silver anniversary season at George M. Steinbrenner Field. As the city of Tampa grew, the Steinbrenners recognized the incentives of relocating operations to their adopted home city, abandoning a longtime spring home in Fort Lauderdale in favor of a massive complex constructed on the footprint of what was once a correctional facility. Originally named Legends Field, the ballpark featured dimensions that mimicked Yankee Stadium circa 1996—318 feet down the left-field line, 408 feet to center field, and 314 to right field. Longtime staffers still chuckle about the day during construction when Steinbrenner ordered an employee onto the snow-covered diamond in the Bronx, counting off steps to make sure the distances were correct.

Situated adjacent to Raymond James Stadium, the home of the NFL's Tampa Bay Buccaneers, Steinbrenner Field boasted seats for more than

11,000 fans. Three practice diamonds allowed the cast of 60 big league players to conduct their hitting and throwing drills efficiently. Another 200 minor leaguers were stationed a half mile away at the player development complex on Himes Avenue. That facility featured a military-style observation tower from which scouts and officials could easily switch their binoculars' gaze between the Double A to Triple A games, keeping tabs on the hottest prospects.

Boone arrived a week early, having loaded his four-door silver Mercedes S560 onto an Amtrak auto train in Lorton, Virginia. As a player, Boone considered seven weeks of spring training to be too much; generally speaking, hitters find their timing by the midpoint, while pitchers need more innings to build stamina. As a manager, Boone welcomed the additional days to roam the practice fields, believing it would give his team more time to fine-tune their fundamentals. "We feel like we've been a championship-caliber team for a few years now," Boone said. "We've been knocking on that door. We just haven't pushed through it yet."

Appropriately, Cole was one of the first players to take the ball when workouts shifted to the big field. A phalanx of photographers captured the righty's methodical preparation as he long-tossed across the right-field grass, then ascended a bullpen mound to pop Sánchez's glove with 25 fastballs and change-ups. "He's going to be a game-changer for us," Hal Steinbrenner raved. "The city's buzzing, and it's continued since the day we signed him."

Following Cole's final pitch, he spoke antimatedly for more than 10 minutes with Boone, pitching coach Matt Blake, and bullpen coach Mike Harkey, lending philosophical weight to the mundane first step toward facing big league hitters. In those early days, Cole dove into detail about the shape of his change-up and the counts he likes to use it in, what his arm action should look like, and what happens when he misses his spots. "He was different than pretty much anybody I've caught," said catcher Kyle Higashioka. "Most guys shake until they throw what they want or they give you total control and never question you. He knows how to pitch guys, but he also acknowledges that there's more than one way to pitch everyone. He wants there to be give and take with the catcher. He's not afraid to ask why."

In camp as a guest instructor, Pettitte said that Cole's intensity reminded him of Roger Clemens' snarl. Boone called the attention to detail "special," saying that the display confirmed everything that the Yankees believed they learned during those four-and-a-half hours in the Newport Beach suite. When Cole emerged from the Steinbrenner Field bullpen a week later, walking toward the mound for his first opportunity to face hitters, his adrenaline spiked with the cheers of about 1,500 sun-splashed fans. Cole had never received a standing ovation for a workout on a non-game day; the Pittsburgh Pirates and Astros didn't draw sizable crowds to their respective Florida spring training sites. In the days that followed, Cole's locker in the Steinbrenner Field clubhouse became a gathering site for teammates curious about the game's finer details. All were welcome—pitcher or hitter. "I feel like he was born for this place," Cashman said. "There's so many similarities to the CC Sabathia acquisition. He can be a transformative figure on the field every five days, and in that clubhouse the other four days, he checks that box. That's what we need in a frontline guy. Now we have to continue to make sure we have enough talent around him to put together a special run."

Cole looked the part, having swapped Astros orange for the Yankees' navy blue, but he still had to contend with his former teammates' actions. The largest cheating scandal to rock the sport since the 1919 Chicago "Black" Sox had stained Houston's triumphs. As whistleblower/pitcher Mike Fiers revealed to The Athletic in November, the Astros used an outfield camera to tip their hitters about incoming pitches. Fiers outlined a scheme in which live game action was monitored on a screen near Minute Maid Park's home dugout. Players and employees would then bang on a trash can to inform the batter if the catcher had called for a breaking ball or change-up.

Major League Baseball's investigation confirmed that the Astros used the system during the 2017 regular season and postseason, plus part of 2018, when Fiers had bounced from the Detroit Tigers to the Oakland A's. MLB granted players immunity in exchange for truthful testimony, limiting fallout to the suspensions and dismissals of Astros general manager Jeff Luhnow and manager A.J. Hinch. Also banned and fired was Red Sox manager Alex Cora, who masterminded the operation as Hinch's bench coach. The only active player named in the report was Carlos Beltran, whom the Mets had hired as their manager in November. Beltran vanished without filling out a single lineup card.

Judge recalled watching MLB Network and ESPN in those days, seeing the sign-stealing scandal overshadow all things sports. He believed more than ever that his team should have advanced to the World Series, especially in 2017, when the ALCS had gone seven games against Houston. That was a series in which the home team had won every game, as Judge and the Yankees lost each of the four contests at Minute Maid Park. Judge believed that he had been robbed.

His first response was of the silent variety. Judge scrolled back in his Instagram feed to November 2017, when he'd congratulated the Astros' Altuve on besting him in the race for the American League's Most Valuable Player award. Judge had a monster season, belting 52 homers and earning unanimous selection as the American League's Rookie of the Year. Still, voters selected Altuve by a wide margin; 27 of 30 first-place votes went to the diminutive middle infielder. Judge had accepted the snub, but only because he believed Altuve's performance was authentic. "I just was so sick to my stomach," Judge said. "I had a lot of respect for those guys and what they did for the city of Houston, an organization and a team that was in last place and eventually got to the World Series. Then to find out that it wasn't earned and they cheated, that didn't sit well with me. I just didn't feel like the post really meant the same anymore."

Suspicions of something hinky in Houston had been whispered throughout the American League, prompting several teams' complaints over the years, including the Yankees. Pitcher Zack Britton said that the players were frustrated by the league office's inaction. MLB had seen and heard no evil until Fiers spoke out, which is part of why Fiers put his name on the issue. That bitterness grew when Jimmy O'Brien dug into the Astros' 2017 video archives. An ardent fan who went by "Jomboy" in online circles, O'Brien rose to online prominence in July 2019—minutes after Boone was ejected from an otherwise sleepy afternoon game against the Tampa Bay Rays. The 30-year-old O'Brien had a knack for reading lips and the know-how to isolate game broadcast audio, both of which came in handy as Boone ranted to home-plate umpire Brennan Miller that his hitters were "savages in that fucking box." It wasn't G-rated, but it was funny, and the fans loved it. So did the players, who were wearing T-shirts emblazoned with "Savages" within days. The Yankees had a new rallying cry.

As the Astros scandal emerged, O'Brien used those skills to scour game videos from Minute Maid Park. One damning episode was from a September 2017 contest, in which Chicago White Sox pitcher Danny Farquhar heard banging from the dugout every time catcher Kevan Smith called for a change-up, a clear advantage for Houston batter Evan Gattis. "The Athletic's article talked about the Farquhar at-bat, and I thought, *That's out there. You can find that*," O'Brien said. "You could hear the banging. I knew it was going to be big, but I didn't realize it was going to leave sports. It reached people from all walks of life that like drama and scandals."

A suspicious Farquhar halted the game, calling Smith to the mound to change the signs. As one of more than five million people to view O'Brien's resulting breakdown, Cashman wondered how his own staffers had not caught on to the scheme. "We knew something was going on and we complained about it, but we didn't have the facts," Cashman said. "We tried every which way. They're doing something; we don't know what they're doing, we don't know how they're getting the signals. But it's clear as day. The whole industry knew about it. We weren't the only team complaining about it. Everybody was. We just could not figure out the intercept, so to speak."

Cole had a fantastic alibi for 2017, when most of the Astros' illicit activities took place—he was still pitching for the Pirates. He claimed to be unaware of any such activities during the '18 or '19 seasons, but the Yankees' suspicions remained high concerning other Astros. Some wondered why Altuve stopped his teammates from tearing off his uniform shirt after the pennant-winning homer. Could an electronic buzzer have tipped Altuve that Aroldis Chapman was about to throw a slider? It seemed far-fetched, but then so did the trash can scheme.

Altuve explained at the time that he was "too shy" to bare his chest in front of the postseason crowd, a comment that prompted snickers from his ballplaying brethren, especially given that Altuve seemed to be okay with posting beach and pool photos on his Instagram feed. Altuve vehemently denied the buzzer accusation through his agent Scott Boras, but some Yankees weren't convinced. Chapman called it "suspicious," and Sánchez delivered an early contender for the spring's best quote in response. "I can tell you that if I hit a homer and I get my team to the World Series," Sánchez said, flashing a broad smile, "they can rip off my pants. They can rip everything off. If I get my team to the World Series, hitting a walk-off homer like that, they can rip anything off."

Torres wondered aloud what would have stopped the Astros from continuing their scheme after winning a championship in 2017. The baby-faced shortstop was speaking from experience. He cheated, too—at video games. In the players' lounge at Steinbrenner Field, the Yankees were getting acquainted with the new version of *MLB 20: The Show* on their shared PlayStation. Torres boasted that he liked to peek at Severino's controller to see if his teammate pressed the buttons for fastball, slider, or change-up. Torres' gaudy digital batting average confirmed that it is much easier to hit if you know what's coming. "If you cheated in 2017 and you won, why wouldn't you do it the next year?" Torres said. "The next time, I'll do the same thing and I'll win. It's easy. That's why I don't believe it when guys say, 'Oh, we felt bad when we went home, so we tried not to do it.' Why would they stop?"

Severino laughed when he was informed of Torres' confession, saying that he had suspected something was awry in their video game showdowns. He was less amused by the Astros' hijinks. Severino was furious when The Athletic's report went live; three fifth-inning runs had chased him from Game 6 of the 2017 ALCS at Houston, a game that the Yankees lost. Now he wondered if Brian McCann's RBI double and Altuve's two-run single had been legitimate. "I remembered how many times I would look in the mirror and do my mechanics to see if I was tipping pitches," Severino said. "When you're pitching against a team that good, you spend hours in the video room looking at yourself, saying, 'What am I doing wrong?'"

In the weeks after Fiers went public, Boone mentally replayed the 2018 and '19 postseasons, wondering if the Astros and Red Sox utilized any devices that altered those series outcomes. During the '19 ALCS, the Yankees complained about hearing a high-pitched whistle coming from the Astros' dugout during Game 1, a claim which Hinch laughed off at the time. It didn't seem so ridiculous now, but to what effect had the scandal changed history? They'd never know for sure. "You're mad, frustrated, disappointed," Boone said. "I've struggled—like I'm sure a lot of people have—with making sense of it all and trying to wrestle my emotions. I don't think I'll ever totally get there. But you also know there's a time to move on. It's time to move on and look forward."

This, Boone said, was that time. As the manager outlined his plans for the upcoming season, he informed his players that there were three expectations: win the American League East, win the pennant, win the World Series. Focusing on the past would not get them closer to any of the three. It was time to power their energies into the future—whatever that might bring.

• CHAPTER 3 •

Shutdown

The cymbal crashes of Frank Sinatra's "Theme From New York, New York" echoed through the loudspeakers at George M. Steinbrenner Field, escorting thousands of fans toward the parking lot. It was March 6, and as the players' cleats clicked on the runway leading toward the home clubhouse, the group of normally-boisterous twentysomethings comprised a subdued bunch.

This exhibition went into the books as a 5–1 loss to the Baltimore Orioles, unquestionably the American League East's softest punching bag and coming off a season in which they'd lost 108 games. The New York Yankees had played in 13 exhibition games, winning eight, preparing for a season opener scheduled 20 days ahead. They'd just watched touted pitching prospect Deivi García cough up a pair of first-inning runs, then roll over as the Yankees' bats could not muster much against a sextet of Baltimore pitchers.

Gene Monahan, the 74-year-old athletic trainer who'd wrapped the aching ankles and elbows of every Yankee from Thurman Munson to Derek Jeter, carried his equipment bag and grunted, offering: "We'll get 'em tomorrow, boys." In a cinder block hallway, a group of reporters nodded toward the silver-haired Monahan, then continued scrolling on glowing smartphones as they awaited for clearance to enter manager Aaron Boone's office. The glass was always half full in the spring, where every player boasted of being in the best shape of his life, and each team remained tied for first place. It was absurd to place stock in the outcome of any single game—especially a Grapefruit League contest between the Yankees, whom Las Vegas frequently touted as a leading World Series contender, and the Orioles, the once-proud franchise of Jim Palmer and Brooks Robinson—now forecast to be hurtling toward a fourth consecutive last-place finish.

Corner a star player in the eighth inning of a spring training game and ask if his team is winning. The response likely will be a shrug. By the halfway point of these contests, most were already back at apartments or rooms rented on the team's dime, bronzing their biceps by the pool. That left the longshots wearing uniform numbers in the 70s and 80s to bust it down the baseline in the late innings, hoping to avoid another summer of riding buses in Triple A.

The clock read 9:29 PM as Boone made a hard right turn into his office and nodded toward Jason Zillo, the director of media relations, who waved at the dozen reporters clutching digital recorders and notepads. They passed through the 25-year-old steel door frame of an office once inhabited by Joe Torre and then Joe Girardi, evidenced by the fading photographs of the five Yankees rosters to claim a championship since 1996.

Now the room belonged to Boone. He kept the office sparsely decorated. The cabinets of a mahogany L-shaped desk were littered with snack food and freebies from the Topps baseball card company, most of which was squirreled away for his four children. Boone conducted his postgame briefings at a circular fiberglass table that could have been procured at any Staples or Office Depot, using his lineup card to nudge aside a national edition of the *New York Post*. The NBA's Brooklyn Nets were about to fire coach Kenny Atkinson, improbably making Boone—hired in December 2017—the longest-tenured manager or coach in New York sports.

Had the newsprint been pointed toward the fluorescent ceiling lights, the group in Boone's office would have eyed some unsettling dispatches. The state of New York had confirmed 89 cases of the mysterious and deadly coronavirus, including a dozen in New York City. The spread was so new that mayor Bill de Blasio rattled off identifying characteristics: a 33-year-old Uber driver from the Rockaways, two Brooklyn women in their 60s and 70s who had cruised to Egypt, a 30-something Brooklyn man who had been to Italy. Nationwide, more than 300 cases were known, including 17 deaths. Offered an opportunity to ease fears, New York governor Andrew Cuomo declined an invitation to ease public fears, telling reporters, "I'm not urging calm. I'm urging reality."

These were warning signs of what was to come. That outside world bled into the happy-happy-springtime vibe via the sizeable dry-erase board mounted on a far wall of Boone's office. The board had been carved into a calendar, denoting the remaining days until the team was supposed to head north for a March 26 opener against the Orioles at Baltimore's Camden Yards. Each box featured a magnet denoting that day's starting pitcher along with any pertinent information that Boone needed—perhaps a VIP who would watch batting practice on the field or a reminder about the annual luncheon to benefit the Tampa branch of the Boys & Girls Club. Someone had scrawled in black marker where a young hurler's name should have appeared. Tonight's Yankees starting pitcher was "Coronavirus."

Following two queries about García's performance and three relating to a passed ball that skipped past catcher Gary Sánchez, *Post* reporter George King rolled his index finger and thumb over the salt-and-pepper stubble that covered his chin. A veteran who worked a clubhouse with a bartender's gruff amiability, King asked if the team had spoken about the virus. Boone confirmed that they had, stating that a doctor had visited the clubhouse before the game to provide a PowerPoint presentation. "They said it was nothing to worry about; please don't be concerned," Gerrit Cole later said. "They said that masks don't do anything, so please just wash your hands, practice good hygiene, and you're going to be okay. We had no idea."

That same day, president Donald Trump visited the Centers for Disease Control in Atlanta, praising scientists for their swift response. Few Americans outside of the government's inner circles understood the magnitude of the situation. Two months earlier, Trump was told by national security adviser Robert C. O'Brien that the coronavirus would comprise his presidency's greatest national security threat, as captured by *The Washington Post* journalist Bob Woodward in his book, *Rage*. The world was facing a health emergency on par with the flu pandemic of 1918, which killed an estimated 50 million people worldwide. In a recorded interview for that book, Trump told

Woodward on February 7, "You just breathe the air, and that's how it's passed. And so that's a very tricky one. That's a very delicate one. It's also more deadly than your…strenuous flus. This is deadly stuff." That information would not be stated publicly for months, and Trump later admitted to downplaying that knowledge to avoid creating panic.

So the marching orders, in Yankees camp at least, were to keep calm and carry on. A different reporter pounced, asking Boone if players were discouraged from signing autographs for fans. Boone stammered, and Zillo interjected, offering that the medical professionals had talked about risks involved in person-to-person contact in any form, including signing credit card receipts at restaurants. If you couldn't use the pen from your server at The Cheesecake Factory, it wasn't a good idea to grab the sweaty blue Sharpies that protruded through the chain-link fences on the practice fields.

Seemingly relieved by the assist, Boone joked that the team had even practiced bumping elbows rather than shaking hands during that game. It felt awkward, just as an exchange had been with one of the coaches that day. As third-base coach Phil Nevin passed from the clubhouse to the coaches' room, the former big leaguer offered a fist bump to Lindsey Adler, the Yankees beat reporter for The Athletic. After the contact, Adler produced a single-use Purell wipe, which she remembers finding in a holiday clearance bin. Nevin was offended, barking, "Oh, is that where we are now?" She replied: "That's definitely where we are now."

"I was kind of a germaphobe to begin with, but that was definitely when it started to get strange," Adler said. "I remember it coming up a lot in the clubhouse."

As Boone bid his questioners farewell for the night, the newsprint on its way to the skipper's desk was growing more concerning. By March 9, Wall Street contended with a 2,000-point drop to the Dow Jones Industrial Index, and cable news viewers inhaled stunning video of empty streets from the nationwide quarantine of Italy. Major League Baseball announced it was joining the National Basketball Association, National Hockey League, and

Major League Soccer in temporarily banning all non-essential personnel from clubhouses, stating that they still intended to play all games as scheduled.

These were developments that Hal Steinbrenner feared were coming. His wife, Christina, lived in Milan for four years and regularly communicated with many friends in Italy's second most populous city. They heard disturbing reports stemming from Fashion Week, an international traveling circus of luxury retailers, deep-pocketed customers, Instagram influencers, executives, and reporters that descended upon Milan in the middle of February. Several designers canceled events, and the tour's conclusion sent scores of well-dressed attendees home to London, Paris, and New York, some undoubtedly carrying more than the latest Gucci bag. "It was just a matter of time to me, based on a lot of conversations my wife had with our friends in Milan about how quickly it spread," Steinbrenner said. "Italians love New York, and they love the fashion aspects of New York as well."

Charged with the unenviable task of enforcing access restrictions, Woody Saylor stood in the bowels of Steinbrenner Field the next morning. Once a postmaster for the United States Postal Service, Saylor's burly build and Fu Manchu mustache offered a remarkable likeness to the Hall of Fame reliever Goose Gossage—now a persona non grata dumped as a guest instructor after one too many get-off-my-lawn tirades about Brian Cashman's army of analytical "nerds" ruining the game. Yet Saylor remained a spring fixture, savoring his security guard title for the access it provided to his favorite team and the bonus of escaping frigid Pennsylvania winters.

Saylor repeatedly held up a hand, denying entry to anyone who wasn't on the Yankees roster. The media was now barred, along with anyone who lacked an ironclad reason to breathe locker room air. The scouts vanished, as did representatives from bat and glove companies. Even the team chef had to find somewhere else to prepare the players' omelettes. "Shit hit the fan," Saylor said. "I couldn't shake hands, couldn't fist bump, elbow bump. They told me *nobody* was permitted."

A Yankees employee counted off six feet in the hallway outside the clubhouse, using retractable belt barriers borrowed from the ticket windows to create an interview rectangle. Club executives sent memorandums urging players and coaches to wash their hands frequently with soap and water, use hand sanitizer that contained at least 60 percent alcohol, and avoid contact with anyone who appeared sick. "I'd like to think," quipped Aaron Hicks, the Bombers' switch-hitting center fielder, "that I was pretty good at washing my hands before this."

By this point, Yankees executives had already received word from Cuomo that their April 2 home opener was in jeopardy. Outside of the ballpark, it seemed to be business as usual: more than 9,000 snowbirds forked over $10 bills to park vehicles on the grassy field outside Raymond James Stadium, home of the NFL's Tampa Bay Buccaneers. There were no masks seen as the fans made a half-mile trek over the highway, filtering through the turnstiles to watch Gerrit Cole take on the Toronto Blue Jays.

The right-hander gave the crowd a good show, bouncing back from a windswept afternoon in Lakeland, Florida, when the Detroit Tigers had made the ace look ordinary by belting four homers—two apiece from Miguel Cabrera and Travis Demeritte. The Detroit start saw Cole at less than 100 percent; he had texted team officials a few days prior, reporting a fever and soreness near the back of his throat. The Yankees tested Cole for strep and advised him not to report to the ballpark; his symptoms dissipated two days later.

At the time, Cole said that he did not believe it was the coronavirus; that would be affirmed by numerous tests later in the year, including those seeking antibodies. Back to full strength, Cole's fastball touched 100 mph twice as he struck out six Jays in three-and-one-third innings—a strong tune-up effort ahead of what would have been his Opening Day start. Saylor said that Cole was the first player he spotted wearing a mask inside Steinbrenner Field. The pitcher explained that he did not want to take any chances with a pregnant wife at home. "It was a scary time for us, especially with the baby on the way," Cole said. "My reaction was probably the same as a lot of people: a lot of uncertainty, a lot of nerves, and a little bit of fear."

Other developments raised suspicion. Cole did not expect to be teamed with backup catcher Kyle Higashioka that day, but Sánchez was absent from camp, having reported a fever that again stoked fears of the coronavirus having infiltrated the clubhouse. Cashman said that Sánchez tested positive for influenza, which doctors said made tests for COVID-19 unnecessary, but the increasing chatter about virology was unnerving for those around the team.

About half of the roster gathered in the parking lot beyond Steinbrenner Field's left-field fence and boarded a pair of chartered buses that evening, shuttling to Florida's Treasure Coast for a two-day trip to play the Miami Marlins in Jupiter and the Washington Nationals in West Palm Beach. Boone and Nevin burned the 195-mile drive by sipping wine and savoring a guilty pleasure, refusing to disembark until the season finale of *The Bachelor* had concluded. Boone laughed about it later, saying that it was "not a good look."

With their broadcast schedule dark, the television and radio teams enjoyed a lengthy dinner at Eddie V's, an upscale steak and seafood restaurant on Tampa's Boy Scout Boulevard. Amid the clinking glasses, there was plenty of shop talk, like whether Cole was a better Cy Young Award candidate than the New York Mets' Jacob deGrom. Michael Kay, the television play-by-play announcer, recalled feeling uneasy. "It must have been like 20 people at the table, all cramped," Kay said. "Part of me didn't want to go because I'd read too much about the coronavirus already. The dinner was a tradition since we started YES [Network] in 2002, and I didn't want to bail on it. Everybody in the restaurant acted like the world was normal, but you just felt like the clock was ticking. That was the last vestige of any normalcy."

Radio announcer John Sterling, 81 years young, sipped from a dirty martini and wondered aloud about the growing health crisis. Sterling was hardly your average cable news consumer; he loved to boast about a New Jersey apartment that augmented its Hudson River views with two television screens—one for live sports and one for films from Hollywood's golden era. Yet current events had infiltrated even Sterling's regimented media diet. "Everyone went around the table; we had a long talk about it," Sterling said.

"Well, we get out of the restaurant—let's say at 10:00 or 11:00—and then the first thing you hear is that the NBA canceled their season."

Had the group been seated within view of the flat-screens at the bar, they may have witnessed the remarkable events taking place, a few clicks of the remote apart. At 9:02 PM, President Trump addressed the nation from the Oval Office, reading from a teleprompter as he spoke of "the coronavirus outbreak that started in China and is now spreading throughout the world."

During Trump's 10-minute address, he announced a ban on all travel from Europe to the United States (except the United Kingdom) beginning on March 13, joining an existing travel ban from China. As the major networks carried Trump's address, ESPN had a broadcast from American Airlines Arena in Dallas, where the Dallas Mavericks hosted the Denver Nuggets. News had been slamming the sports world all day—the Golden State Warriors were preparing to play without fans in attendance, as were several college conferences. A game between the Utah Jazz and Oklahoma City Thunder was postponed without explanation. Ryan Ruocco, a familiar voice to Yankees fans as part of the YES Network's revolving door of announcers, partnered with Doris Burke to call the Denver–Dallas matchup for ESPN in an atmosphere that he described as "surreal." "Doris and I had the feeling going into the game that it was going to be the last time we were broadcasting a game the way we normally did," Ruocco said. "I thought maybe our next broadcast would be from the studio, or there wouldn't be fans. We both went into it thinking, *Let's enjoy tonight because it feels like things are about to change.*"

Their broadcast was in the second quarter when reports circulated that Utah Jazz center Rudy Gobert had tested positive for COVID-19, days after the 27-year-old big man flippantly touched microphones and recorders following a news conference. The ball bounced out of bounds, and Ruocco prepared to send the broadcast to a commercial when producer Ian Grucka's voice crackled into his earpiece: "Ten, nine, Ryan, tease we have *major* breaking NBA news on the other side of the break, three, two, one."

Ruocco directed the broadcast back to the studio, where insider Adrian Wojnarowski announced that the NBA was suspending the season indefinitely.

Mark Cuban's eyes bulged as he stared into the glowing screen of his cell phone, as the Mavericks owner was captured on video from his courtside seat with his mouth agape. Ruocco and Burke fidgeted at the announcers' table, realizing that the game in front of them had shifted into a shocking news story. The unseen enemy was closer than they knew; uncharacteristically fatigued that day, Burke was diagnosed with COVID-19 shortly thereafter. "It felt like the planet was shifting off its axis," Ruocco said. "We felt the weight of that uncertainty and trying to appropriately steer the broadcast that night, knowing that it wasn't your normal NBA broadcast. It was a historic event. When we got done, we were emotionally shaken and drained."

Twitter had transformed into even more of a raging dumpster fire than usual, so it seemed appropriate that a photograph of a plastic garbage can accompanied the next domino to fall. Actor Tom Hanks announced on social media that he and wife Rita Wilson tested positive for the coronavirus, having experienced fatigue, colds, and body aches while traveling in Australia. "Well, now," Hanks wrote in the caption of the photo, which showed a used surgical glove resting atop a plastic bag. "What to do next?"

Indeed, what to do? Major League Baseball remained silent, so those Yankees not on the travel rosters pointed their vehicles toward Steinbrenner Field at sunrise. Brett Gardner shagged a few fly balls and called it a half-day, saying that the steamy weather probably had the fish biting. Gardner's preferred version of social distancing was being alone on a boat in the middle of Tampa Bay. Erik Kratz brought his sons out to watch their dad hit in the batting cage. Approaching age 40 and in camp as a non-roster invitee, the journeyman catcher recognized that he would not have many more opportunities to share a moment like that with his boys. "But I didn't know that we were going to be shut down for months and I wouldn't be able to get back on the field with them," Kratz said.

Cole followed his usual routine, ascending the bullpen mound and pumping fastballs to prepare for an Opening Day start that no longer seemed guaranteed. Across the state in West Palm Beach, the other half of the Yankees laced their spikes and prepared to face the Nationals. As more than 8,000 fans lathered in sunscreen and filtered into the seats of the Ballpark of the Palm Beaches, Cashman clicked off the Fleetwood Mac-heavy playlist filling his rental car—"Me, myself, and I, just singing away," he said—and milled in the seats near his team's dugout. The GM knew more than he was letting on. The team had already made coronavirus-related decisions in their scouting ranks, sending their professional scouts home and barring amateur scouts from booking flights. There would soon be no games for them to watch. "I was told before the game that the announcement was coming, that they were going to shut down after that day's game," Cashman said. "They told us, 'You can play that game and then be done.'"

Boone watched his team hit on the field in West Palm, sensing that he was staring at the last nine innings he'd manage for a while. Boone trotted toward the dugout as batting practice concluded and saw numerous hands outstretched, seeking autographs or handshakes. Peering through blue sunglasses, Boone thought about offering a hand, then told a fan: "Come on, man! The NBA just canceled last night."

As the Yankees finished off their 6–3 victory, MLB announced that it would cancel the remainder of spring training and delay the beginning of the regular season by "at least two weeks." Boone huddled with his coaches on the bus ride back to Tampa, swapping thoughts on how they could keep their pitchers' arms in motion over what they figured would be a brief delay. As an active player, Boone woke in a Chicago hotel room on the morning of September 11, 2001, turning on the television to learn that the world had changed. Seven days after one of the darkest events in American history, Boone was back in his Cincinnati Reds uniform, pounding a glove at third base. Boone believed that baseball would answer the coronavirus shutdown with a similar return to normalcy. "At that point, I didn't really understand," Boone said.

The next morning, the players gathered at Steinbrenner Field to discuss their options. Fresh from a conference call that included Dan Halem, the league's deputy commissioner, managing general partner Hal Steinbrenner and Cashman entered the room. Cashman cleared his throat and glumly relayed that there was no foreseeable restart date for camp, a comment that generated disbelief among the players. *How could they not know?* If they wished, the players could stay in Tampa, where Steinbrenner pledged to keep the ballpark operational on a limited basis. They could also return to their respective homes. The least desirable option for all involved, given the increasing outbreak in New York City, was to fly north and train at Yankee Stadium. "That was just a tough meeting," Steinbrenner said. "You could see the disappointment in their faces. We had such high hopes for the season, and my goodness—at that point, we had no idea if there would be a season or not."

One of the players piped up, asking Steinbrenner for guidance. "I remember one of the questions was: 'Would you prefer that we stay here and work out?'" Steinbrenner said. "And I said, 'Absolutely.' Because I knew it was going to be safe here. Whatever gyms they were going to, we didn't know what it was going to be, where it was going to be. I made it clear to them that as long as MLB was okay with using weight rooms and non-formal workouts, I was more than happy to keep this as the safest place in Tampa."

The players unanimously agreed that they should remain together, holding informal workouts at Steinbrenner Field. Doing so, they believed, would give them an advantage if play resumed quickly. Pulling double duty as the team's representative for the MLB Players' Association, Zack Britton said that the players understood that the situation was more serious than anything they had experienced in their careers, but there seemed to be no panic. Given the team's wealth of resources in the area, including connections with hospitals and medical professionals, Tampa was where they wanted to be. "Once Steinbrenner addressed the team, we were like, 'We're just going to hang tight,'" Britton said. "We all wanted to stay together. I think everyone was unsure about what was going on and how severe it was. We were thinking that maybe somebody would get a handle on it in a few weeks and we'd be back."

The position players usually complain that spring training runs two weeks too long under normal circumstances, and now the Yankees had signed up for a camp with no end date. They'd arrive around 8:00 AM to hit in the indoor cages, toss from bullpen mounds, pump iron, and receive treatment before clocking out around noon, rolling the clock back to the free-form days before pitchers and catchers reported. All the while, they would keep their cell phones close by, scanning social media for the latest updates.

The rhythms of baseball provided a sense of normalcy until they ventured away from the stadium. When pitcher Masahiro Tanaka visited a grocery store with his wife, Mai, the couple was stunned to see barren shelves. Walmart and Target looked like scenes out of Florida's hurricane preparation playbook, as harried shoppers piled their carts high with bottled water, toilet paper, and canned goods. "I don't know what to do. I don't think anybody does," Tanaka said.

Each player had an app on their cell phone called Teamworks, generally used by bench coach Carlos Mendoza to distribute the expected report times and workout plans. Software originally intended to make sure players didn't miss batting practice was swiftly repurposed, now pushing files with titles like "How to Make Hand Sanitizer.PDF."

The unified Camp Yankee unraveled within 72 hours, shaken when one of the organization's minor leaguers tested positive for the coronavirus—the first known case to impact professional baseball. It was Denny Larrondo, a 17-year-old pitcher from Cuba who pitched 32⅓ innings in the Gulf Coast League the previous year. Larrondo had spent a quiet night in his hotel, ordering a pizza for dinner, then awoke complaining of fever and fatigue. When tests for influenza and strep were negative, Larrondo was sent to Tampa General Hospital, where he received the organization's first coronavirus test. A laboratory in Tallahassee confirmed the positive result within 48 hours. Larrondo's roommate, outfielder Estevan Florial, had been with the Yankees on their trip to Florida's East Coast. "I rushed over to the minor league facility and said, 'Get him off the field,'" Cashman said. "I met with Florial and said, 'We need to take you to get tested. It could be nothing, but we need to be sure.'"

Florial's test was negative, but the Hillsborough County Department of Health advised the organization to shutter both Steinbrenner Field and the minor league complex. This was a time in which players and coaches were still joking about social distance. "Hey, six feet! You're too close to me!" Nevin announced during a workout in early March, laughing. That changed quickly.

Though the team said that Larrondo had not interacted with any players on the big league roster—Larrondo hadn't even set foot inside Steinbrenner Field—some players still were concerned about possible exposure. "The flu goes around spring training, and guys always have colds because there are so many people in contact," Britton said. "I was worried. If you're saying there are cases in our system, guys go back and forth to minor league camp all the time."

In camp as a non-roster invitee, Kratz, the veteran catcher, remembers being at the practice fields when that directive came down. "I was still supposed to get one more at-bat, and they pulled us off the field, 'Let's go. We've got to get out of here,'" Kratz said. "They just told us we have to go, so we left. It felt like, 'Oh, man, something bad happened.'"

The Yankees hired an outside firm to douse all player areas at both complexes with two coats of a disinfecting bleach-like mist, which Cashman called "due diligence." More than two decades at the beck and call of the unpredictable, combustible George Steinbrenner helped Cashman navigate this latest crisis with a cool touch, shelving his usual duties of roster management to contain the latest developments. The task grew more challenging when a second minor leaguer was also diagnosed with COVID-19. Cashman's take in the moment proved prescient. "Whether it's in our personal world or professional world," Cashman said, "I think we all are going to experience that someone you know might have it."

The team ordered all minor leaguers, coaches, and staff to self-quarantine for two weeks. Most of the players scattered in four hotels near the ballpark; a few rented apartments. Eschewing his usual workday uniform of a tucked-in polo and khakis in favor of flip-flops and a T-shirt, Cashman made the rounds with employees, delivering pre-packaged meals in the parking lots each morning. "The food was really good, to be quite honest," Cashman said. "I took some for myself every now and then." The most popular man at those stops was Ben Tuliebitz, the Yankees' traveling secretary. Tuliebitz doled out cash each morning, handing $75 to each player—their usual meal money plus a $50 quarantine bonus.

Most of the minor leaguers plunged into Netflix marathons and online game tournaments. Jake Agnos, a 22-year-old lefty from Virginia, killed hours in his rented Airbnb by watching YouTube clips that taught him to play the ukulele. Others participated in what they dubbed the "Quarantine Workout Challenge," sharing videos with family members back home that included races against ducks and pushing pickup trucks through vacant parking lots.

As COVID-19 cases rose nationwide, MLB issued another directive, instructing players to avoid all activities where they assembled in "significant numbers" or would be unable to practice social distancing protocols. Cashman requested another head count, seeking to determine how many players intended to keep reporting to Steinbrenner Field. Rumors of an imminent nationwide travel ban circulated amongst the players, and the attendance record dwindled. Five days of batting practice and ground balls with no games were enough for Luke Voit; the first baseman loaded his pickup truck and steered toward his Missouri home. "We were trying to stay, but Tampa was becoming a hot spot," Voit said. "It just kept getting worse and worse."

The exodus had begun. Riding the elevator to the fifth floor of the Lantower Westshore apartment complex, pitcher Jordan Montgomery wrestled with his options. As he clutched the leash attached to the collar of his golden retriever, Tuck, Montgomery did some quick math. It was only a seven-hour drive to his hometown of Sumter, South Carolina, one they could probably make on two tanks of gasoline and a few bathroom breaks. But what to do then? The gyms at home were almost certainly shuttered, as were the ballfields of local high schools and colleges. "I'm not going to have anyone to throw to," Montgomery lamented.

Montgomery eventually decided to join the caravan of trucks and SUVs hitting the interstate. Relaying guidance from the MLBPA, Britton told his teammates that they should go wherever they'd be most comfortable for four to six weeks. Aaron Judge, Giancarlo Stanton, DJ LeMahieu, and Luis Severino were among the few who pledged to stick it out at Steinbrenner Field.

Even a baseball lifer like Boone felt the pull of home. There were no more lineup cards to fill out, and his wife Laura could use the backup with their four children entering the brave new world of online schooling. Behind the wheel of his Mercedes once more, Boone fiddled with the radio, landing on the mellow soft rock of his favorite SiriusXM station: The Bridge. He rolled toward Dr. Martin Luther King Boulevard, tapped the turn signal, and held his left index and middle fingers up in a peace sign, intending to reach North Carolina before nightfall. "Stay safe, y'all," the manager said, depressing his right foot to the accelerator.

• CHAPTER 4 •

QUARANTINE

About 1,100 miles from Steinbrenner Field's padlocked gates, the trees were still bare outside the property line of Gerrit Cole's new two-acre lot in Greenwich, Connecticut. Pedestrians passed beyond a three-foot stone wall as the New York Yankees ace wore a glove on his left hand, lobbing to his new throwing partner on a sunny 40-degree Sunday afternoon. Twenty-six weeks pregnant with their first child, Amy Cole stood about 60 feet away, urging her husband to air his arm out.

Come on, she said, flashing the competitiveness that had once earned a roster spot on the UCLA Bruins softball squad. A younger sister of San Francisco Giants shortstop Brandon Crawford, Amy was no stranger to the ballfield, having played the sport since age five. Cole increased velocity as his wife danced across their yellowed blades of grass, snaring the ball and returning fire with increasingly loud pops. Observing from a safe distance, Aaron Boone chuckled and dug into his pants pocket. This was too good not to document, Boone thought, clutching his smartphone and pressing record on a clip that would swiftly go viral. "Let's tighten up your footwork there, Gerrit," Boone teased.

It was March 22, and the schedule said that Boone should have been in a dugout for the final Florida exhibition of the spring, playing host to the Detroit Tigers. Boone and his coaches would have been debating how many pitchers they should carry on the Opening Day roster and reminding players that they needed to present their passports to Canadian customs officials when the flight touched down for a two-game exhibition series against the Toronto Blue Jays in Montreal.

Instead, the manager and his most valuable pitcher were in a suburban neighborhood near Putnam Lake, a few miles from where the Merritt Parkway passes the Burning Tree Country Club. Boone landed in the area after being hired by the Yankees in 2017, relocating his family from Scottsdale, Arizona. As such, Boone could advise the young couple on topics of interest, like school systems or the best local coffee shops. Unfortunately, Boone came up empty when his ace wondered when—or if—the season would get underway. "Overall, it really sucked," Boone said. "But there were a lot of good things about being home, being around family, cooking a lot of meals together. We'd be out in the driveway, shooting hoops. We played a lot of H-O-R-S-E. We got a Peloton bike, so I was riding that a lot. To watch the seasons change from my front porch was kind of cool; that's one part I really enjoyed."

Thirty miles southeast of where Boone stood, New York City was the epicenter of the coronavirus pandemic, where shuttered bars and boutiques lined what should have been lively streetscapes. There were no matinees on Broadway; all the shows closed on March 12. Public schools emptied on March 16. More than 10,000 New Yorkers had tested positive for COVID-19, accounting for nearly half of the United States' confirmed cases. There was no St. Patrick's Day's parade, the flow of green beer stanched by an order barring bars and restaurants from in-person dining. In scenes to be repeated in other cities, New York hospital officials expressed alarm about shortages of masks and ventilators.

Governor Andrew Cuomo ordered the Empire State's businesses to keep non-essential workers at home. That included Yankee Stadium, where the ground crew should have been dragging the infield for an April 2 home opener against the Blue Jays. Back on March 11, after the World Health Organization first declared COVID-19 to be a global pandemic, team employees had been told that they should work from home through the weekend so crews could disinfect the ballpark. That was only part of the story; the team had hired an outside firm to conduct pathogen testing throughout the clubhouse and the offices.

Told that their existing setup was lacking, the team invested in hospital-quality CASPR in-duct units that pumped small amounts of hydrogen peroxide, killing viruses in the air and on surfaces. It was months before the Yankees reactivated the employee access cards, leaving office plants to wither. Lunches and snacks perished in the refrigerators, and one worker lamented the unopened boxes of Girl Scout cookies on his desk, as the Thin Mints and Caramel deLites gathered dust. "The week of Friday the 13th—great day, right?—I told most of the staff to only come in as necessary," said Lonn Trost, the Yankees' chief operating officer. "Everybody had to be out by the 13th because we were disinfecting the stadium. I came in to pick up 13 or 14 bankers boxes of files, began to work at home, and everyone else did the same thing."

In the days since Zack Britton told the players to go where they would be most comfortable for the next four to six weeks, the Yankees' roster had scattered. A small number remained at Steinbrenner Field, where DJ LeMahieu thought that the practice routines were keeping him "sane." LeMahieu reasoned that the virus stats did not seem any better in his home state of Michigan. Tyler Wade was in a similar circumstance; unwilling to board a flight to his home state of California, Wade saw no logic in a cross-country drive to the Los Angeles suburbs, where Governor Gavin Newsom had already announced a statewide lockdown. "We prepared like we were going to pick back up the next day," Wade said. "If I didn't think there was going to be a season, I would have gone home and spent time with my family. I just had a gut feeling. I was like, 'No way we don't play a single game this year.'"

Some Yankees made their year-round homes in the Tampa, Florida, area, like left-hander J.A. Happ, who had discovered Clearwater's celebrated white sand beaches a decade prior while with the Philadelphia Phillies. Hitting coach Marcus Thames also lived in Clearwater, regularly making the 20-minute drive over the Courtney Campbell Causeway in a pickup truck. Once inside Steinbrenner Field, Thames would snap on a pair of surgical gloves, then cover them with batting gloves to lob meaty fastballs to hitters. Thames wore a cloth mask as he aired his arm out, sometimes grooving pitches to infielder Miguel Andújar, who opted for a black balaclava—the hooded article of clothing that big leaguers occasionally sport during frigid April or October games. It was almost certainly the first time one was worn on a Florida diamond. "With the very few guys that were at the facility, there were some sad weeks," said bench coach Carlos Mendoza. "We didn't even want to be playing. We were going to the stadium and doing workouts, but there was no energy. Guys still came in and did the work, but they were like, 'Why am I throwing a side or taking 80 swings?' We didn't know when Opening Day was going to be, so it was just weird."

When their workdays were complete, some of the players found outdoor activities in the sunshine, like boat fishing excursions and Clearwater Beach visits. With their complex sealed, the few minor leaguers remaining in Tampa occasionally donned their team-issued T-shirts to toss baseballs across vacant parking lots, finding one such location between an Extended Stay America and a shuttered dance club. Few noticed. The Tampa Bay area was in the early stages of its Tom Brady frenzy, as some fans peeked over the walls of a rented Davis Islands mansion, whose landlord was Derek Jeter, in hopes of spotting the future Super Bowl LV MVP. Brian Cashman remained on the ground in Florida, handling fallout from the positive minor league tests, but most of the staff had dispersed.

Unable to conduct their regular face-to-face meetings, the team grew familiar with Zoom. A cloud-based software platform founded in 2011, Zoom was advertised as a user-friendly teleconferencing solution, making it an indispensable tool during the pandemic. Boone participated in daily Zoom calls with analysts, coaches, front-office members, and scouts for three weeks, comparing notes on each player in the system. Bench coach Phil Nevin was the first to crack up the other participants by altering his virtual backgrounds, and Boone sometimes kept the mood light by wearing a football helmet. On one occasion, the players attended what Boone described as his "State of the Union address," a session that swiftly devolved into the smack talking and ribbing usually heard within the clubhouse walls. It was a friendly reminder of the camaraderie that seemed to be building before the team departed camp. "That was a lot of fun," Boone said, "just to get on and see guys making fun of one another."

Unable to observe his pupils in person, Matt Blake leaned upon his previous experience running a pitching academy in Sudbury, Massachusetts. The neophyte pitching coach created a Google Sheets document and shared the private link with Yankees players and staff members, requesting that hurlers input their actions every day so the team could keep tabs on their progress. Relievers threw twice a week to remain sharp while starting pitchers settled back into their offseason programs.

When Britton threw 25 fastballs and change-ups in his Austin, Texas, gymnasium, zipping them past a dummy planted in the batter's box, the workload went into the spreadsheet. The same was true when Deivi García tossed 20 pitches to his brother across an empty Dominican Republic road. Aroldis Chapman popped a friend's glove outside his Miami mansion; Chad Green threw into a net in a Louisville, Kentucky, public park. Jonathan Loaisiga latched on with a pro team in his native Nicaragua, appearing in four games. Clarke Schmidt and his father Dwight scanned the shelves of The Home Depot in the Atlanta area, finding the necessary tools to construct a backyard mound. "We ended up looking on Pinterest, and there was a diagram," Schmidt said. "It took probably five or six hours. My dad was an engineer in college, so he knows what he's doing. It was really good. We still have it in the backyard. I still use it."

The Google document kept a space for pitchers to leave notes where they might mention what their focus had been that day or their estimated intensity level. "The guys that had technology available like Rapsodo—that gave us even better understanding of what was coming out of their hands," Blake said. "We didn't know when we were going to start, but we knew we had to stay ready. That centralized document allowed the guys to see what the others were doing, so they could crowdsource about what the throwing program should look like."

Recent advances in technology also proved invaluable for the media members covering the team. Before the shutdown, Meredith Marakovits had ordered a ring light and lavalier microphones for her Clearwater, Florida, condominium, testing the equipment with happy hour segments on her social media channels. It was supposed to provide a fun diversion when the YES Network was dark, but Marakovits was ahead of the curve. Her living room became a makeshift television studio, checking in for light-hearted chats with players and coaches. "We called it *YES: We're Here*," Marakovits said. "We started off just saying hello to people and letting them know we were going to provide them with entertainment of some sort during the pandemic. I'm doing this all off my laptop and I realized we could do TV like this. It doesn't look the same, but it's still getting done, and we're giving people content to take their minds off what's going on in the world."

Still unpacking boxes in his new home, Cole enjoyed frequent visits from Amazon delivery drivers, having been about a week ahead of a nationwide crush that emptied the e-commerce powerhouse's shelves of gym equipment. His search queries included a workout bench, cables, dumbbells, box jumps, step-ups, and a rubber floor mat—everything he'd need to keep his body fine-tuned without venturing outside the property line.

There were numerous days that Cole knocked on Adam Ottavino's door, stealing a few minutes on the hurler's portable outdoor mound. Driving his two-seater Porsche north on Interstate 95 following camp, Ottavino had been chatting with Cole on speakerphone when he mentioned his budding pitching laboratory. That was catnip for a self-professed pitching nut like Cole. Steps from where his young daughters kept *Frozen II* on a perpetual loop, Ottavino proudly showcased his collection of high-tech gizmos, measuring data like spin rate and spin efficiency, to the intrigued Cole. They called upon bullpen catcher Radley Haddad to squat behind the plate, providing a target. "We'd just trade off inning by inning, trying to keep it like a game situation," Cole said. "It was a balance of trying to keep your arm going, but not wasting bullets."

Boone and assistant hitting coach P.J. Pilittere liked to swing by in the afternoons to watch, occasionally standing in as hitters. Boone collected 1,017 hits during a 12-year career in the big leagues, and Pilittere played eight seasons in the Yankees' minor league system. Still, they would have struggled to make decent contact against either hurler, whose repertoires seemed to be close to top form. "It was pretty humbling," Pilittere said. "Standing in there with these guys letting it rip, it just further reinforced to me how difficult it is to hit. That gave me a great perspective in trying to coach our guys."

Cole repaid the Ottavinos for their hospitality by cooking several dinners. An aspiring chef specializing in Italian cuisine, Cole learned the importance of an excellent red sauce from his mother, Sharon. She would routinely pluck meals from *The Best Recipe* cookbook on weeknights, summoning Gerrit and his younger sister Erin to the kitchen for help. Their father, Mark, took the reins for a more involved dinner on Sundays. The routine of being around the table, usually with a good bottle of wine uncorked, was deeply ingrained. "My mom was big on everybody sitting down for dinner," Cole said.

From his home in the Cleveland suburbs, Blake couldn't partake in the pasta party, but the rookie pitching coach feasted on the resulting data. Yet to make so much as a regular-season mound visit, Blake said that there were days that the lines between reality and fantasy seemed to blur, wondering if he was actually a big league pitching coach. "It was like one of those weird dreams where you're about to do something cool and then you wake up," Blake said.

Most of the pitchers found empty ballfields and volunteers to squat behind the plate. In Japan, Masahiro Tanaka did so, having submitted to a mandatory 14-day quarantine after returning to his native country. Tanaka later acknowledged that he experienced situations during his time in Florida that made the pitcher concerned for the safety of his wife, Mai, and their one-year-old child. The spread of COVID-19 created a surge of anti-Asian racism across the United States. President Trump's March fixation upon referring to the virus as the "China virus" or "kung flu" did not help. The *South Florida Sun-Sentinel* detailed the actions of "virus vigilantes" who harassed Asian American shoppers at a The Home Depot location in Sarasota and sunbathers in Bradenton, Florida. Tanaka declined to elaborate on the specific incidents that he experienced. "The biggest thing was about family for me," Tanaka said. "There were some incidents, and someone had to make the decision of what we were going to do. Considering everything, I thought that going back to Japan would make the most sense for our family."

Keeping skills sharp was more difficult for the position players. Mike Tauchman purchased a net to take swings in his Illinois backyard. Kyle Higashioka set up shop on his father-in-law's sixty-acre ranch in Oregon, where his wife Alyse fed balls into a pitching machine. Clint Frazier shopped online for a virtual reality hitting experience, hovering the mouse over a top-of-the-line model before deciding to stick with his usual routine of seeing high-velocity pitches in an Atlanta-area cage. "There's a brand that you can put the goggles on, and they have real bats to track the pitches," Frazier said. "I didn't know where we stood with the season, so I didn't want to spend $2,500 on something that I might not use."

Gio Urshela remained in Florida, buddying with the Cleveland Indians' Francisco Lindor to keep their legs in shape with lengthy bike rides through Orlando's side streets five days a week. Gary Sánchez returned to the Dominican Republic, though the work to retool his defense continued at the private facility where he performed his offseason workouts. Sánchez practiced his new one-knee-down approach on videos he would email to catching coach Tanner Swanson, who reviewed the footage between home projects in Swanson's tiny hometown of Roslyn, Washington, which once served as Alaska's stand-in for the TV series *Northern Exposure*. When a new video arrived, Swanson would set down his circular saw, then gauge Sánchez's progress in stealing strikes. "As things shut down, he physically felt comfortable, but we hadn't solved how he was going to move to his left or right," Swanson said. "We focused on receiving early in spring training, but those other skills are critical as well. He was back home trying to play with different modifications, and I'd give him feedback as best I could. We were trying to maintain progress and not take a step backward."

At his family's farm in Holly Hill, South Carolina, Brett Gardner scanned 2,600 acres of corn, soybeans, and cotton, remarking how it was the first spring he'd spent on that soil in 15 years. Gardner got his hands dirty in that familiar two-stoplight town, piling into a pickup truck to help his father and uncle with their usual rounds. The solitude suited Gardner, who once pointed his car south from New York City at the end of a baseball season and drove more than 300 miles in the middle of the night, reaching Richmond, Virginia, before realizing that the radio was still off. "I unplugged and got away," Gardner said. "I was around as few people as possible, to be honest."

It wasn't all work. Like the rest of the U.S., the players and coaches spent a sizable portion of their idle time Netflix and chilling, ripping through the streaming pop culture of the moment. The true-crime docudrama *Tiger King: Murder, Mayhem and Madness* inspired a text message chain on which the players cackled at the miniseries' crass anti-hero, Joe Exotic, swapping theories about the 1997 disappearance of Carole Baskin's then-husband, Don Lewis, which is still an open investigation in the Yankees' Florida backyard of Hillsborough County. "When we look back on this in 10 or 20 years, that'll be one of the images of the coronavirus, the *Tiger King*," said Boone, whom at one point was so starved for sports programming that he delved into YouTube's archive of World Series games from the 1970s and 1980s. For Boone, *The Last Dance*, ESPN's 10-part miniseries focusing on Michael Jordan's 1997–98 season with the Chicago Bulls, served as a godsend, reminding him how much he missed the thrill of competition.

The Yankees also played video games—lots and lots of video games. That was true even before the shutdown, when right-hander Tommy Kahnle arrived in camp clutching a copy of *Madden NFL 20* to proclaim himself as the commissioner of the National Savages League. A dozen teams were formed, and as play continued through the end of March and into April, Ben Heller's Indianapolis Colts upset Kahnle's beloved Philadelphia Eagles in the inaugural Super Bowl. The online games provided a fun avenue for the players to remain in contact. Tons of trash talking ensued over those microphones, especially when Frazier, Aaron Judge, and Luke Voit revealed themselves to be the league's bottom feeders. The group played five seasons, drafting each year's real-life college class until their rosters started to fill with generic high school players. Some of the teams were not human-controlled, creating a competitive loophole that required a new rule to be enacted. Judge was the most flagrant offender; he'd go back and play the computer multiple times before saving his progress, trying to fatten his statistics. "All our team does is play video games," said outfielder Aaron Hicks. "I'm not too worried about our guys going out and getting wild. They like their video games."

While others mashed their thumbs playing games like *Call of Duty: Warzone* and *Rocket League*, Voit kept busy outdoors, savoring his first spring in Wildwood, Missouri, since his senior year at Lafayette High School. The slugging first baseman joked that he was embracing his inner redneck; he planted trees and bushes, set a trap to snare a troublesome mole, and then fired up his backyard smoker with chicken, fish, and a whole turkey that produced some killer gumbo. "Clean eating" was Voit's newfound mantra, easing his consumption of alcohol and late-night snacks with assistance from his wife, Victoria. Voit's husky frame matched the boisterous personality that once prompted Cashman to compare him to professional wrestler Jerry "The King" Lawler, but Voit wanted to be lighter on his feet when play resumed. He incorporated a cardio regimen, beginning each workout with a one-and-a-half mile run through his neighborhood. "Luke looked great," said P.J. Pilittere, the Yankees' assistant hitting coach. "He loves the weight room, and to see him come in really toned up was impressive. Kudos to him. He worked his tail off and had his mind wrapped around the things you need to do to improve."

The players were safe, but the coronavirus rocked New York's baseball world early in the pandemic. Anthony Causi, a photographer for the *New York Post*, developed symptoms after returning from an assignment shooting the New York Mets' spring training in Port St. Lucie, Florida. A barrel-chested, bearded Brooklynite with a booming laugh, Causi was beloved throughout the sport. If you've seen Causi's iconic photo of Mariano Rivera exiting the Yankee Stadium bullpen for a postseason save opportunity with

No. 42 on his back, allow yourself a moment to consider how it was taken. Photographers are not permitted in the bullpens, so the team granted Causi special access during one of their most important games. That trust does not develop overnight.

In 2017, mercurial Mets outfielder Yoenis Cespedes invited Causi to his Florida ranch, dressing in cowboy gear for a photoshoot. Didi Gregorius counted photography among a bevy of extracurricular interests, and the Yankees shortstop frequently asked Causi for pointers on lighting and shutter speeds. From a bed at North Shore University Hospital in Manhasset, New York, Causi announced that he had been diagnosed with COVID-19, saying in a March 22 Instagram post, "I never thought I would get something like this. I thought I was indestructible. If I do make it out of here, I promise you this: the world's not going to know what hit it."

Placed on a ventilator shortly after that post, Causi fought for nearly three weeks. He passed away on April 12 at age 48, leaving behind a young wife, Romina, and two young children, John and Mia. The *Post* mourned Causi's death with its entire front page, a black-and-white photograph of Causi holding his telescopic lens accompanied by the headline: "Our eyes, our heart, and our city's loss."

"I got back from spring training on a Friday and texted Causi, not knowing how sick he was," said George King, the *Post*'s Yankees beat writer. "He said, 'Horrible. Thanks for asking.' Professionally, he was terrific. He was just great to work with. I still wait for the phone to ring with a joke or something really funny."

With sirens wailing throughout New York's avenues amid grim visuals of refrigerated trucks waiting for bodies, it was clear that the Yankees were not returning to the Bronx anytime soon. With each passing week, the original schedule grew more unplayable. Major League Baseball scrambled, sketching scenarios where players would reconvene to their spring camps and begin the regular season in a bubble.

An Arizona plan and a Florida plan made the rounds, wherein the traditional American League and National Leagues would be abandoned, dividing teams into the Cactus League and Grapefruit League. A Texas hub was also among five suggested sites that boasted the facilities and resources to host big league teams. The Florida plan held some appeal for the Yankees, who would have been able to play the Phillies (Clearwater), Pittsburgh Pirates (Bradenton), and Tigers (Lakeland) without traveling more than an hour by bus. Yet other aspects of the plans were unworkable. Some of the spring ballparks were rickety compared to their big league counterparts, offering unappealing visuals for a made for TV sports experience. The suggestion of sequestering players for an indeterminate period with no family member access was also problematic. "There were a lot of email chains and text messages with me and my counterparts around the league," said Ben Tuliebitz, the Yankees' traveling secretary. "We'd say speculatively, 'Okay, what kinds of hotels could we use here? How are we going to prioritize?' There were always some of us that were like, 'Man, that'd be really hard to pull off.' In the end, we all realized it probably wouldn't work."

As he pulled out of the players' parking lot at Steinbrenner Field on a clear and sunny April afternoon, his 6'7" frame compressed into a white BMW i8 roadster, Judge admitted that he'd already gone stir crazy. He'd spent the first part of the shutdown transforming his Tampa apartment into a gallery of autographed sports jerseys and was out of decorating challenges to tackle. A ballplayer's life is scripted for nine months of the year, an endless series of report times, first pitches, bus rides, charter flights, and check-ins. Having endless hours to stare at his walls was not an issue that Judge ever anticipated. It seemed as though time had paused with the last spring training game. Was this March 45th? March 60th? Who could say for sure? "The days kind of blend together in quarantine," Judge said.

CHAPTER 5

TELL US WHEN AND WHERE

Weeks before Dr. Anthony Fauci and Dr. Deborah Birx became daily fixtures on United States television screens as they helped navigate the nation's worst public health catastrophe in 102 years, Zack Britton was killing time by flipping through his Netflix recommendations. The Yankees pitcher stumbled across a compelling title: *Pandemic: How to Prevent an Outbreak.* The six-part documentary was released in January 2020, featuring several notable public health experts offering warnings of a hypothetical respiratory virus that could overwhelm the globe in a matter of months. From his rented spring apartment, Britton watched with rapt interest, never dreaming that the subject matter would supplant his day job of tossing sinkers and sliders.

Fielding phone calls, text messages, and Zoom invitations from his Texas home, Britton frequently thought about the documentary, marveling at its prescience and relevance. As a union player representative, Britton served as a conduit between Major League Baseball, the New York Yankees, and the MLB Players Association. His services were in high demand as the league negotiated how—or if—they would get back on the field. "I definitely did not feel like a baseball player," Britton said. "I kept thinking, *This is what it would feel like working a normal job.* I was on the phone all day with the union, trying to communicate with every player on our team. I was getting texts from guys all day, trying to do the best I could with the information I had, which a lot of times wasn't much."

MLB and the MLBPA eventually found common ground, but not before an ugly war of words left both sides with black eyes, a battle between millionaires and billionaires that no one cared to referee amidst a once-in-a-century pandemic. While claims for unemployment assistance skyrocketed nationwide, the league and union engaged in a distasteful game of financial Ping-Pong, pushing the more relevant discussions of player safety to the back burners.

Britton served as the Yankees' traffic cop, attempting to slow the spread of misinformation while hoping that cooler heads would prevail. His understanding of the challenges players faced was boosted by Scott Boras, who offered a presentation on the health and safety aspects of playing through a pandemic. Years before he became the sport's power broker, Boras completed a pharmacology degree at University of the Pacific in Stockton, California. That background proved useful as Boras sought to gauge the risks COVID-19 presented for professional athletes in their 20s and 30s. "I buried myself in the medical dynamic to illustrate that this was safe for players to do," Boras said. "At the time that we were telling players this, it was not a popular commentary. Our point was: if you do this, you've got to really isolate yourself from your grandparents and your parents. This is about the virus, and it's something that fortunately protects that age group."

For that presentation, Boras also crunched the statistics for players who sat out for an entire year and then returned; they weren't promising. Beyond the virology, storm clouds were on the horizon concerning a financial battle to come. The league's Collective Bargaining Agreement was set to expire after the 2021 season. The pandemic pushed those discussions into the present. MLB and the MLBPA agreed on March 27 to prorate salaries in the event of a shortened season, assuring players that they would receive partial advances and concessions regarding service time.

That agreement became a point of contention. MLB portrayed it as a starting point for negotiations, asking players to accept additional pay reductions because the season would be played in closed ballparks. The players disagreed, believing the March 27 pact settled that matter. The league's owners approved a revenue-sharing plan on May 11, speaking optimistically about an 82-game season that would begin on or around July 4. That stalled when the players demanded to see financial statements to support the claim that all 30 teams would be unprofitable without fans in the seats. Also swiftly rejected was the owners' May 26 proposal, which outlined an expanded postseason and a sliding scale that would pay between 20 and 72.5 percent of players' salaries based upon their original contracts. The players shot that down in the time it took an Aroldis Chapman fastball to cross home plate. They countered five days later, suggesting a 114-game season with full per-game pay.

By this point, Britton said that some of the Yankees were beginning to express anxiety. Players are effectively seasonal employees only paid during the baseball season, and based on their salaries, most didn't exactly qualify for the $1,200 coronavirus stimulus checks issued by the federal government in April. It fell upon Britton's shoulders to reassure them that—despite what they were reading in the news—there would be a 2020 season. "Guys started panicking, like, 'Are we going to play? Do I have any checks coming in?'" Britton said. "I didn't have a ton of answers. Financially, I'm in a different spot than a young guy who is just cracking the big leagues, when that salary is so important. I just told them to be patient and to save their money, to lay low for a little bit."

The talks went back and forth. Commissioner Rob Manfred and players union head Tony Clark conducted discussions over Zoom, then telephone, then in terse emails. Manfred appeared on MLB Network on June 10, stating there would "100 percent" be a 2020 season, painting a rosy picture as the league prepared to hold its pandemic-shortened draft—shaved from its usual 40 rounds to just five.

With few high school and college games to watch in person, the Yankees' scouts scoured the Internet for video of at-bats and innings from the preseason or the fall of 2019, adjusting to the unfamiliar routine of being afforded a chance to sleep in their home beds for weeks on end. When evaluating players in person, scouts look past raw statistics, gauging maturity and temperament through interactions with teammates. They can observe how a player positions himself before a pitch or clock a runner down the baseline without wondering if the video glitched.

Physical changes are noted; a good scout can tell if a player is spending his extra hours pumping iron at the gym or pounding beers at the campus frat house. Many prospects showcased videos on social media channels or uploaded them to a portal maintained by MLB, but Damon Oppenheimer thought those were deceiving—the same way a celebrity's glamorous Instagram feed does not provide a complete image of their daily life. "If they threw a bullpen and it didn't go well, they wouldn't post it," said Oppenheimer, the Yankees' senior vice president of domestic amateur scouting. "We'd see the ones that are all really good. The ones that aren't, I wouldn't post them either."

That made the evaluation process something of a guessing game. Instead of ringing doorbells and meeting prospects in living rooms, scouts dialed in for Zoom calls with potential draft picks and their parents. By doing so, they discovered that many in baseball's next generation seemed to be more at ease with communicating online than in person, likely a reflection of their frequent smartphone usage. "It was hard," Oppenheimer said. "The fact that you didn't get to see them with your eyes interact with their teammates, how much they'd grown or put on weight from the time you made your evaluations on them in the summer. We did the best we could with it."

The Yanks' draft class consisted of only three players, having lost their second and fifth-round selections as compensation for signing Gerrit Cole the previous winter. As negotiations began with the team's top pick, University of Arizona catcher Austin Wells, Manfred and Clark continued to haggle over much higher stakes.

When Manfred's June 12 offer asked players to accept reduced pay to make a 72-game season possible, Clark replied that further negotiations with the league would be "futile," adding: "It's time to get back to work. Tell us when and where." The quote became a rallying cry, as many players posted "when and where" on their social media channels. Frustrated, Manfred walked back his comments from five days prior, telling ESPN that he was "not confident" that the league would play a single game in 2020. It was posturing; Manfred had the authority to impose a season without the union's approval as long as the players received prorated pay from their original contract. "Any time those kinds of negotiations spill out into the public, they leave a bad taste in the fans' mouths and on both sides of the line," Cole said. "When the public is used to create leverage against one side or another, it's not going to be pretty. It's especially not pretty under the backdrop of a pandemic."

So there was waiting, and wondering, and then more waiting. While the league bickered with its players, several stars turned their attention to the ongoing protests against police brutality and racism. Giancarlo Stanton was among those spurred to step out of his comfort zone, transfixed in horror by the eight minutes and 46 seconds of George Floyd pleading for his life. Stanton's heart rate pulsed as he saw Floyd, an unarmed Black man, with his neck under the left knee of Derek Chauvin, a 19-year veteran of the Minneapolis Police Department.

A pedestrian outside a convenience store took the video on May 25, capturing what would be Floyd's final moments. More revelations emerged in the days to come—that Floyd, an unarmed Black man, had been detained after allegedly attempting to use a counterfeit $20 bill. Chauvin, the most prominent officer on the scene, had a reputation for being overly aggressive and had a trail of misconduct complaints. Stanton had none of those details at hand upon his first viewing of the Floyd video, but they solidified his resolve as he took in hours of cable news coverage. Interspersed with more than 20 cries of "I can't breathe!," the choppy footage seemed all too familiar to many, including Stanton.

Growing up in Los Angeles, Stanton frequently rolled through the Foothill Boulevard exit off Interstate 210, near his mother's house. It was the spot where a group of Los Angeles Police Department officers savagely beat motorist Rodney King on March 3, 1991. Fifteen months old at the time of the incident, Stanton later learned about the six days of riots and civil unrest that engulfed his home city in April and May of 1992, when a trial jury failed to convict four officers of using excessive force. Stanton felt as though he was witnessing the same scene—the names and faces had changed over three decades, but the story sadly had not.

As protesters mobilized in Minneapolis and other cities across the United States, filling city streets in marches that turned violent in some instances, Stanton felt the need to speak. Until then, Stanton primarily used his Instagram social media account as an occasional diversion. His most recent posts had been video of a 2015 home run that exited Dodger Stadium, a gap-toothed Cinco de Mayo karaoke video in which he displayed the lasting damage from being hit by a Mike Fiers fastball in 2014, and a throwback photo wearing football pads in a black and red No. 36 jersey at Verdugo Hills High School.

Stanton was aware of current events. In the early days of the pandemic, he donated 15,000 reusable face shields to healthcare workers in New York and Los Angeles. But like many of his baseball brethren, he was reluctant to wade in politicized waters. The Floyd killing crystallized right and wrong, and Stanton wanted to be part of the solution. "I feel like the door's been opened that should have been opened a long time ago," Stanton said. "We've always talked about it amongst ourselves: the cities where we hear things that we shouldn't in the outfield. Now's the time to let it be known that this needs to stop."

Within days, Stanton participated in a video that supported the Black Lives Matter movement. Produced by Coleture Group, the video was edited by Brandon Mihm, an assistant director of original content in the Yankees' scoreboard department. Aaron Judge and Aaron Hicks lent their voices to the project, as did CC Sabathia. "We've been told that our peaceful pleas were not made at the right time, at the right place, and the right way," the players said. "We've been told to wait, but we remember when Dr. Martin Luther King Jr. warned us that the word 'wait' has almost always meant 'never.' We will wait no longer. We will make our voices louder for all of us who can and for all of those who could not. Eight minutes and 46 seconds is enough time to lift a knee. To do what is right. To say something to acknowledge the pain of the Black community. You have cheered for us, but we need you to cheer with us now when we need you the most. Black Lives Matter."

Hicks said that he was inspired by the movement, even making efforts to wear black clothing and support Black-owned restaurants. According to one estimate by *The New York Times*, Black Lives Matter may have been the largest movement in United States history. More than 15 to 26 million participated nationwide. Stanton believed that the resulting political and social movement would be lasting, pointing to the participants' range of skin tones. "That's why this time might be different," Stanton said. "It's not just people of color out protesting at these rallies. There's a lot of white people, younger white people, advocating for us. I think that's the only way it's going to change."

Still uncomfortable with air travel, Brian Cashman drove to Tampa to oversee the draft, using the trip as an opportunity to gauge his team's social awareness. Joined by senior director of player development Kevin Reese and director of player development Eric Schmitt at the minor league complex, Cashman quizzed players, opening doors to difficult conversations that were taking place in many businesses and walks of life. Some of the minor leaguers expressed dissatisfaction that the team had not publicly acknowledged the Floyd killing for eight days, by which time most organizations in the four major sports had done so.

The Yankees had their social media team amplify a quote attributed to Nelson Mandela, the South African anti-apartheid revolutionary: "No one is born hating another person because of the color of his skin, or his background, or his religion. People must learn to hate, and if they can learn to hate, they can be taught to love. For love comes more naturally to the human heart than its opposite."

The front office believed that the quote was significant and accompanied it with a photograph of Mandela smiling in a Yankees warm-up jacket during a June 1990 rally in his honor. Mandela had been a friend of the Steinbrenner family, and a plaque bearing his name was dedicated in Monument Park during the 2014 season. To some players, it had been a safe choice, lacking the force that the moment demanded. Two Black minor leaguers—first baseman Chris Gittens and outfielder Canaan Smith-Njigba—voiced that opinion privately and on social media. They lobbied to Reese, stating: "We need to hear you say 'Black Lives Matter.'"

Cashman said that the discussion opened his eyes to the differences that permeated daily life. For example, when Cashman taught his daughter Grace how to drive, he coached her on what fuel types to buy and how to merge onto a busy highway. They never discussed what to do if stopped by the police, a topic that was a high priority when Sabathia performed the same duties with his teenage son. "It was a very real circumstance for part of our employee population," Cashman said. "Trying to pretend it wasn't would not have been an effective way to go about your business. You try to run toward it and have conversations about it to the degree you can. We had some very uncomfortable conversations with people opening up and really sharing what they're thinking, feeling, their experiences, and why they feel the way they do."

While serious clubhouse discussions accompanied the demonstrations in the streets, the league struggled to resuscitate its stalled season. Yankees president Randy Levine attempted to play peacemaker, publicly urging Manfred and Clark to cease their electronic exchanges and sit six feet apart in the same room until they reached a deal. Levine went so far as to describe the players as "patriots," suggesting that it was within their duties as red-blooded Americans to lace their spikes and swing for the fences. "It became obvious that we had to play," Levine said. "The country was getting more and more depressed, and sports would be a good thing to bring back. From baseball's point of view, we had to play because two years off would really hurt the game. We thought that we could be an example to bring back other companies."

A hard-nosed attorney from Brooklyn, Levine was known in baseball circles as a bulldog, having sharpened his teeth as Rudy Giuliani's deputy mayor before moving his office to the Bronx. Levine relished a good clash; he once called a news conference to gloat after the team defeated relief pitcher Dellin Betances in an arbitration hearing, crowing that he was "not an astronaut, and Dellin Betances is not a closer based on statistics." The arbitrator agreed, but the pitcher fumed, vowing that free agency would be easier for him in the future.

Levine's pleas for Manfred and Clark to speak face to face were acknowledged. Manfred boarded a commercial airliner bound for Arizona, where he and Clark held a productive meeting at a Scottsdale resort. The league proposed a 60-game season with full prorated salaries and an expanded postseason with 16 teams. The players voted against the plan by a 33–5 margin on June 22, prompting Manfred to fire the lone arrow left in his quiver, unilaterally imposing a 60-game season with a July 1 report date. The players zipped their bags, expecting that there would eventually be grievances filed for lost pay covering 30 to 40 more games that could have been played while the sides dithered. "We stood our ground and we fought for what we believed in," said James Paxton, who was involved as a member of the MLBPA's executive subcommittee. "We knew what we wanted. We knew what we thought was fair and we stuck to that."

It would be a season unlike any in baseball history—the shortest regular season since 1878 and the most postseason games ever played in a year. To reduce travel, teams would see only their geographic division and interleague games against the corresponding division, meaning the Yankees would be limited to games in the American League East and National League East. The National League temporarily adopted the designated hitter, a change that the American League had implemented in 1973. With no active minor league affiliates, teams established a 60-man player pool and would begin the season with a 30-man active roster, soon reduced to 28. "Eliminating the travel cross-country gave the guys some reassurance, staying out of the air for long periods," Britton said. "Once we got that plan, the majority of guys felt pretty comfortable that there was going to be enough testing available and we were going to be able to play a safe season."

The players had their when, having agreed to MLB's proposed health and safety protocols. Now it was on to where, and Hal Steinbrenner's vision was to have his players reconvene at Steinbrenner Field for "Spring Training 2.0," later re-dubbed "Summer Camp." MLB even found a sponsor, obtaining the support of Camping World—a retailer offering recreational vehicles for outdoor escapes, a tailor-made fit for a pandemic. Several other teams considered holding camps in their home cities. That idea held little appeal to Steinbrenner, who had stood before his players in March and vowed to keep the Tampa facility open for as long as necessary. Several players were still using the field regularly, and Steinbrenner Field boasted three baseball diamonds plus four more at the player development—ample space for 60 players to rev up while maintaining social distance.

In his first year as the Yankees' performance coach, Eric Cressey took the players' need for live reps to another level, hosting secret sandlot workouts for his clients at Palm Beach Gardens High School in Palm Beach, Florida. The star-studded group featured Justin Verlander, Max Scherzer, Corey Kluber, and Paul Goldschmidt facing off in games where the final scores did not matter. It was a 2020 version of Ray Kinsella's Iowa farm from *Field of Dreams*. Stanton was there, but his name wouldn't have appeared in a box score had there been one kept. "I was down there working out with them, but I wasn't a part of that game," said Stanton, who was still mending his right calf injury at the time. "But it was cool being down there, getting work in, and seeing a diverse group of guys all going to different camps and getting ready in their own aspects."

Stanton expected to spend a few more weeks in Florida, occasionally commuting between Tampa and Cressey's hub in West Palm Beach. That plan evaporated when positive coronavirus tests skyrocketed in the Sunshine State, which had been among the nation's first to re-open. One month after governor Ron DeSantis prematurely celebrated Florida's victory over COVID-19, jabbing on May 20 that the state had succeeded "and I think that people just don't want to recognize it," the state's total caseload swelled past 90,000 with more than 3,100 deaths attributed to the coronavirus.

Florida's case numbers were likely underreported, but even at face value, Steinbrenner viewed the statistics as a neon blinking sign that the Yankees could not reassemble in Tampa. When several teams announced new positive coronavirus tests, including the Yanks' Grapefruit League neighbors, the

Toronto Blue Jays and Philadelphia Phillies, MLB shuttered all 30 spring training facilities. Reluctantly, Steinbrenner decided that his team must pivot to the Bronx. "It was damn close," Steinbrenner said. "From my perspective we had geared up again with the cleaning, getting everything ready. Tampa and Hillsborough County were still pretty low at that time in cases, low in fatalities. Then the beaches opened back up, all the bars on Howard Avenue. As soon as that all started going again, you could just see that it was going to happen. And unfortunately it did."

* * *

The phone rang in Doug Behar's office. Intimately familiar with every nook and cranny of the 1.3 million square-foot cathedral, Behar, the Yankees' senior vice president of stadium operations, keeps Yankee Stadium humming 365 days a year. As Behar listened to Steinbrenner's voice on the other end of the receiver, he nodded, performing mental calculations that seemed nearly impossible to fathom.

The Yankees had not held a training camp in the northeast since World War II, when travel restrictions prompted the Bombers to make Asbury Park, New Jersey, their chilly spring home prior to the 1943 season. Joe McCarthy's squad upgraded their digs to Atlantic City, New Jersey, during the springs of '44 and '45 before returning to Florida in 1946. Now, with a few days' notice, Behar would have to convert Yankee Stadium from a 45,000 seat entertainment venue into a training ground for 60 big league players—all while abiding by league and local protocols.

Behar was not afraid to roll up his sleeves and grind; on the eve of the Stadium's opener in 2009, Behar pulled an all-nighter, even shining door-knobs and scrubbing rubber drink trays in the luxury suites. The difference was: he had a team at his disposal then. As one of the few people permitted in the stadium, Behar doubled up on masks and gloves to clean out the office pantries that had been stocked with dairy products back in March, all long past their expiration date.

Chunky milk and yogurt were the least of the team's concerns. Employees were challenged to view Yankee Stadium more as a hospital facility than a baseball stadium. For example, when players completed their turns pumping iron in the weight room, workers would conduct terminal cleaning on all of the equipment—the same as a hospital might do to prepare an operating room for its next patient. "We always prepare for the worst and hope for the best," Behar said. "Despite all of our best planning efforts throughout the years, this was something that we didn't have a manual to pull out and say, 'Okay, here's what we need to do.' It was certainly an education. You could imagine the hundreds, if not thousands, of emails that we got."

The quick shift was assisted by New York governor Andrew Cuomo and New York City mayor Bill de Blasio, who welcomed the Yankees home with open arms. In a conference call with Steinbrenner and Levine, Cuomo expressed his desire to see baseball resume. The governor believed that the public needed to see their teams back on the field—even if the stadiums remained closed to fans.

As the players returned to a tri-state area that bore little resemblance to the workplace they left behind in October, they searched for facilities to ply their trade. That was how Judge, Hicks, and Mike Ford wound up on a Ramsey, New Jersey, high school ballfield, belting moonshots into the northern red oaks beyond the chain-link outfield fence. Hicks connected with Jason Ferber, an amateur baseball coach, asking for leads on available diamonds where the players could work out privately. Ferber suggested the field at Don Bosco Prep, a Catholic school for boys in grades nine through 12. The ballfield had never seen talent like this. Some school administrators nudged their young children to shag fly balls in the outfield, as the big leaguers gave the locals a workout. The players beamed, happy to be doing what they were supposed to. The boys were back in town.

• CHAPTER 6 •

SUMMER CAMP

One hundred and twelve days after Major League Baseball vanished from the sports landscape, two silver chartered buses wedged below the elevated railroad tracks near the intersection of East 161st Street and River Avenue with their four-way flashers blinking. The drivers sported pale blue surgical masks as they flung open the doors of the chartered Van Hool coaches, unloading the Yankees onto the New York City streets. Baseball was back in the Bronx, though it looked and felt nothing like any of the team's previous 97 seasons in the borough.

As uniformed NYPD sergeants ushered Clint Frazier, Gleyber Torres, and Gio Urshela toward a stadium entrance, each player wore cloth masks over their noses and mouths while sporting shaggier haircuts than the last time they'd been seen in public. James Paxton flashed a peace sign, steering his black pickup into the underground parking lot, where he was greeted by a staffer wearing a disposable full-body protective suit. Gerrit Cole beamed as he drove past a photograph of retired New York Yankees great Bernie Williams, acknowledging a few pedestrians on the sidewalk from the safety of his rolled-up window. "It's been a long summer for everybody," Cole said that day. "As a country, as a world, we've had to overcome a lot of challenges to get to this point. I'm thrilled to get back on the field. To see my teammates, it was just kind of a nice stress relief. It was good to see a lot of people smile."

The players and coaches received their formal introduction to the new normal in the Legends Club, the swanky bi-level hangout behind home plate where Cole had proudly hoisted his "TODAY TOMORROW FOREVER" placard seven months prior. It felt like seven years had passed. They received instructions from the medical staff and submitted to intake testing, including blood work on the first day and the less-invasive PCR saliva testing every other day.

MLB had those vials shipped to the Sports Medicine Research and Testing Laboratory in South Jordan, Utah, which was usually in service to flag performance-enhancing drug cheats. At a reported expense of more than $1.5 million, the league converted the lab to run coronavirus tests. It took time to work out the kinks; delays in testing during the Independence Day weekend prompted the cancellation of five workouts league-wide, and MLB later added a second lab at Rutgers University in New Jersey to keep up with demand.

Temperature checks, symptom screenings, and saliva tests were administered from a tent in the loading dock, manned by workers in face shields, masks, and full-body PPE. The players had strict 25-minute windows and could not eat or drink 30 minutes before arriving at the stadium. They had to spit into plastic cylinders for their PCR tests, filling it to a certain line. Some of the guys tried to keep quiet on the bus rides so they'd be able to spit in one shot. Otherwise, they'd have to spit four or five times. Some later said they'd place their cell phones on do not disturb mode, preferring to silently work up the quarter teaspoon needed to fill the vial in one shot. When the players rode buses later in the season, they made a gross game out of baiting a teammate to talk, which would force them to start collecting saliva from scratch. Still, it was preferable to receiving a brain-tickling nasal swab every other day. "I feel like the organization did a really good job of making everybody feel safe," said infielder Tyler Wade. "It felt pretty normal—besides all of the testing and protocols we had to do."

DJ LeMahieu wished that he could have been there to shoot the spit with his teammates. With more than 355,000 new cases reported nationwide during that first week of July, the coronavirus was surging across America. Those statistics hit home when the Yankees saw two empty lockers in their clubhouse. LeMahieu and pitcher Luis Cessa had tested positive for COVID-19 in the weeks prior and were self-quarantining at their respective homes.

When Florida's rising caseload shuttered Steinbrenner Field, LeMahieu traveled to Birmingham, Michigan, envisioning a quiet evening on the back porch with his father, Tom. The most stoic Yankee wanted nothing more than to sit a few miles from the school where he'd won back-to-back honors as the state's best baseball player, listening to the crickets and cracking a cold beverage or three.

LeMahieu visited a clinic and requested a COVID-19 test, telling the doctor that he had no symptoms but had spent the previous five months in Tampa. He was stunned when his cell phone rang a few days later with a positive result. LeMahieu grew frustrated as he submitted to no fewer than nine additional swabs, trying to collect the required consecutive negative results at least 24 hours apart before he'd be cleared to wear a big league uniform. "It was just shocking news to get," LeMahieu said. "When you have something that there's no cure for, it's obviously scary. But after those first few days, I was feeling fine. I had so much support from my teammates and family. So after a couple weeks, I was ready to go again."

Cessa was in a similar position, having traveled to his Arizona home with his girlfriend, Telemundo television reporter Nancy Arreola. They would both test positive for COVID-19; Arreola complained of a fever and body aches, while Cessa lost his senses of smell and taste. The right-hander remained strong enough to toss a bucket of balls into a backyard net, piecing together a quarantine workout by jogging through his neighborhood's empty streets at night.

"We tried to figure out where we got the virus; we didn't really know," Cessa said. "Maybe it was in a supermarket when we went out to buy something. We didn't have contact with anybody. Thank God I never had [severe] symptoms."

Aaron Boone acknowledged the absences as he strapped a mask over his ears, repeating chunks of the address he had given in Tampa months prior. The circumstances had undoubtedly changed, and the challenges were greater, but the mission remained the same. As Cole said early in camp, "There is only going to be one coronavirus World Series champion. That's unique in and of itself. I don't see why you wouldn't want to take that trophy home."

It was a message that Boone had to repeat at least three times because social distancing protocols prevented all 60 players from gathering in a room. On a normal game night, two rosters of 26 players plus the managers, coaches, and other staff members utilize the home and road clubhouses at Yankee Stadium. To spread out players as much as possible, they were assigned lockers in all areas of the home, road, and auxiliary clubhouses. Couches were removed from the lounge area, reducing the appeal of what had once been a favorite hangout.

"I believed we would pull off the season, but probably a little naively," Boone said. "For me, it was: 'Okay, here's the plan, here's what we've got.' That's what I lived, and that's what I focused on. I never looked too far ahead. My prayer life got a little stronger, and I leaned on my coaching staff a lot. In a lot of ways, we became even closer."

The players mostly believed that the instituted protocols would be sufficient to keep them safe from the coronavirus, but MLB's 113-page operations manual outlining the changes presented an ice cream headache. It was hardly light reading. Rooted in a period during which many Americans were bathing grocery deliveries with Clorox and Lysol, the comprehensive document included healthy doses of hygiene theater. "The first time it hit my inbox, I didn't get very far into it," said Doug Behar, the Yankees' senior vice president of stadium operations. "I had to pause and say, 'Boy, this is going to be hard.' The further I got into it, the more angsty I felt. Once you started piecing it out and engaging others, you realized it was going to take a lot of effort, but we could certainly do it."

The team held meetings to outline aspects of the girthy document, hammering home the importance of wearing masks to avoid air transmission of the virus. One guest speaker included Dr. Paul Lee of NewYork-Presbyterian Hospital, who has served as the team's internist since 2007. Lee was on the front lines during New York's worst days of the pandemic in March and April and he warned the players that MLB's plan to resume could be on shaky ground. "All it takes is one person being careless, bringing it into the clubhouse, and the whole team is going to get it," Lee said. "That was the first thing I said: that the team really needs to work together to make sure that there is no weak link that jeopardizes this whole season."

Enforcement was entrusted to Mark Kafalas, who accepted the role of the club's COVID-19 compliance officer. A burly former NYPD detective who sports a flat-top haircut and stands at eye level with Aaron Judge and Giancarlo Stanton, Kafalas is one of the security guards who travels with the team and protects players from overeager fans. His new responsibility was to keep the players apart from each other. "Look, I'm not here to debate whether or not you believe in the pandemic," Kafalas told the team. "You might think you have tiger blood and you're immune, but there are guys on the team that are concerned about the virus, whether it be personally or for their families. They will follow the protocols and wear the masks and do everything we ask. If you don't think it's a worry for you, out of respect to your teammates, wear the mask and follow the protocols."

That made sense to Judge. Continuing to grow in his role as a clubhouse leader, Judge told his teammates that there would be no one to watch the players when they left Yankee Stadium, so it was incumbent upon them to make smart decisions. "Fellas, we've got four months of locking it in, four months of going through everything in the procedures to keep everybody safe," Judge said. "Hold off on going out to places. You can spit, do sunflower seeds, and go to a restaurant when this is all over."

Frazier was listening. The outfielder arrived at Summer Camp intending to wear a mask on the field, one of the few big leaguers to do so. Frazier said he'd spoken about it with his girlfriend, Kaylee Gambadoro, who was studying to become a pediatric physician's assistant. When she explained that masks were an assumed part of her workday, Frazier said he would make it part of his, too. He believed that the healthiest team would finish on top, calling the season "survival of the fittest," and hoped that his act might provide a positive public example.

"There's a lot of people that have had this impact them," Frazier said. "I want to make sure that I'm not the reason why it spreads to anybody. It's the right thing to protect myself and others around me."

Frazier experimented with a blue surgical mask before switching to a Gaiter face covering that featured the Yankees' colors and his No. 77, wearing it for his at-bats and in the field. There was some brushback on social media, where Frazier saw a few tweets calling him a "sheep" or wondering about his political leanings—"I'm surprised ur a Democrat," one wrote—but Frazier disregarded those. His restraint served as evidence that the 25 year old had matured since the 2019 episode in Toronto that prompted Reggie Jackson to roll his eyes. "We have a big platform, and the Yankees make the platform two times as big," Frazier said. "A lot of people are watching. If wearing a mask upsets some people, I'm not really too worried about that."

As for the rest of the roster, they were mostly on the same page, but a smattering of mask-related slipups transpired. In those instances, Zack Britton said that he felt eyes looking toward him for enforcement. The reliever expressed irritation with the added responsibilities. "I'm not going to be your dad. I'm not the police," Britton said. "If you chose to be here, then these are the rules that we're going to follow. If you don't want to be here, you can go home. There was an opportunity for people to opt out. We felt like, if you can't follow these rules, then go home. It was a privilege just to play with the way the world was."

Despite those changes, there was laughter and camaraderie among the players, who enjoyed their unencumbered space. Catcher Kyle Higashioka said that there was more messing around and trash talking than in previous years, when the players had to guard against their commentary appearing in the next day's newspapers. "No slight to the media, but we had the whole clubhouse to ourselves," Higashioka said. "That was actually kind of fun. It brought us back to our minor league days."

The Yanks' preparation resembled the spring's early-morning routines, when teammates faced off in live batting practice or simulated games. Nearly all of Summer Camp took place in that fashion with squads denoted as the

"Clippers" and the "Bombers"—nicknames usually issued to the Old-Timers' Day lineups each summer. The Yankees wore their navy blue uniform jerseys from the spring, still bearing a sleeve patch celebrating Steinbrenner Field's 25th anniversary.

Thus, Cole's first assignment on the Yankee Stadium mound was to stare down a hitting group that featured Judge, Aaron Hicks, and Luke Voit. The righty's Amazon.com spending spree and stolen moments on Adam Ottavino's portable mound paid dividends. His fastball touched 99 mph on the radar gun while generating a series of overmatched at-bats. As Judge dug into the batter's box to face Cole, he winked, as though to say: "Hey G, how's it going?" "He just looked right through me," Judge said. "That shows you what type of competitor he is. It doesn't matter if it's practice, live BP, or the game, he's the real deal."

Embracing the mound personality of a steely assassin, Cole reverted into a gooey proud papa each day upon return to his Connecticut home, when he'd relieve his wife Amy after a long day of diaper changes and bottle feed-ings. The couple welcomed Caden Gerrit Cole on the evening of June 30, and he clocked in at seven pounds and 13 ounces. Wowed by the newborn's blue eyes, Cole announced the arrival minutes into his first visit to the Yankee Stadium Zoom Room. "We had to wait a little while to share this beauti-ful baby with the family," Cole later said. "You wished that Grandma and Grandpa could say hello, but I was back at Summer Camp, and Mom was resting comfortably at the house, so the baby was good. We were just trying to get adjusted to life in 2020 with a newborn."

When the Yankees designed their new Stadium before its 2009 opening, they placed a well-lit conference area, capable of seating hundreds of media members, near the home clubhouse on the basement level. When the manager or a player entered, cameras rolled, and a wireless microphone was handed around by a staffer, allowing interested parties to take turns asking questions. That practice was obsolete in the COVID-19 world, which saw baseball adopt a caste system in which on-field personnel like players and coaches were des-ignated as Tier 1 VIPs and granted access to all areas. Select executives were labeled Tier 2. That included Brian Cashman, for example, since he required occasional contact with people on the field. The reporters credentialed for each workout or game were Tier 3, and their access was limited to avoid face-to-face interaction with any Tier 1 person.

As most of America had already learned, the solution was Zoom, the must-have app of the pandemic. Zoom made investors rich as its user base exploded from 10 million daily participants in December 2019 to more than 300 million by April 2020. The San Jose, California, company's usual business clientele was shoved aside by elementary schoolers chatting with grandparents and millennials gulping down quarantinis in their online happy hours.

The Yankees were among their new customers, converting the press conference room into a makeshift Zoom studio. The media relations staff cycled relevant players in front of a high-definition camera for a daily interview buffet with reporters clicking a raise hand button to enter the question queue. A 95-inch flat-screen television allowed the player or coach to make eye contact with his questioners, which often lingered on the last person who had asked a question. On one occasion, Boone jolted a veteran Yankees radio reporter to attention by yelping in a sing-song voice, "Swe-e-n-y Murti, you're on the scr-e-e-n!"

"We were seeing them, but it wasn't the same as looking somebody in the eye," said the YES Network's Meredith Marakovits, who covered Summer Camp from her Upper East Side apartment. "It was harder for me personally to focus; I'm sitting in my living room with running tights and slippers. Top half, I look professional. Bottom half, I look like I'm ready to take a nap."

For on-field activities, YES continued with remote coverage for much of Summer Camp, experimenting with robotic cameras with commentary provided by off-site talent like Marakovits, David Cone, John Flaherty, and Michael Kay. It was a dry run for how road games would be produced during the regular season, and for a content-starved audience still quarantined at home, the coverage provided a welcome diversion. "We had the idea that we were going to try and show as much as we could," said John J. Filippelli, YES' president of production and programming. "Some of this was Aaron Judge trying to bunt, which was actually entertaining by itself on a lot of levels. The fact is: the viewers just wanted to see players in uniforms with the interlocking 'NY.' Why wait until the season officially started?"

The team granted stadium access to a maximum of 35 accredited photographers and reporters each day. Guards stationed outside the Great Hall administered forehead temperature checks, then read a series of questions, asking in the past 72 hours if they or anyone they lived with experienced shortness of breath, cough, fever, headache, chills, loss of taste or smell, muscle pain, vomiting, diarrhea, upset stomach, chest pain, or abdominal pain.

Assuming the answer was no to all, they passed through a metal detector and collected day passes from an employee in what used to be an advance ticket window. A few globs of hand sanitizer later, they rode the elevator to the stadium's 200 level, walking through barren concourses to the press box. Dystopian and post-apocalyptic were two adjectives that fit best. The Wi-Fi was still blazing fast, but half of the seats had vanished, and work desks were taped off with large blue Xs. The only refreshments provided were plastic bottles of Poland Spring water. "It was like barbecue chicken without the barbecue sauce," said George King of the *New York Post*. "It was in front of you. We saw it, we were there, but we couldn't touch it. We couldn't do what we do, which is talk to players, coaches, managers. You had this whole thing that you've watched forever and fills up your whole summer, but it wasn't really all there."

The first formal workout took place on Independence Day, offering a sobering reminder that even a typical baseball season could present challenges. Facing hitters for the first time in months, Masahiro Tanaka tossed a pitch that hovered in the heart of the strike zone to Giancarlo Stanton. One of the majors' most powerful hitters, Stanton flicked his wrists and immediately crouched. He knew that Tanaka had no chance to avoid the projectile, which rocketed off the sweet spot of Stanton's bat at 112 mph and smashed into the right side of the pitcher's skull.

Tanaka crumpled to the mound clay as his cap flew off and hovered in the air for several seconds. The infielders hesitated, wondering how it was possible to help their fallen teammate and maintain social distancing at the same time. They reverted to the old playbook: crowding around as head athletic trainer Tim Lentych checked Tanaka's vitals. From the grass behind home plate, Judge gestured toward a camera operator on the 200 level, telling him to stop recording. Judge received no reaction; the workout was being televised live on YES. Although the broadcast was not overly gratuitous, swiftly cutting to a wide angle, a few fans recorded clips of the ball's impact and shared them widely. Judge and Torres expressed frustration when their social media feeds filled with replays. "I get that everyone has a job to do, but continuing to film and zoom in on someone hurt and down in the stadium doesn't sit well with me," Judge later said.

Four tense minutes passed, and Tanaka was helped to his feet, walking off the field en route to NewYork-Presbyterian Hospital, a short ride across the Harlem River in upper Manhattan. Incredibly, Tanaka was in decent condition. He had sustained a concussion, as expected, but a CT scan revealed no fracture of his skull. Discharged that evening, Tanaka soon was acting as though nothing had happened. A few days later, the pitcher completed a throwing session in right field and intentionally fired a baseball into the second deck beyond first base, cackling as the boom of ball against an empty seat startled a photographer. Tanaka even admitted to laughing as he watched replays of Stanton's liner many times. "I'm never able to see other pitchers in the same situation get struck in their head. That kind of frightens me," Tanaka said. "But for some reason, I'm able to see myself get struck in the head by a ball. I don't know why. It's kind of weird."

Seeing it in real time had been enough for Stanton, who was relieved by his teammate's quick recovery. While playing for the Miami Marlins in September 2014, Stanton sustained one of the more gruesome on-field injuries in recent memory, when a Mike Fiers fastball hit him in the face. Stanton later described the sensation of trying not to choke on the blood, teeth, and bone fragments swimming in his mouth as he writhed at home plate.

Stanton's anger now surges with any pitch up and in, and he felt great concern as Tanaka flailed. "You see it in slow-mo," Stanton said. "You want that ball to keep veering off, and it didn't. Kind of like when I got hit, everything's slow-mo. You look at how fast it all happened later."

With Summer Camp on an accelerated schedule, the Yankees played their first intrasquad scrimmage on July 7. The players were accustomed to hearing cheers as they bounded onto the field and seeing kids clutching baseballs, begging for autographs. Instead, there was silence. Voit said the conditions reminded him of his time playing sparsely-attended fall games at Missouri State University. "I felt really good to be back out there, but it felt like a practice," Voit said. "The weirdest part is walking out of the dugout. When you're walking out to stretch, there's no ovation. You're used to the guys out in right-center field and right field yelling at you."

In the first inning of one of the early intrasquad games, Brett Gardner stood in left field and sneezed, listening as his *achoo!* echoed throughout the empty seats. In the press box, one scribe stifled the urge to reply, "Bless you!"

When some of the pitchers complained about hearing dugout chit-chat from the mound, soft music was piped through the speakers for a few games. That ended when an iPad—supplied to all 30 teams by Major League Baseball—with artificial crowd noise arrived at Yankee Stadium. Referred to as a "noise bed," its sounds were sampled from the video game *MLB The Show 20*. Greg Colello, the senior director of scoreboard and video, mastered the art of thinking ahead with game situations, deploying small, medium, and loud cheers.

The soundboard contained build-up noises, like the crescendo that a human crowd would create with a two-strike count, trying to will a pitcher to a strikeout. Notably, there was no booing option; it had disappointed noises, but those were akin to the sighs you would hear if an umpire made a call against the home team. Boone said it sounded like the static of an AM radio, and Cole compared it to a white noise machine, but they agreed that it was better than nothing.

"I didn't think we needed the fake crowd noise, but when I would go back and watch the games on replay, it sounded real," Kay said. "Maybe it brought people closer to what they feel is normal."

The rules were schoolyard loose; they'd play five or six innings until every pitcher had seen enough time on the mound, and by the end, there might be only one outfielder patrolling the grass. In one of the first intrasquad games, Cole struck out Mike Tauchman, prompting catcher Gary Sánchez to fire the ball toward third base as part of an around the horn celebration. When the ball returned to Cole, bullpen catcher Radley Haddad—serving as the home-plate umpire—waved it out of play, barking that it had touched too many hands. Cole reluctantly accepted a replacement, which Miguel Andújar swatted into the right-field seats. "We weren't exactly sure if we were supposed to keep it or not," Cole said. "I probably should have kept it."

The league' coronavirus protocols forbade activities considered to be part of baseball's fabric, including the act of spitting. A 2016 New York City ordinance banned the use of smokeless tobacco at Yankee Stadium and Citi Field, but its enforcement seemed to be on the level of how umpires treat pine tar use by pitchers—technically against the rules, though only a blatant case like the smudge on Michael Pineda's neck demanded action.

Now you weren't even supposed to chew gum; the ever-present tubs of Dubble Bubble and ranch-flavored David sunflower seeds vanished from the dugout. The team provided wet rags that pitchers could stash in their back pockets for moisture, a substitute for licking fingers. Each reliever was issued a set of warmup balls and had to carry their own rosin bag to the mound. The hot tubs and cold tubs used for injury therapy were drained, and even the postgame shower seemed foreign. "Bringing our own stuff to the shower was weird; there was no communal soap or shampoo or anything like that," Ottavino said. "The first two times I went to clean myself up, I forgot it and had to go back to my locker."

The game's rhythms were upended in other ways. It is drummed into a player's head that they should get to the ballpark early—get a lift in, watch TV, play cards, just be around. The new protocols nixed the practice of showing up seven hours before a game, as players were shuttled in and out and hustled through workouts on an inflexible schedule. Days passed without many teammates crossing paths. "Baseball is a weird sport where we're at the field for so long," Britton said. "It's one of those things ingrained in you coming up through the minors, that you get to the field and just kind of hang out. I think guys realized that they didn't really need that. We could show up to the field at 4:00, get dressed, and do our stuff. There wasn't nearly as much downtime. Maybe that's something that's going to carry over into future years."

The alternate site players worked out first, followed by the big leaguers. Most intrasquad games were scheduled for early evening to simulate the conditions players would experience during the regular season. During the first spring training, players like Judge could crank up the high-velocity machine and gorge on sliders or curves, but space limitations in the Bronx made that a challenge. After one intrasquad game, Judge received permission to stay on the field for approximately 30 more minutes, smacking balls into the vacant bleachers. It felt like a win.

"That was kind of what we were missing with all the time off: having the ability to just work on things, get your reps in," Judge said.

No Yankees were among the 22 big leaguers who opted out of the season, but several wrestled with the loneliness of their ballpark-hotel-ballpark routine. J.A. Happ considered bringing his wife and two young children to New York, ultimately deciding against it. Instead, the veteran returned to Manhattan after each workout, his schedule clear until the next day's activity. Britton discussed a similar trip, but the reliever opted to keep his pregnant wife and three children in Texas. Technology made the distance more tolerable—imagine if the pandemic had taken place 30 years prior in the age of rotary telephones—but there was no substitute for being present. "You can only FaceTime so much," Britton said. "They keep asking when I'll be home or if they can see me. I signed up for it. We felt like it was the right thing to do, but I knew it was going to be hard."

Britton was the only Yankee with any experience applicable to what the rest of the league was about to encounter. In 2015, Britton's Baltimore Orioles hosted the Chicago White Sox at Camden Yards for the first closed-admission game in big league history. Civil unrest made a ballgame frivolous; sirens wailed and smoke rose over the Inner Harbor after Freddie Gray, a 25-year-old Black man, had died in the Baltimore Police Department's custody. The events sparked an unlikely open conversation in the Orioles' clubhouse concerning racial equality. Outfielder Adam Jones explained that he had dealt with the same issues being protested in Baltimore's streets. Britton never forgot that, nor hearing announcer Gary Thorne's distinctive baritone from the press level, describing each of Britton's pitches to the television audience during the final inning of Baltimore's 8–2 victory. "I distinctly remember saying after the game, 'I hope I never have to do this again,'" Britton said. "That was tough. Obviously, it was a completely different circumstance, but it wasn't fun to not have your home crowd there. It felt like a back-field spring training game."

The first intrasquad games provided a semblance of normalcy, but the repetitive matchups between the same hitters and pitchers grew tired. Coaches tried to keep it fresh by shuffling the lineup and experimenting with defensive alignments. During one game, Hicks, an outfielder, trotted into the infield to test a five-man infield. It was a concept that Boone toyed with during the previous season, hoping to take advantage of Britton's propensity for inducing grounders with his heavy bowling ball sinker.

There were sweeping changes made behind the scenes. The dining area was relocated to the Legends Club. Each day, players and coaches could use the Teamworks app on their smartphone to pre-order the next day's meal, and it offered choices of salads, meats, and desserts prepared in an individually packed box with disposable utensils. That was arguably the most relaxed place in the ballpark, where players could let their guards—and masks—down to eat at a safe distance.

Most of the conversation revolved around baseball, though several players were newly interested in the stock market, recovering from its most devastating crash since 1929. Rookie pitcher Michael King recalled one after-noon in which he'd been discussing several airlines with a teammate, having funneled some of his spare cash into a Robinhood investment account. (This was months before an army of day traders organized on Reddit, using Robinhood and similar apps to send the pandemic-distressed stocks of companies like GameStop and AMC Theatres to insane heights.) King, an outgoing right-hander from New England, heard LeMahieu mumble from six feet away. "DJ is looking at me, and he says, 'Did you just say something about the stock market?'" King said. "DJ talks so quietly that I didn't know I could crack into him, but we ended up having a good conversation. He liked Rocket Mortgage. He and his buddies were all big into it during the shut-down. It ended up being a thing where if one of us found a new company that we thought could blow up soon, we started talking about it."

When they weren't cheerleading for businesses like Starbucks and Square, the players wandered into other areas of Yankee Stadium that they had never before had reason to explore. Unable to hold meetings in the usual clubhouse spaces, the players rode a service elevator up to the suite level—four passen-gers at a time with tape on the floor denoting boxes to stand in—to access the FedEx banquet and conference center above right field. Intended to accommo-date up to 125 guests in a dinner or classroom setting, the 2,400 square-foot area with a projector screen smoothly transitioned for the hitters and pitchers to conduct their meetings. "Credit to everybody because the players were on board from the beginning," said bench coach Carlos Mendoza. "You're used to getting out of your locker and going next door for a meeting. Now you've got to walk all the way outside, get on an elevator, and go sit in a meeting, then come back down, and get ready to play the game."

Despite the chaos of the outside world, Yankee Stadium felt like a bubble of safety, where the players could hit, run, and throw without concern. That popped on the afternoon of July 11, as Boone lowered himself into the Zoom Room chair to announce that the Yankees had another positive coronavirus test. Though Aroldis Chapman had passed his intake testing and participated in six days of workouts, even throwing from the bullpen mound to Sánchez, he was now being placed on the COVID-19 injured list.

The coronavirus' non-uniform incubation period—believed to be anywhere from two to 14 days—may have played a role in Chapman's delayed diagnosis. No one could say with certainty if Chapman was exposed in Miami, a COVID-19 hotspot at the time, or in New York. Instead, contact tracing focused upon revealing how many players or coaches had interacted with Chapman since his arrival. To great relief, the case did not spell a clubhouse domino effect; other teams would not be as fortunate in the weeks to come. "At that time, I was thinking, *We're not going to get through Spring Training 2.0*," Britton said. "The symptoms didn't seem to be very severe for the guys on our team. So that gave guys some peace of mind, but that didn't mean it wasn't going to impact somebody else differently."

With other clubs around the league already seeing cases in an isolated format, some wondered if the numbers would explode when nine-inning games filled the schedule seven days a week. According to Dr. Zachary Binney, an epidemiologist at Emory University in Atlanta, baseball's intrinsic social distance worked in its favor. The sport requires less man-to-man contact than, say, basketball or football, putting it more on the level of golf or cross-country.

The batter-catcher-umpire trio would stand closer than the six feet of suggested distance being hammered home by the Centers for Disease Control, but Binney said that baseball's outdoor nature and COVID-19's tendency to dissipate in air reduced the chances of transmission between teams. That was something baseball would soon gamble upon when the coronavirus-stricken Marlins played an ill-advised game against the Philadelphia Phillies. Baseball's more considerable challenge would be traveling between cities, having discarded bubble plans like the one that the NBA was arranging at Walt Disney World to complete its playoffs. "I was skeptical," Binney said. "They were the first major professional sport in the U.S. to attempt a comeback outside of a bubble. They would be interacting with people in the community who could be infected, then bringing that into the team. That could spread rapidly through a MLB clubhouse."

Hungry to test their skills against new faces, the Yankees were thrilled when MLB approved three exhibitions before the opener, including nine innings against the New York Mets at Citi Field. For Subway Series games in years past, NYPD cruisers and motorcycles escorted the Yankees' buses across the Robert F. Kennedy Bridge to Queens, a commute that the cops could reduce to fewer than 10 minutes. On those jaunts, motorists frequently parked on the shoulder, waving at the passing ballplayers. This was different; with police resources spread thin and the Grand Central Parkway clear of fan traffic, the Yankees simply drove their cars to the big ballpark in the shadows of LaGuardia Airport.

The change of scenery was welcome. From his position in left field, the artificial crowd noise and canned chants of "Let's Go Mets!" momentarily allowed Frazier to forget he was playing in a pandemic. When the center-field video board showed a well-timed 2019 clip of fans going wild, Frazier remarked, "I thought that was actually going on in the game."

That first game produced a victory, and the players weren't sure how to react; eschewing the usual handshakes on the infield grass, they opted for a series of fist bumps and elbow taps that Boone called "really weird and awkward." Beyond postgame attaboys, those dry runs served as a learning experience, allowing teams to grow familiar with gameday routines.

Philadelphia's visit to the Bronx marked Joe Girardi's first time in the ballpark since his dismissal three years prior, and it produced one of Summer Camp's oddest moments. When the Phillies recorded the third out of the fifth inning, Girardi waved his team back to the field, wanting pitcher Vince Velasquez to reach an allotted pitch count. Judge shrugged and entered the batter's box, slugging Velasquez's next pitch into the right-field bullpen. Velasquez scowled and stalked off the field, and Judge rounded the bases for a confusing home run that the teams decided should count in the official spring training statistics.

With that episode of bizarro baseball, Summer Camp was a wrap. The Yankees maintained a text message chain among their players on which Gardner correctly predicted that they would play the season opener against the Nationals in Washington, D.C. ESPN owned the broadcast rights for the first game, and the network always viewed the Yankees as a ratings giant. Send them up against the defending World Series champions with a splash of patriotic symbolism, and it made too much sense not to happen. "It's been a long road, a long journey to get to Opening Day," Judge said at the time. "It's been a crazy year, affecting a lot of people, a lot of families. I'm just excited to get back on the field and start playing the game that I love. I know our team is ready."

• CHAPTER 7 •

IRREGULAR SEASON

A parade of players and coaches in jeans, untucked button-down shirts, and sneakers passed through the marble concourses of New York's Pennsylvania Station on the morning of July 22—the eve of the season opener. Sporting a mask bearing the New York Yankees' interlocking "NY" logo, Aaron Boone raised his right fist while descending the escalator to the tracks below. All aboard, indeed.

Their chosen transportation method was an early signal that this 60-game schedule would present many new experiences, especially for a ballclub generally accustomed to jetting around the nation at 35,000 feet. Instead, the Yankees had an Amtrak Acela train all to themselves, enjoying the freedom to roam between cars as they harkened back to simpler times in which the likes of Babe Ruth and Lou Gehrig rumbled through the northeast corridor. That comfort overpowered any trepidation about being back on the road in the middle of a pandemic.

"Leaving that bubble was a little bit difficult, but this is what we signed up for," Aaron Judge said. "We wouldn't have signed up for this if we weren't aware of the risk and what we would have to face. The Yankees prepared us; they gave us the dos and don'ts to do our best to keep everybody safe."

As the train squealed into Washington's Union Station, the players grabbed their bags and passed through turn-of-the-century marble archways, boarding buses that ferried them to the Navy Yards neighborhood of the nation's capital. Constructed alongside the Anacostia River, Nationals Park opened in 2008 and was eight months removed from hosting Games 3, 4, and 5 of the World Series between the Washington Nationals and Houston

Astros, a Fall Classic won by Washington in seven games and the first World Series in which the home team lost each contest.

With the United States Capitol in view beyond the left-field wall, bats cracked and gloves popped during the Yankees' brief workout, as the players returned to the visiting clubhouse for their first pre-series meeting of the year. The hitters hurried through a scouting report on opposing ace Max Scherzer—mostly fastballs, sliders, and change-ups, but be aware of the cutter and curve—and the pitchers deconstructed a lineup headlined by left fielder Juan Soto, already one of the National League's most talented hitters at age 21.

That day, the Yankees also conducted an open forum regarding the racial strife roiling the nation. The team agreed that they would make a statement, but they grappled with executing it properly. In response to the George Floyd killing, the Philadelphia Phillies' Andrew McCutchen floated the concept of a unity ribbon, a 200-yard swath of black fabric that would be held by players on both teams. Major League Baseball and the MLB Players Association swiftly signed off on McCutchen's idea, which would have the black fabric extend from left field to home plate, and then back out to right field. The Yankees liked it, too, but Judge and Giancarlo Stanton were among those who suggested that they should also kneel. Stanton spoke passionately during the meeting, sharing his encounters with inequality and racism while growing up in the Los Angeles area. "A lot of my teammates and coaches haven't experienced some of the things that I have," Stanton said. "You heard a lot of, 'You have to be exaggerating,' or 'It couldn't have been that bad.' Now that things have come to light and there's more video cameras, there's more evidence of what's going on. It's easier to give stories and to explain what's going on."

San Francisco Giants manager Gabe Kapler and several of his players took a knee before their exhibition game against the Oakland A's one night prior, and Judge pushed for the Yankees to show that their support. Judge sensed baseball would be more receptive than it had seemed in September 2017, when A's catcher Bruce Maxwell channeled San Francisco 49ers quarterback Colin Kaepernick and became the first big leaguer to kneel during the anthem. "When Bruce Maxwell took a knee, we just didn't have the support yet," Judge said. "I don't think we were able to get the message together of staying unified. Having uncomfortable conversations with our teammates is the way to start this. I don't have all the answers now, but I like where we're going with this."

It was a sensitive issue, baked into a period when the president was chastising Minneapolis city leaders for the prolonged unrest that followed Floyd's May 25 death. Clear-eyed and honest, Stanton explained that he wanted to show support for those who have faced "racial injustice and for Black lives in general," and not necessarily the Black Lives Matter organization. "Giancarlo spoke and really showed some great leadership," said general manager Brian Cashman. "He's a strong man, a quiet man. But whenever he chooses to speak, I think he's got a very strong voice."

The players ultimately decided upon kneeling for 60 seconds, clutching the unity cloth. They would then stand through the Players Alliance video, a recorded narration from actor Morgan Freeman that emphasized equality and empathy, and a pre-recorded version of "The Star-Spangled Banner." The Yankees relayed their intention to the Nationals, who enthusiastically agreed to participate. When Boone met the media via Zoom that afternoon, he sported a black Nike T-shirt with "BLACK LIVES MATTER" printed in large white text across the front, saying that he understood "the heartache that's gone on in our country, in our world on so many levels." Several players wore identical shirts during batting practice, and the league permitted on-field personnel to wear uniform patches bearing the logos of United for Change or Black Lives Matter.

There were other changes in motion, as the league pieced the puzzle together in slapdash fashion. Hours before first pitch, MLB reached an agreement to expand the postseason field from 10 teams to 16, announcing the creation of a best-of-three wild-card series. Favored not only to win their division but also to reach the World Series, the Yankees' views were mixed; they appreciated the safety net, but believed there should be more of a premium placed upon winning the division. Relief pitcher Zack Britton said that he thought the expanded playoffs would be good for the sport, but felt the format was "kind of rushed." "It's good for the game to create more excitement, but I wasn't a big fan of the division winners not being rewarded," Britton said. "If you win your division, you should be given a bye or something to show that you won your division."

Not much seemed to be on solid ground. Six days before the opener, the Nationals were forced to consider moving the games to a minor league park, receiving pushback as the District of Columbia refused to waive a mandatory 14-day quarantine for any players, coaches, or employees potentially exposed to COVID-19, including visiting teams. D.C. officials relented before the league seriously explored relocating the festivities to the Nationals' properties in Fredericksburg, Virginia or West Palm Beach, Florida.

Filling out his first lineup card of the year, Boone wrestled with including the team's best overall hitter in DJ LeMahieu, who had been limited to a handful of Summer Camp at-bats after returning from the coronavirus. Boone decided to start Tyler Wade at second base instead, telling LeMahieu that he would play in the season's second game. The Yankees noticed that the Nationals were late providing their lineup. Washington bench coach Tim Bogar apologized, telling bench coach Carlos Mendoza that they were "working through some things."

The Nats' internal discussions were soon revealed: Soto, Washington's dazzling young outfielder, had tested positive for COVID-19. Soto would miss nearly two weeks of the season, later believing that his test had been a false positive, but neither team knew that in the moment. It was not encouraging to have a high-profile opponent flagged for the virus before the first pitch. Might other members of the Nationals also be infected? Boone nudged a few of his players, reminding them to be mindful of unnecessary interactions. Under normal circumstances, Boone wouldn't have thought twice about wandering across the field to exchange pleasantries with his Nats counterpart Davey Martinez. Soto's test provided pause.

As Scherzer and Cole worked up lathers in their respective bullpens, the Nationals prepared to raise their 2019 championship banner in the center-field plaza. When the Yankees celebrated their most recent title, the 2010 home opener had been an extraordinary gala attended by legends like Yogi Berra and Whitey Ford. The fans made that afternoon special. More than 49,000 of them roared as World Series MVP Hideki Matsui emerged from the visiting dugout to claim his ring, dressed in Angels red and enveloped lovingly by his former teammates. The ceremonial first pitch had been tossed by former outfielder Bernie Williams, whose graceful service made him a fan favorite over 16 years in the Bronx.

The Nationals would have liked a similar event to cap the first championship in franchise history, perhaps something that incorporated their previous life as the Montreal Expos or paid homage to the long-gone Washington Senators, whose banner from a 1924 triumph again fluttered in the breeze. Instead, the players heard only computerized applause as they jogged to their respective baselines. "It definitely felt odd," Judge said. "It was good to have some real baseball back, but it was strange with a team celebrating the World Series championship, and none of their fans were there. You look forward to the opening ceremonies, hearing the boos, cheers, everything like that."

The star of the pregame ceremony was Dr. Anthony Fauci, the director of the National Institute of Allergy and Infectious Diseases. A self-described Nats "superfan," the 79-year-old immunologist had once pledged his allegiance to the Yankees. Growing up in the Bensonhurst neighborhood of Brooklyn, Fauci debated the merits of Mickey Mantle and Yogi Berra against pals who favored Duke Snider and Roy Campanella.

In the early days of the pandemic, Fauci had predicted that professional sports would return, albeit with social distancing, protective masks, and spectator-less games. That proved prescient as Fauci walked to the mound, waving at imaginary occupants in the vacant blue seats. The red Nationals mask covering Fauci's nose and mouth would later land in the National Baseball Hall of Fame's archives.

The Nationals' decision to invite Fauci seemed to irk the president. About two-and-a-half miles away at the White House, Trump stood in the press briefing room and claimed that he, too, had been invited to throw out a first pitch—by the Yankees. Calling team president Randy Levine "a great friend of mine," Trump said he would appear on the Yankee Stadium mound before the Yankees–Red Sox game on August 15. The announcement surprised both Yankees officials and White House staffers; Trump did have a standing invitation from the team, as would any president, but no specific date was discussed. Trump backed away three days later, tweeting that he could not visit Yankee Stadium because of scheduled meetings on a potential coronavirus vaccine, the economy, "and much else." Though his official schedule was clear except for a 5:00 PM news conference and a roundtable with supporters, Trump wound up spending that date at a golf club in Bedminster, New Jersey.

Wearing a Nationals jersey with his surname and No. 19 stitched on the back, Fauci eyed reliever Sean Doolittle squatting behind home plate, then went into his right-handed windup. The heave missed its target by about 15 feet, bouncing toward photographers stationed near the first-base on-deck circle. Fauci told *The Wall Street Journal* that he had "completely destroyed" his arm in an overenthusiastic game of catch two days prior. Though the errant toss brought levity, Fauci's stadium visit did not escape scrutiny. While seated between his wife and a friend during the game, Fauci was photographed with a mask lowered beneath his mouth. He'd call the ensuing criticism "mischievous," claiming that he had lowered the mask to drink from a water bottle.

The professionals could finally take over. Cole described the moment in which he walked through the visiting clubhouse, seeing his teammates dressed in their crisp road grays with "NEW YORK" stitched across the chest in navy blue and white. "It just hit me," Cole said, "that this was for real."

And so was the Yankees' potent offense, which Stanton touted as "unmatched in the league." Facing Scherzer, Judge laced a liner into left field for the season's first hit, and Stanton tucked an early lead into Cole's back pocket, smashing a cutter over the wall in left-center field for a two-run homer. Stanton admired the blast as it traveled 459 feet toward a beer garden, coming to rest under a table top.

Cole retired the first batter he faced in his new uniform, inducing Trea Turner to fly out before leaving a fastball over home plate to Adam Eaton, who swatted the first of 14 homers that Cole would permit during the regular season. When the inning ended, Cole barked into his glove while stalking off the field, providing the Yanks with a glimpse of their ace's persona in a game that mattered. "This was his favorite team growing up as a kid," Judge said. "To come full circle from being a fan to pitching Opening Day for the Yankees against the reigning champs, that was special for him. He was excited. You could just see in his preparation throughout the day that he was ready to roll; he wanted this."

A three-time Cy Young Award winner and an All-Star in seven consecutive seasons, Scherzer was dazzling at times, striking out 11. But the Yankees picked their spots, notching four runs and six hits. Judge raked a run-scoring double in the third inning, sending Wade sprinting home from first base, and Stanton struck again for an opposite-field RBI single in the fifth. Meanwhile, Cole seemed to get better as the night went on, retiring 10 straight batters through one stretch.

Eaton's first-inning homer served as the only blemish on Cole's line, having permitted one run and one hit through five innings with a walk and five strikeouts. The Yankees held a 4–1 lead and were threatening for more in the sixth inning, placing runners at the corners with one out. With Wade due to face Scherzer, lightning flashed, and the skies opened with deafening thundercracks, prompting the umpires to halt play. The teams scurried to their respective clubhouses as a torrential downpour ensued, flooding the concourses and dugouts. "It was just a terrifying D.C. summer thunderstorm, truly the most intense I've ever sat through," said Lindsey Adler, who covered that game for The Athletic. "It was very funny to me that we waited months for the season to resume, and then here we are in the end of July, and it lasted five innings."

The delay stretched nearly two hours before the field was deemed unplayable, and it felt every minute of that for the players, who didn't even have couches—removed as a social distancing measure—to relax on. Cole thought that he had at least two more innings in the tank, but as the West Coast game between the Los Angeles Dodgers and San Francisco Giants flickered on the television, he recognized that Mother Nature had capped his Yankees debut at 75 pitches. He fished his cell phone out of his locker, placing a FaceTime call to his wife, Amy, exclaiming: "I can't believe I'm going to get a complete-game, one-hitter in the debut! That's just ridiculous."

There was a scheduled off day between the first and second games, which typically would have provided an opportunity for the players to explore and sample new restaurants. Instead, Cole and Brett Gardner footed the bill for a socially distanced dinner in the gallery ballroom of the Park Hyatt Washington. Flat-screen televisions were tuned to the other games around the majors as the players savored juicy steaks. The room got loud when the Matt Olson of the A's slugged a walk-off grand slam, sinking the Los Angeles Angels of Anaheim in extra innings. Even in a pandemic, watching sports on TV remained fun. "It was a nice way to relax," said reliever Chad Green said. "It was good to just talk baseball, get other guys' opinions, have a nice dinner. And I can't complain about a good steak."

The clubs returned to Nationals Park for a Saturday matinee. Stanton found Cashman and Boone in the visiting clubhouse, telling them that the unity ribbon ceremony had not been enough in his view. Stanton explained that he wanted to make his stance against social injustice clear, saying that he was "for basic human rights in America." He told Cashman and Boone that he planned to kneel for the anthem before the Yankees' second game; Aaron Hicks also pledged to do so. "I'm for equality and for us all to have a fair shake," Stanton said. "There's a lot of things in the system that can be changed, and it's just a way to bring light to that."

Technically, kneeling violated team policy—just as if a player took the field with a full beard. Cashman promised that the players there would be no discipline, viewing the demonstration as a response to a nation that was "broken in certain aspects and not all together as we should be." Boone also approved, understanding that it was an issue the players considered heavy on their hearts. Ownership was on board, but Hal Steinbrenner wished the situation could have played out differently. "Do I wish that kneeling wasn't one of the ways that they manifested their feelings? Yes, I do wish that," Steinbrenner said. "But at the same time, I understood it wasn't a decision they took lightly. And I understand that they truly believed that in order to enact the change they believed needs to happen, that was something they had to do. It didn't happen every game, obviously, but we tried from the very beginning to be as understanding as we could."

Hats over their chests, Hicks and Stanton dropped to their left knees near the foul line in shallow left field. LeMahieu stood nearby; as the song concluded, he tapped Hicks and Stanton on their shoulders, a wordless gesture that LeMahieu said was intended to convey his support. "I didn't want them to be out there by themselves doing that," LeMahieu said.

Hicks' voice quivered as he discussed the moment, inadvertently echoing Martin Luther King Jr.'s famous "I Have a Dream" speech from 1963 when he stated that he overwhelmingly desired to be judged by his character and not his skin tone. "It's not easy for a Black man growing up," Hicks said. "I just want people to know that, even though we're kneeling, we understand that there's great people in the world. They may not understand, but they've got our backs. That's all we ask for. We just—I just—want to be treated right."

There was backlash. Rudy Giuliani, the former New York City mayor and an ardent Yankees fan who frequently sports a World Series ring on his left hand, called the players' actions "hypocritical." The Yankees received many letters from fans vowing that they would tune out, as Giuliani claimed that he did. Stanton said that he could deal with whatever backlash stemmed from his actions. "It upset a lot of fans, but I think a lot of fans also understood," Steinbrenner said.

Once Stanton rose to take his at-bats as the Yanks' designated hitter and Hicks reported to center field, the D.C. visit continued with a flop. Pitcher James Paxton had spent the shutdown at his home in Eau Claire, Wisconsin, performing throwing sessions five days a week in what used to be a vending machine warehouse. It was a strange place to rehab from back surgery, lacking the resources and oversight that the left-hander might have otherwise had in a more formal setting.

Less than six months removed from going under the knife, Paxton could not generate sufficient velocity on his fastball and recorded only three outs in a 9–2 loss. That strained the bullpen, and Boone needed five relievers to clean up the mess. The Yankees needed a fresh arm, which prompted a difficult conversation the next morning when Clint Frazier was summoned to Boone's office. Frazier had done absolutely nothing wrong—in fact, Boone saw him as brimming with confidence after being one of the team's more potent hitters during Summer Camp—but they did not need a spare outfielder at the moment.

The Yankees set up their alternate site camp in Moosic, Pennsylvania, the home of the Triple A Scranton/Wilkes-Barre RailRiders, but this would be unlike any of Frazier's previous demotions. There were no scheduled games to play in; Frazier envisioned a series of instructional league workouts in which he'd face inexperienced hurlers in their early 20s, showcasing sizzling fastballs and little control. Frazier confronted Boone and Cashman in a raw exchange that spanned about 15 minutes, asking if he had a future in the organization. "It was frustrating," Frazier said. "I got to ask some questions and I got some answers. We were just passionate about it, like grown-ups in there. It was kind of like, 'What am I? What is expected of me? Where's my place on this team?' I feel like I'm ready and I'm hoping that I can make the most of an opportunity. It's hard to make the most of something if you're not given that chance."

Boone characterized Frazier's demeanor that morning as "very honest, direct, and mature." In a similar situation the previous June, Frazier had rankled the organization by taking the full allotted 72 hours to travel from Chicago to Scranton. This time, he hustled. Frazier told himself that he needed to stay ready—whether for the Yankees or one of the other 29 teams—a mind-set that he credited to his agent, Seth Levinson, who sent him lengthy motivational text messages each day.

With Frazier on the way to Pennsylvania, the Yankees' lineup could have used his help through six innings. Left-hander Patrick Corbin silenced them, economically retiring 18 of the first 19 batters. Corbin looked every bit the stud that Cashman had once courted, holding what had once been his favorite franchise scoreless until Gleyber Torres mashed a 403-foot homer over the left-field wall. Luke Voit tied the game with his first home run of the year, a solo shot off reliever Will Harris, and Torres gave New York the lead with a go-ahead single in the eighth. Tommy Kahnle pitched around a Torres throwing error in the home half of that inning, using a stellar change-up to strike out Eric Thames and pin the bases loaded. Kahnle pumped his fist and whirled off the mound, unaware that it would prove to be his only appearance of the year. "Tommy brought such great energy to the guys," Britton said. "He's like your biggest hype man with that infectious positive personality. He was a guy that we missed at the end of the season. Tommy was a big help getting us through some of that initial uncertainty."

A 30-year-old right-hander who'd recorded a 3.67 ERA in 72 appearances the previous year, Kahnle joined a substantial roster of pitchers who sustained injuries in the early weeks of the 2020 season. He underwent reconstructive Tommy John surgery on his right ulnar collateral ligament, and the stockpile of shelved arms made many wonder if the three-and-a-half week restart had been too hurried. "Unfortunately, it was not unexpected just given the circumstances we were pressed into," pitching coach Matt Blake said. "Some teams were a little bit more laissez-faire with how they approached the ramp-ups; some teams were really on top of it and came in guns blazing. A lot of these guys were put in circumstances that didn't foster success for them."

The bullpen was now without Kahnle and Aroldis Chapman, who was still recovering from COVID-19 in his Manhattan apartment. Otherwise, the Yankees were satisfied with the opening series as they boarded six buses in the underbelly of Nationals Park. Each game in the shortened season was the equivalent of 2.7 over a 162-game campaign, so if you wanted to get funky with the math, they'd won 5.4 of their first 8.1 games. As Voit said, "Every game is like a sweep."

Three down, 57 to go. But the events that followed over the next several days would prompt the Yankees to wonder how—or if—they'd ever get 60 in the books.

• CHAPTER 8 •

Best-Laid Plans

Sixty stories above street level, the New York Yankees savored one of the most lavish breakfast arrangements they'd see all year on the morning of July 27, taking in the view from the JG Skyhigh Lounge of the Four Seasons Philadelphia. Over plates piled high with eggs and bacon, the players and coaches sipped their premium Blue Bottle coffee and gazed at the fluffy clouds over Center City, feeling as though the world was burning below them.

Having traveled from Washington, D.C., to Philadelphia the previous evening, the players were surprised to learn that their game against the Phillies was postponed. It was—on what was forecast to be a sunny day with temperatures in the high 90s—the first of numerous delays and postponements the Yankees would endure, and most had nothing to do with the weather.

While the Yankees concluded their series with the Washington Nationals, the Miami Marlins were wrapping up an 11–6 victory against the Phillies at Citizens Bank Park. The next morning, the Marlins had become baseball's first test case on how to handle an outbreak, as 18 players and two coaches tested positive for the coronavirus. The contagion wrecked MLB's revised 60-game schedule, which had remained intact for all of four days. Miami used 45 players to get through its first 10 games, including 27 pitchers. "When that happened with the Marlins and Phillies, I said, 'We're not finishing the season,'" said outfielder Aaron Hicks. "It just seemed like more and more teams were coming out of nowhere with COVID."

Fortunately, most of the Marlins' cases were asymptomatic or had mild symptoms, like those exhibited by shortstop Miguel Rojas, who reported a fever and cough. All of the infected players had to be quarantined and loaded onto buses pointed back to South Florida. Marlins chief operating officer Derek Jeter acknowledged that his players let their guards down on a two-game visit to Atlanta prior to the series opener, getting together in groups and not wearing masks. "We're battling something that's invisible here," Jeter said. "You can't see it. You don't know where it starts. You don't know how it gets there, but once it gets there, it has an opportunity to spread quickly. And we've seen that."

Instead of preparing to play their next game, the Phillies were instructed to report to Citizens Bank Park for drive-through coronavirus testing. All players and staff members, including manager Joe Girardi, were greeted by a worker in full PPE gear. They'd roll down their car windows, fill a saliva vial, then go home. The Yankees and Baltimore Orioles—who were supposed to play Philadelphia and Miami, respectively—just had to sit and wait.

Told that they could not enter the ballpark, none of the Yankees complained. They understood that episodes like this would be part of the season's backdrop and did not seem eager to occupy a visiting clubhouse where the Marlins had just spent a weekend dressing and showering. Because one of the visiting clubhouse workers tested positive for COVID-19, likely by transmission from one of the Marlins, the Yankees summoned their staff down Interstate 95 from New York.

Naysayers pointed to the ordeal as evidence that MLB's plan to play in 30 different stadiums was doomed, but Rob Manfred didn't agree. The commissioner said that he didn't consider Miami's outbreak to be in the nightmare category, explaining that protocols allowed play to continue. That was why teams were given secondary training sites, and the Marlins would have to call upon that depth to bring in 17 new players as their season paused for a week. Manfred placed the blame on the players, saying that they "need to be better," but he vowed that the season would continue. "I am not a quitter in general," Manfred said. "And there is no reason to quit now."

Sidelined through no fault of their own, the Yankees could do little but enjoy the Four Seasons' 300 thread count sheets and wait for the league to sort the mess out. The Yankees had the place to themselves, and they described top-notch treatment from employees thrilled to have customers back in the rooms. "There was a sincere sense of joy of the staff being back to work," said Ben Tuliebitz, the Yankees' director of team travel and player services. "Even the bell staff opening the doors and guys busing the tables after the team finished their meals, they were smiling, so happy to be back to work. It was a genuine appreciation for normal life."

In a three-story lounge that previously played host to weddings, banquets, and bar mitzvahs, areas were set aside for players to pick up their individually-boxed meals. There was also an outdoor terrace with tables separated by at least six feet. From the 60th floor, one staffer gestured toward a window washer dangling from an adjacent building and joked: "It could be worse. We could be that guy."

"We had food at every time you would want food," said reliever Adam Ottavino. "If the food is lousy, then you're kind of stuck, so I felt like they did a good job."

That was also one of the first stops where the Yankees had a game area set up, allowing their players to blow off steam with table tennis, foosball, and electronic dartboards. Brett Gardner swiftly earned a reputation as the guy that you did not want to see across the net with a Ping-Pong paddle. "That was right up Gardy's alley, just competing 24 hours a day," said P.J. Pilittere, the team's assistant hitting coach. "Gardy is the hustler. He's going to act like he's not good at anything: 'Oh, I haven't played this in forever. I'm not very good.' And then he just mops the floor with you."

Gardner wasn't the most talented table tennis player on the roster. That was probably Jonathan Holder, a relief pitcher who sometimes tried to coach his teammates on how they could spin the ball like a professional. But Gardner was consistent, returning the ball defensively and forcing opponents to make mistakes. Teammates wanted to beat him—bad—and they couldn't.

"I don't think I've ever tried so hard to embarrass somebody on a Ping-Pong table," said infielder Tyler Wade. "He had my number. I felt like that was my one time with people around to bury him. He didn't let me."

The Yankees were among the few clubs to provide such amenities for their players on the road; some others simply instructed their players to stay in their rooms, and at least one team refused to foot the bill for room service. Players were permitted to use DoorDash or Grubhub to order from local restaurants on their own dime, but since the team provided meals, many did not. Rooms were set aside for massage therapy, and players could sign up for time blocks to utilize the gym. Space was devoted to pregame meetings and video review, making it easier for players to prepare without being at the stadium.

But with players strongly discouraged from leaving the building, even luxurious four-star accommodations began to feel like a gilded cage. DJ LeMahieu said that he spent most of the time with his cell phone in hand, participating in the team's group text message and wondering what the next move would be.

After two nights in Philadelphia with no games, the Yankees made plans to return to New York, wheeling their equipment from the visiting clubhouse at Citizens Bank Park. The buses were about 45 minutes from pointing north when general manager Brian Cashman called manager Aaron Boone, asking what he thought about the idea of going to Baltimore instead. The Orioles were similarly marooned; they'd flown to Miami in anticipation of opening a series against the Marlins and now were set to re-board their plane and travel back to Maryland.

Boone told Cashman that he was all for the idea, but that it would be up to the players. Britton pinged Tuliebitz's phone with an urgent S.O.S., saying that the players needed to assemble immediately. They gathered in a lounge on the 58th floor just after noon, as Britton explained the development and took a head count. Aaron Judge remarked that it felt like "backyard baseball." *Hey, we heard there's a team down the street ready to play. Who wants next?* "That was such a mess," Britton said. "We had to sit in the hotel and we were like, 'What is going on?' Everything was so inconsistent."

The Yankees voted unanimously not to go home, altering the schedule to play two games in Baltimore instead. The Orioles had a similar gathering in

During his introductory press conference in December of 2019, Gerrit Cole holds the sign he used as a young New York Yankees fan. Team owner Hal Steinbrenner (left) and his wife Amy Cole (right) join him at the podium.

Gio Urshela bats during a March 8, 2020 spring training game against the Atlanta Braves at George M. Steinbrenner Field in Tampa, Florida, before baseball—and the entire country—shut down.

During spring training 2.0 or Summer Camp, manager Aaron Boone celebrates with his players after defeating the New York Mets on July 18, 2020 in New York.

Director of the National Institute of Allergy and Infectious Diseases Dr. Anthony Fauci (in white jersey) stands for the national anthem before throwing out the ceremonial first pitch at Opening Day between the New York Yankees and the Washington Nationals on July 23, 2020 in Washington, D.C.

In normal times, the New York Yankees' home opener versus the rival Boston Red Sox would be a festive and raucous affair. But having no fans made for a much different atmosphere on July 31, 2020.

*New York Yankees relievers Chad Green (left) and Adam Ottavino (right) show
their support for social justice before the Opening Day game.*

*Giancarlo Stanton, one of the team's more outspoken social justice advocates, kneels
for the national anthem before a game against the Boston Red Sox on September 18,
2020.*

While trotting the bases after hitting a solo home run during the fifth inning—his ninth homer in the New York Yankees' first 17 games—of an August 11 game against the Atlanta Braves, slugger Aaron Judge started to labor because of a calf injury.

Aaron Judge's injury paved the way for Clint Frazier, who jogs down the third-base line after hitting a solo home run in his first game back with the New York Yankees on August 12, 2020.

Tampa Bay Rays slugger Mike Brosseau yells at Aroldis Chapman after the reliever's first pitch—a 100.5 mph fastball—buzzed over his head. That at-bat on September 1, 2020 underscored the bad blood between the Rays and New York Yankees.

Part of a 20–6 drubbing of the Toronto Blue Jays amidst a 10-game win streak, Luke Voit hits a three-run home run on September 15, 2020 to help get the New York Yankees back on track.

Though fans couldn't attend the New York Yankees' postseason games, the players did receive support from their girlfriends and wives, who were able to sit in a luxury suite high above right field. (Courtesy Nancy Arreola)

During a 10–9, Game 2 victory that spanned four hours and 50 minutes to win the wild-card series against the Cleveland Indians, Gio Urshela flips his bat after hitting the first postseason grand slam ever hit by a New York Yankees third baseman.

Deivi García throws during Game 2 of the ALDS, making him the New York Yankees' youngest starting pitcher ever in a postseason contest. The decision to use him as an opener was a controversial one.

Closer Aroldis Chapman allows a tiebreaking home run to Tampa Bay Rays slugger Mike Brosseau in the eighth inning of Game 5 of the ALDS.

After Gio Urshela flies out for the final out of Game 5 of the ALDS, catcher Michael Perez and the rest of the Tampa Bay Rays celebrate winning the series.

Miami, voting to return home and face the Yankees. Chris Marinak, MLB's executive vice president of strategy, technology, and innovation, was responsible for shoehorning the games into the schedule. Marinak said that the league was prepared for those challenges, having expected positive tests and accompanying postponements throughout the season. Having teams play division rivals 10 times mixed with 20 games against their corresponding division helped; chances of finding a workable geographical match were higher.

Once MLB approved the change, Tuliebitz sprang into motion, rifling through his digital Rolodex in search of a block of Baltimore rooms. Big league clubs usually reserve their accommodations about eight months in advance, and Tuliebitz now had to get the Yankees settled in a matter of hours. Overlooking the Inner Harbor adjacent to the National Aquarium and a performing arts center, the Four Seasons was the team's preferred go-to in Baltimore. Tuliebitz was relieved to learn that the hotel had about 70 rooms available since the pandemic had decreased business and leisure travel. Tuliebitz explained MLB's new protocols and heard assurances that they could make it work.

The buses made the right turn onto Philadelphia's Market Street around 5:30 PM, beginning the 101-mile trek. Staffers hurried to delete scouting reports on Phillies players from the iPads used by coaches and players, substituting Orioles data. By 8:00 PM, the Yankees had the lights flicked on at Camden Yards underneath a portrait-quality red sky, finally able to hit and throw once again. Boone lauded the players' flexibility, saying that they had remained "in the athletic position" throughout the uncertain episode. "We just took a nice little weekend trip to Philly to check out the Four Seasons," Judge said.

Gerrit Cole was back on the mound when play resumed on July 29, notching his second victory in as many starts behind homers from LeMahieu, Judge, and Hicks. Paired with Gary Sánchez, Cole lauded his catcher's familiarity with the Orioles' lineup for helping him retire 14 consecutive batters and 19 of 20. Perhaps it felt fresh for Cole, but beating up on Baltimore was old hat for the rest of the Yankees. The next day, they won their 18th consecutive game over the Orioles, an inconceivable run of dominance at the game's highest level.

The Birds led late, taking advantage of a mushy J.A. Happ effort. But Lucy pulled the football from Charlie Brown as Judge launched a titanic three-run homer, powering a comeback that also featured Luke Voit's first career grand slam. Gardner, a Yankee since 2008, pulled his jeans on and said that it had been the strangest road trip of his decade-plus compiling big league service time. "Going to Philadelphia, staying there for two days, and basically not leaving the hotel, not playing Philly, then going to Baltimore, and extending the road trip," Gardner said, "a lot of guys were wearing clothes for the second or third time through those last couple of days."

As Boone eyed the Yankee Stadium home opener on the schedule, the manager said he held only an "impression" of the upcoming timetable. After the Philadelphia debacle, it was best not to get too locked into plans. The postponed games against the Phillies were to be played the next week, followed by a weekend trip to play the Tampa Bay Rays that now included a Saturday doubleheader.

At that time, the league had not finalized a decision to reduce double-headers to seven-inning games, a request made by the Major League Baseball Players Association to minimize the time in the stadium while lightening pitchers' workloads. They'd sort that out soon. For the moment, they could just be pleased that there more games were on the calendar. The Boston Red Sox were next. "If there is one thing 2020 taught us," Boone said, "it was not to look too far ahead."

CHAPTER 9

HOME SWEET HOME

Aaron Judge's spikes crunched into Yankee Stadium's right-handed batter's box as the slugger waggled his black 35-inch, 33-ounce Chandler bat, finally logging an at-bat in his home park that would count in the statistics. He tapped the glossy hunk of maple on home plate and acknowledged Christian Vazquez of the Boston Red Sox, his eyes darting toward the decks of empty blue seats. "Imagine," Judge told the catcher, "how rocking this place would have been."

Vazquez could not disagree. The New York Yankees' home opener was supposed to be against the Philadelphia Phillies, but with those games rescheduled, the schedule-makers delivered the rich tradition of rivalry with the club's New England neighbors. This weakened Red Sox roster bore only passing resemblance to one that had ended Judge's season two years prior, having traded star outfielder Mookie Betts and other vital pieces. The clash of classic uniforms would have to carry the weight.

The home opener is always a noteworthy date on the baseball calendar. When the Yankees opened 2019, hosting the Baltimore Orioles for a March 28 matinee, nearly 47,000 fans filtered through the stadium's gates on a breezy 48-degree afternoon for the pageantry of an Opening Day in the South Bronx. The atmospheric conditions were more pleasant on a 79-degree midsummer evening, but the only witnesses in the seating bowl were a few television camera operators and an authenticator who trudged after foul balls in Sisyphean fashion. Without the fans, Yankees–Red Sox just wasn't the same. "I definitely noticed it the first time we played the Red Sox," Aaron Boone said. "You know what those games bring in energy and edge for our fanbase. Whether you're at Fenway Park or in the Bronx, you notice it. You certainly miss that because it's a special thing to be a part of."

As first pitch neared, Suzyn Waldman cleared her throat and performed vocal exercises in the broadcast booth to keep a promise she had once made to Gerrit Cole. During a casual 2018 conversation outside Yankee Stadium's visiting clubhouse, the veteran radio broadcaster and reporter offhandedly mentioned to Cole—then a member of the Houston Astros—that he would make a great Yankee once he reached free agency. "If I do," Cole replied, "you have to sing the National Anthem on Opening Day."

Waldman chuckled, replying something along the lines of, "We'll see." A trained Broadway performer, she had performed "The Star-Spangled Banner" before sports events on many occasions. At the original Yankee Stadium, Waldman especially liked to sing against the Red Sox so her parents could watch on television from New England. Cole remembered the exchange, reminding Waldman following the formal portion of his December news conference: "Don't you forget: you promised me!"

"I thought that was never going to happen because they do everything except shoot cannons off on Opening Day here," Waldman said. "But since they don't want to let anybody in the park, maybe I'm the only one left."

Indeed, it would be a home opener devoid of the usual pomp and circumstance. Even the red, white, and blue bunting that usually draped each level prior to big games was absent; the stadium's only accoutrements were large tarpaulins covering the field-level seats, bearing sponsor logos like those of Bank of America and Delta Air Lines. Some teams placed weatherproof cutouts of smiling fans in their empty seats; the Yankees did not. "Every park had its own view. We just thought it was silly," said Lonn Trost, the Yankees' chief operating officer. "Did you ever try to clean wet cardboard?"

Besides, the Yankees were quietly continuing to pursue the possibility of having fans in attendance. Hal Steinbrenner said that the team had Ticketmaster produce a limited-admission seating diagram of Yankee Stadium, which would have reduced capacity to about 25 percent; the team's largest announced crowd of the 2019 season was 48,101. "We had it all set up in the orientation of how everything would go, row by row, seat by seat," Steinbrenner said. "It would probably have been 12,000 to 15,000."

The league eventually took that decision out of their hands, stating that there would be no in-person attendance until the postseason. After thousands of innings in the current stadium, this would be Waldman's first time singing for an audience there—albeit one limited to on-field personnel and a smattering of media. Since her Tier 3 credential did not permit field access, she clutched a wireless microphone in the broadcast booth, locking eyes with the mural of George M. Steinbrenner that towers beyond the right-field wall. "It was like singing into a nightclub microphone," Waldman said. "I was in the broadcast booth, and there was no feedback. I could hear everything, and I looked out there. The first thing you see out there as you look out there is George. George would have loved that."

Cole scarcely contained a grin throughout the song, doffing his cap toward the press level in appreciation at its conclusion. Cole lauded Waldman's pace, saying that she had "nailed it." For months, Waldman fielded requests from fans and friends who wanted to hear the rendition again. She'd link with a New York-based composer to benefit Citymeals on Wheels in the Bronx, capturing the vocals with her home computer before sending the audio file off for mixing.

Members of both rosters stood in front of their respective dugouts to bang large metal pans, as New Yorkers did each evening at 7:00 PM in recognition of healthcare industry workers across the metropolitan area. Even Steinbrenner participated. Sporting a mask as he drummed a spoon on kitchenware, the managing general partner scanned the barren ballpark and marveled at a scene he called "absolutely surreal." "It's not just what you see on the field and the fact that you can hear all the players rooting for each other," Steinbrenner said. "It's just walking around the office level, not seeing ticket takers and security and ushers. It felt like it was me and five other people in the stadium. I got used to it, amazingly enough, but boy—it's not the same."

The ceremonial first pitch honors were entrusted to CC Sabathia. COVID-19 limitations created a limited pool from which the Yankees could draw, but the retired hurler would have been a sharp choice even in the Before Times, returning to the mound where he blew out his left shoulder in Game 4 of the previous year's American League Championship Series. Cole was tabbed for the receiving honors, as the pair owned a friendship that stretched back more than a decade.

An agent offered Cole, then a high school standout, the opportunity to enjoy lunch with Sabathia, then a Cleveland Indians star in town for a series against the Los Angeles Angels of Anaheim. Cole accepted instantly. They dined at the Fashion Island shopping plaza in Newport Beach, the same hub where Cole would gush over meeting Andy Pettitte years later. Cole could see that retirement and quarantine had been good for Sabathia, who appeared svelte in a tight-fitting T-shirt, lobbing an easy toss that Cole scooped from the left-handed batter's box. "That's the furthest I've thrown a ball since that playoff game," Sabathia said. "It just reinforces my decision to retire."

Playing through the myriad issues of 2020 also held little appeal for Sabathia, whose gregarious personality was a unifying presence over his 11 seasons in New York. Sabathia loved to invite teammates to backyard barbecues, pool parties, and share his courtside seats for basketball games at Madison Square Garden, all of which were impossible in the COVID-19 environment. Sabathia said that he would "be such a bad teammate right now; I'd be complaining about everything."

The current Yankees took care of business on the field, posting a 5–1 victory. Judge took aim at the short porch in right field and rounded the bases for a two-run homer, his third consecutive game with a long ball. Judge also did it on defense that night, snaring a J.D. Martinez liner in the third inning and rifling a strong throw to first base that doubled off Kevin Pillar, supporting Jordan Montgomery's first victory in more than two years. He couldn't help glancing at his vacant Judge's Chambers, imagining what the reaction would have been. "I was sitting on the bench talking with DJ [LeMahieu], just saying, we knew this place would have been packed," Judge said. "It was a little different, but the game still goes on. Life goes on."

They were rolling, but five-and-a-half miles south at the league office, MLB was scrambling to keep its season alive. Commissioner Rob Manfred was issuing warnings that afternoon that baseball could shut down within days if the players did not do a better job of following protocols. Manfred was distressed by the magnitude of the Miami Marlins outbreak, as well as 18 positive tests in the St. Louis Cardinals clubhouse. Manfred would later acknowledge that baseball had "some pretty nervous days" where a shut-down appeared imminent. "This virus is unpredictable and unmanageable," Manfred said. "Despite all of the preparations and efforts in advance, we had to respond really quickly to developments that were simply not foreseeable."

St. Louis did not play for 16 days. Manager Mike Shildt said that multiple Cardinals had gone to the emergency room with COVID-related symptoms, and pitcher Carlos Martinez later revealed that his symptoms were so distressing that he had been to the hospital "three or four times." TV networks were alerted to secure alternate programming, and eight teams saw their schedules interrupted over the season's first nine days.

The Cardinals' outbreak was the latest in a series of frazzling circumstances for baseball's medical director, Dr. Gary Green. Each evening around 10:00 PM, Green received an email with the day's coronavirus test results, the opening of which he described as "like defusing a bomb." In response to the outbreaks, the league installed compliance officers who essentially acted like hall monitors. "Rob [Manfred] was great about it," Steinbrenner said. "We had an owners call almost every week and sometimes twice a week. It was clear how much work MLB was putting into all of this with the doctors they were talking to and infectious disease people. With all the preparation that was put into it, I was at least confident we had a fighting chance of finishing the season."

The Yankees focused on what was within their control, which was beating up on Boston. The next night, Judge crushed a 455-foot drive toward the back of the left-field bleachers, where the ball rolled down three steps before coming to rest. Gio Urshela hit his first career grand slam, and rookie reliever Nick Nelson tossed three scoreless innings, earning the victory in his big league debut. In the series finale, Judge continued to sizzle, homering twice and driving in five runs. It was Judge's fifth consecutive game with a homer, including a tie-breaking, jaw-dropping 468-foot shot that powered the Yankees' 9–7 victory.

Judge leaned on the aw-shucks routine that endeared him to fans during his charge to unanimous selection as the American League's 2017 Rookie of the Year, saying he was "not locked in yet, still trying to find it." Luke Voit said that the display was a reminder of what Judge could do when he was healthy, saying that Judge was "a guy that you don't want to take your eyes off when he's hitting."

"He was a man on a mission," said infielder Tyler Wade. "I think the whole world saw what a mission this guy was on. Dude, it was contagious. I thought he was going to win MVP. I would have put all my money on him winning MVP just from his mind-set and all the hard work he put in."

The last game of the Boston series was carried by ESPN, and Alex Rodriguez and Matt Vasgersian called the game from a Bristol, Connecticut, studio. The Worldwide Leader received more than it bargained for by planting a microphone on Yankees third-base coach Phil Nevin. If anyone wondered what coaches talk about during games, Nevin's between-innings bench commentary provided a sample. "Did you have that Greek chicken?" Nevin asked someone, his face covered by a mask bearing the interlocking "NY" logo. "Whew. I'm going to have to ask somebody else. I can't stop burping it up."

The homestand continued with a series against the Phillies. Coming off an idle week in which they had no new coronavirus cases, Joe Girardi's club was cleared to return to action. Their welcome back gift was the challenge of facing the sizzling Cole, who was pulling on his pinstriped uniform for the first time in a game. Cole's first home start in pinstripes generated a strong line, holding the Phils to a run on five hits in a 91-pitch effort. Cole said that he was impressed by how aggressive the Phils were despite the long layoff and fed them a steady diet of curveballs to counter their approach of hunting for fastballs. "I was thinking about the things that I can control," Cole said. "I was excited. It was special to put on the uniform, it was special to warm up in that bullpen, and and it was special to take the field. You don't dream about pitching in a stadium without any fans, but I guess we were kind of getting used to it at that point."

LeMahieu slugged a leadoff homer, and Brett Gardner started the home third inning by clearing the left-field wall for the first over-the-wall, opposite-field home run of his career. Watching on television from Southern California, former Yankees pitcher and prolific tweeter Phil Hughes reached for his cell phone and tapped out: "Gardy is my boy, but if he's going oppo the league has a baseball problem." Someone in the clubhouse printed the message and left it on Gardner's chair, where it rested when he returned to his locker following the Yanks' 6–3 victory—their seventh straight.

Gardner would dish out plenty of retribution in the weeks to come. His favorite target was Wade, and he frequently dumped baby powder on the chair in front of the 25-year-old infielder's locker. Wade would stew as he cleaned his chair, asking teammates who had done it. They remained tight-lipped and shrugged, passing the secret around: *Gardner did this to Wade. Wade doesn't know. Don't tell him.* During the season Wade received a bottle of Tajín chili lime salt from his parents in California. He loved to put it on fruit and would urge his teammates to try it. Of course, Gardner dumped that on Wade's chair as well, adding baby powder and hand sanitizer for good measure. "Every time I would walk out to BP, he would dump like half of it on my chair," Wade said. "It was just Gardy being Gardy. I had got some stuff in mind that I wanted to get him back with, but that's playing with fire."

Wade concocted a scheme in which he could sneak into Gardner's room and place timers, which would go off at odd hours. It never happened, but Judge did help out his buddy on one occasion. Judge dumped a container of baby powder on Gardner's chair, then left a trail leading to Giancarlo Stanton's locker, knowing that Gardner would have little interest in confronting the 6'6" slugger.

With eight wins in their first nine games, the Yankees were playing well and having fun doing it. The last thing anyone wanted was another postponement, but Hurricane Isaias' approach nixed the next night of action. The Phillies didn't even bother checking into their New York hotel, busing from Philadelphia to Yankee Stadium and back the same day. The situation prompted Girardi to recall the line Joe Pesci delivers to Marisa Tomei in his favorite movie, *My Cousin Vinny*: "Is there any more shit we can pile on?"

A doubleheader was set for August 5 at Citizens Bank Park, though each game would only last seven innings. The Yankees would be the "home team" for one game but wear their gray road uniforms to ease the laundry load. It was weird. A Yankees hype video played on the left-field scoreboard, and Dan Baker—in his 48th summer as the Phillies' public-address announcer—spoke words he'd never thought he'd say in that ballpark: "Your New York Yankees." A small group of fans outside the stadium, identifying themselves as the "Phandemic Krew," booed that announcement.

Yankees hitters heard their walk-up music at the plate—along with ringing cowbells and banging drums from beyond the center-field gates; the outskirts of Ashburn Alley were the closest any fans could get to a regular-season game. They were at least closer than the Yankees' television and radio teams, who did not travel to any of the road games. Most called the action from separate broadcast booths at Yankee Stadium. Michael Kay compared that scene to *I Am Legend*, a 2007 post-apocalyptic film in which Will Smith is the last human in New York City.

"Being in that ballpark and doing a game somewhere else, with all the stadium lights off, it felt extraordinarily dystopian to me," Kay said. "It was spooky, especially for night games. We'd look around and go, 'Is this really happening?' Baseball is really hard to do if it's not in front of you."

Kay, David Cone, and Meredith Marakovits were in separate booths at Yankee Stadium, as were John Sterling, Waldman, and Rickie Ricardo on the radio side. Paul O'Neill was more than 500 miles away, performing color commentary from his Ohio basement. Incorporating the former outfielder into the broadcast was a challenge. Kay, Cone, and Marakovits were never sure when O'Neill might interject, and after a few stumbles, Kay suggested that they keep one video monitor trained on O'Neill. Like a schoolchild, O'Neill would raise his hand if he wished to speak. As they grew more comfortable with the arrangement, O'Neill volunteered to perform nightly show-and-tell from his extensive memorabilia collection, a segment he could never have shared if he were at the ballpark. "He had the silver bat from his 1994 batting title under his couch," Kay said with a laugh. "He started pulling things out of his closet: a Hank Aaron ball, a Joe DiMaggio bat, just some amazing stuff. It became part of the fun of the broadcast, and we'd build around it: 'Paul, what do you have today?'"

Judge hit his seventh homer in the first game of the doubleheader, but a late surge against the Phils' porous bullpen fell short. The Yankees had the lingering feeling that they'd run out of at-bats in the seven-inning contest; if the Phillies had needed to get six more outs, Philadelphia's 11–7 lead might not have held. In the second game, Voit hit an early homer off Aaron Nola, who held the Yanks to three hits while striking out 12 over six innings. Then Girardi turned to the bullpen; Stanton and Voit greeted Tommy Hunter with consecutive singles, and Mike Tauchman lined a double to right-center field to give New York the lead. Urshela added another run-scoring hit, helping secure the doubleheader split.

The first opportunity to see the extra-inning rule in practice generated mixed reviews. Boone understood why it was in place for the pandemic-shortened season, believing that it would help teams avoid burning out their pitching staffs in extraordinary long games—in fact, no regular-season game would go longer than 13 innings in 2020. But Boone thought that it tipped the scales in favor of the home team. Relief pitchers feared being marginalized out of the game and especially hated seeing the automatic runner at second base. "Every game matters, and just to throw a guy on second base is not the answer," Chad Green said. "It's not something that you would want to do in the postseason when every game matters. Personally, I'm not a big fan of it."

The active roster reduced from 30 players to 28, where it would remain for the rest of the regular season. The Philadelphia visit wrapped with a loss, wasting Gary Sánchez's long homer. That game featured a brief interruption as Boone complained about an air horn blasted by fans outside. Boone suggested that the game should be treated "like a golf environment," but the umpires shrugged and told Boone there was not much they could do. Play resumed after a Philadelphia police cruiser rolled by to silence the air horns.

The Tampa Bay Rays were the next team on the schedule, representing the first trip of the season in which the Yankees would travel by air. Even on a chartered jet larger than the one the team usually reserved, it was not exactly luxurious. Surgical or N-95 masks were mandatory throughout the two-and-a-half hour flight to Tampa International Airport, and players had to eat pre-packaged food. They were told to avoid eating simultaneously with the person across their row and could only leave their seat to visit the restroom. Solo Netflix marathons replaced the usual card games and lively banter. Though Tampa was a second home for many in the traveling party, the Marlins and Cardinals' recent outbreaks scuttled initial plans to permit players to stay off-campus. Unable to go home, bench coach Carlos Mendoza had his wife and children visit, but their access was strictly limited. "They had to get tested twice before they were able to come into the hotel, but then they couldn't use anything," Mendoza said. "When I went to the stadium, they couldn't use the pool. If I found an hour in the morning or an hour and a half after the game, that was it."

The Yankees' only chance to soak in the sunshine came on bus rides to Tropicana Field, the dingy dome pinned by Interstate 275 in St. Petersburg. Originally constructed to lure the San Francisco Giants in the early 1990s, the Trop and the ensuing visits there had become easy pickings for the Yankees. New York was a dominant steamroller in 1998, the same year that the Tampa Bay Devil Rays joined the American League, sporting a grotesque purple and green color scheme that matched their woeful on-field performance.

Over their first decade, Tampa Bay was a laughingstock, averaging 97 losses per season—a relief to Yankees manager Joe Torre since George Steinbrenner took any defeat to his neighbors across the Howard Frankland Bridge as a personal affront. Those losing ways turned with Joe Maddon's hire as manager in 2005, sparking the franchise's embrace of analytics just as a young and talented core rose through the farm system. They shed their "Devil" moniker before the 2008 season, swapping in a sharp navy blue and light blue scheme, adding a bright yellow sunburst intended to convey life in the Sunshine State.

There were ugly clashes between the clubs, dating to a spring 2008 game when Tampa Bay's Elliot Johnson trucked the Yankees' Francisco Cervelli at Steinbrenner Field, fracturing the catcher's right wrist. New York's Shelley Duncan drew blood a few days later at sleepy old Al Lang Field in St. Petersburg, sliding spikes high into Rays second baseman Akinori Iwamura and setting off a bench-clearing brawl. Maddon called the play "borderline criminal," then got the last laugh with a trip to the World Series that autumn, falling in five games to a powerhouse Phillies squad. "I don't want to overdramatize that and say that one incident is why the Rays turned it around," said Marc Topkin of the *Tampa Bay Times*, "but that was the first time they were able to step out a little bit against the Yankees. It was a one-sided rivalry; they would trudge out of Yankee Stadium old and new, having lost almost every season series. They were never comfortable being there."

Over the years, the faces changed, but the tension remained. Sabathia saw to that, playing a starring role in the intensifying rivalry. The Yankees never forgot reliever Andrew Kittredge's high-and-tight fastball that buzzed Austin Romine in a September 2018 game. Sabathia responded by drilling catcher Jesus Sucre with his first pitch of the next half-inning, prompting an ejection. It was Sabathia's final start of the season, and he exited the field two innings shy of reaching a contract incentive worth $500,000. He got his money's worth, gesturing toward Kittredge on the Tampa Bay bench and shouting: "That's for you, bitch!" The Yankees quietly paid the bonus anyway.

In May 2019, Voit was hit in the left shoulder by Yonny Chirinos immediately following a LeMahieu homer, which Voit called "sketchy." Sabathia called it "stupid," then fired a pitch that nearly drilled outfielder Austin Meadows. Sabathia finished the inning and, as he walked to the dugout, announced: "I was definitely trying to hit his ass." Sabathia was also at the center of a bench-clearing incident in July 2019, staring down outfielder Avisail García after a generous third-strike call. Shortstop Didi Gregorius had to restrain his much larger teammate as the benches cleared.

Sabathia said that there was "no love lost" between the clubs, and Rays ace Blake Snell said that they "party harder" after wins against the Yankees. Snell got to celebrate after a well-pitched series opener. Each team was limited to two hits in a Tampa Bay victory decided by an eighth-inning sacrifice fly. Next up was another seven-inning doubleheader and another split. Cole was crisp, striking out 10 before fatiguing in an 8–4 victory. Mike Ford, Stanton, and Judge all homered, a performance that prompted Voit to boast about his teammates. "There's no limp in the lineup," Voit said. "Everyone can hit the deep ball, get on base, walk, has good approaches, doesn't swing at balls. It's lots of damage throughout. You look up in the third or fourth inning, and the pitcher's at 60-plus pitches. This lineup is just tremendous, deadly. We're called the Bronx Bombers for a reason."

Stanton's homer came off left-hander Sean Gilmartin, the husband of White House press secretary Kayleigh McEnany. That did not escape some of the writers, who noted Stanton's enthusiastic support of the Black Lives Matter movement. The afterglow wouldn't last long. Back on the field about 40 minutes later, the injury bug caught Stanton, who had been feeling so good earlier in the week that he recorded his first stolen base in nearly two years. Now, Stanton experienced tightness in his left hamstring, grimacing after sliding into second base on a wild pitch. Stanton was able to stay on the bases, scoring on a Voit single, but he gingerly moved down the dugout steps and told Boone: "Have somebody ready."

It was yet another installment in Stanton's maddening litany of injuries. With Stanton limited to 18 regular-season contests in 2019 due to a left biceps strain, a left shoulder strain, a left calf strain, a strain of his right posterior cruciate ligament, and a strained right quadriceps, Yankees lineups with his name had become a novelty. The hulking strongman who once bench pressed supermodel Adriana Lima during a winter workout simply could not stay on the field.

"Words can't really describe the disappointment I've had over this," Stanton said. "I put a lot into this. It's unbelievable. It's a tough spot, but people have been in worse. There can always be light at the end of the tunnel."

The game, a 5–3 Yankees loss, also featured a new chapter in the ongoing beef with the Rays. Tempers flared after a handful of high and tight pitches, prompting the ejections of Boone and hitting coach Marcus Thames. Boone said that the Yankees counted four pitches during the four-game series that were dangerously close to Urshela and LeMahieu. Most notably, they were irked by a high and tight heater that forced LeMahieu to stumble away from the batter's box. The pitch was thrown by Kittredge, the 30-year-old right-hander who'd also thrown a heater too close to Romine's neck two years earlier. "It was more just about the history," Judge said. "You don't usually forget stuff like that. Then to continue to throw up and in, that's tough. We've got a lot of big hitters up there. We know they're going to throw in, but to miss that far up and in, you're going to get a little barking from the dugout."

The Yankees had grown tired of the usual excuses, as pitchers like Kittredge rubber stamped the claim that a pitch had gotten away. Sure, control could evaporate on an off night—the Yankees experienced that against the Rays in 2014, when a left-hander named Cesar Cabral allowed two hits and drilled three batters without recording an out, prompting disgusted home-plate umpire Joe West to eject Cabral for the Rays' safety. But this was too frequent to be a fluke. The tension carried over into the series finale, which featured more chirping in a 4–3 Yanks loss—each word amplified with no fans in the stands to drown them out.

James Paxton was cruising, thinking ahead to a happy flight with 11 strikeouts in the books, throwing only 77 pitches. Boone had no qualms about giving Paxton the ball to begin the seventh inning, a decision that would be second-guessed when Mike Brosseau launched a two-run homer. Boone hesitated, leaving Paxton in to face Brandon Lowe, who launched a game-tying blast. Lowe rounded the bases, hearing a torrent of insults from the third-base dugout. When Tampa Bay's dugout clapped back later, identifying Nevin as an instigator, the Yanks took exception. Lowe, who typically doesn't say much worth filling reporters' notebooks, called the Yanks' display "a little childish." "They've been chirping the whole weekend," Lowe said. "We chirped at them once, and they kind of got upset about it. They've kind of been loud about everything. We did it back, and they didn't like it."

Zack Britton surrendered a walk-off single to Michael Perez, completing the disheartening series in which the Yanks lost three of four to their division rivals. They scored 14 runs over the four games, but eight of those came in the first game of the Saturday doubleheader. The weekend had been a bust. "I've been here a long time, and as long as I can remember, they've always played us tough, especially at the Trop," Gardner said. "They're just a good team, and they have been for a while."

As the Yanks zipped their bags and prepared for the socially-distanced flight back to New York, Judge poked his head into the trainers' office, mentioning tightness in his lower legs. Boone displayed concern, having already lost Stanton to the injured list during the series.

Judge mentioned that he probably should have worn tennis shoes rather than spikes on the Trop's artificial surface, promising the manager that he would rest during the upcoming off day and be ready for the next game. As Judge exited the room, Boone measured his slugger's gait suspiciously, hoping that it was indeed nothing to be concerned about.

• CHAPTER 10 •

DERAILED

The shuttle bus came each morning around the same time, welcomed by a driver whose job description typically included ferrying sleepy commuters to regional flights out of Wilkes-Barre/Scranton International Airport. Instead of traveling to cities like Charlotte, Chicago, or Washington, D.C., these passengers were headed right down the road to PNC Field, home of the Triple A Scranton/Wilkes-Barre RailRiders.

Clint Frazier slumped into a seat by the window, watching the Pennsylvania scenery pass en route to the New York Yankees' alternate training site. It had once been home to the Philadelphia Phillies' top farm club, then a concrete bowl with artificial turf that bore reminders of long-gone Veterans Stadium. A $43.3 million facelift before the 2013 season opener elevated the building, situated two-and-a-half hours northwest of Yankee Stadium in the lush Pocono Mountains, to rank among the best ballparks in the International League.

Frazier knew the surroundings well—too well, really. It had been his first stop after being acquired by the Yankees in a blockbuster July 2016 trade with the Cleveland Indians, a deal punctuated when general manager Brian Cashman lauded the then-21 year old for his "legendary" bat speed. Privately, Cashman thought the Yankees were rushing Frazier by assigning him to Triple A, but Cleveland had already advanced him to that level, and Cashman didn't want to complicate the transaction by adding a demotion.

Frazier opened 2017 patrolling the outfield in Triple A, homering in his big league debut against the Houston Astros that July. The subsequent years brought a costly 2018 concussion and a ticket on the "Scranton shuttle," bouncing between New York and the top farm club depending on need. When Frazier was bounced from the active roster after the 2020 season's second game, he felt bitterness, wondering if that walk out of Nationals Park marked the end of his Yankees tenure. "That thought crossed my mind a few times, being down in the alternate site for a few weeks," Frazier said. "It was tough. I wondered, *Am I going to make it back? Am I going to get a chance, or am I just going to kind of hang out?*"

With the minor league season spiked, the alternate site players shifted into a similar mode to the early days of Summer Camp. Because the 30 alternate sites didn't intermingle, the almost-Yankees faced off in games of five or six innings where the final scores weren't tallied and nine-on-nine matchups never happened. Both clubhouses were used, and the players split into two groups of pitchers and two groups of position players. The coaches did what they could to make the action feel realistic, focusing on showdowns between batters and pitchers, which were video-logged and accessible by the decision-makers in New York. At any moment, Cashman or Aaron Boone could check to see how Frazier was doing with his new batting stance—front leg coiled, allowing him to keep his hands behind the ball and swing as hard as possible—against young pitchers like Luis Medina and Clarke Schmidt. "After a while, he wore out a number of guys," Cashman said. "It's the hitters' advantage because they're seeing the same pitchers over and over again."

Frazier boasted that he probably hit .900 at the alternate site, making loud contact that echoed beyond the right-field wall, where Conor Foley perched behind trees and shrubs. With the ballpark closed to fans and media, it was the best vantage point available for Foley, who covered the RailRiders for *The Scranton Times-Tribune*. Most afternoons, Foley would steer his black Hyundai Elantra sedan into the parking lot of a shuttered 20-screen multiplex, using binoculars to determine who was tossing from the mound or swinging in the batting cage. Sometimes Foley couldn't see where the balls landed, but he discovered that if he stood in foul territory beyond the right-field wall, he could sneak looks at the high-tech data fed to the left-field scoreboard—velocities, extension, spin rates, and more. For the most part,

Foley had the place all to himself. "I never saw any other reporters," Foley said. "One dad and son showed up because they were big Aroldis Chapman fans. It was pretty much live batting practice with some base running. They knew how many pitchers needed to throw each day and worked around that."

Frazier believed that he belonged in the majors, felt it in his bones, but he resolved that he was "done playing GM." Early in his Yankees tenure, Frazier had reacted with anger or surprise when bypassed for promotion before learning that Major League Baseball is a business. Every time he stepped in the batter's box, whether it was at Yankee Stadium or in Moosic, Pennsylvania, he was playing for the other 29 teams as well. That was true for all in the alternate site group, from 21-year-old right-hander Deivi García to 40-year-old catcher Erik Kratz. They called themselves "the JV team" or "Field 2," a reference to the spare diamond at the Florida training site.

They were the lucky ones: only about 10 percent of the professional baseball world was actually on a field. The rest of the minor leaguers were home, collecting weekly $400 stipends. One of them, left-hander T.J. Sikkema, supplemented that income by making DoorDash food deliveries in Davenport, Iowa.

Given the number of pitchers who needed reps, Kratz's days were busy. Most of the players bunked at hotels in the Scranton area, but Kratz opted to beat up a rental car to sleep in his own bed about 90 miles away in the Philadelphia suburb of Souderton. The grind wasn't for everyone. Veteran catcher Chris Iannetta opted out and quietly retired after the first week, and the players who remained battled boredom, discouraged from visiting their teammates' rooms. Entertainment options were scarce; a few slipped away to hit golf balls at a nearby range. If they walked outside, there was a Starbucks open for grab-and-go, a Pancheros Mexican Grill offering take-out or delivery...and that was about it. Kratz found joy in the rhythm of defensive work, batting practice, and the loosely-scheduled games. He'd loudly call balls and strikes from behind the plate, his bellows reaching an appreciative Foley in the parking lot. "I had a good time, but I didn't spend a ton of time there," Kratz said. "For other guys, the luster wore off a little bit. We had a good mix of young guys who wanted to learn and older guys who knew how to get their work in."

Many of those reinforcements would have chances to contribute. Back in New York on August 11, the Yankees continued their winning ways with a 9–6 victory against the Atlanta Braves, an outcome tempered by Aaron Judge's early exit. His legs were still sore from the previous weekend at Tropicana Field, but you couldn't tell by Judge's monstrous fifth-inning homer off Bryse Wilson, which pelted a Toyota advertising board over the right-field bullpen. It was Judge's ninth homer in the Yanks' first 17 games; Luke Voit marveled that it had been struck so well that he was surprised that the sign was not damaged. "Judge was so hot and locked in," said P.J. Pilittere, the assistant hitting coach. "At that point, we were joking that he was going to hit 30 homers. To be honest, he might have."

Judge galloped into his home-run trot, and eagle-eyed television viewers noticed a slight grimace near second base. Judge returned to his position in right field to play the top of the sixth inning, but he was absent when his turn in the batting order came around in the home half. Judge watched from the dugout railing as pinch-hitter Mike Tauchman worked a seven-pitch walk, then disappeared into the clubhouse. Quizzed about Judge's departure, Boone was publicly evasive, saying that he wanted to give him a few innings of rest after playing four games in three days on the Tropicana Field surface. In the dugout, however, Boone spoke more candidly. Judge had appeared slow while tracking an Adam Duvall fly ball near the right-field line, prompting the manager to nudge bench coach Carlos Mendoza: "He's not moving like he should." Mendoza agreed.

Judge had grown sensitive and secretive regarding injury-related matters since a fractured right wrist in July 2018, incurred when he was hit by a pitch from Jakob Junis of the Kansas City Royals. The Yankees provided a laughably optimistic timetable, forecasting Judge's estimated return to action in three weeks. Judge needed seven-and-a-half weeks to heal and he tired of reporters visiting his locker to seek updates on his progress. Even more, Judge especially detested the suggestion that he had become an injury-prone player, but he acknowledged that "one piece of the puzzle is staying on the field."

Boone claimed that Judge was only receiving treatment, but plans were already in motion to have the slugger's lower half stuffed into a tube for testing. Given the Yankees' injury woes of the past few years, they would have benefited from those frequent customer punch cards used by sandwich shops: buy nine MRIs, get the 10th free. Judge's exam revealed a strain of the soleus muscle in his right calf, classified as Grade 1—the least severe of the three grades.

Frustrated and desperate, Judge implored Boone, Cashman, team doctors, trainers, and anyone else who would listen not to place him on the injured list, promising that he could play through the injury. He swore that he felt good enough to run, jump, swing a bat—any activity that would be required to complete a nine-inning game. He also reminded them that his most recent swing had launched a missile into the right-field bullpen. "Just give me a couple of days," Judge pleaded. "I don't need 10 days to be feeling good."

They understood, and Boone hated to lose one of his productive hitters from the lineup card, but any further injury would prompt a more prolonged absence in a season that was already short. Frazier's cell phone buzzed on the morning of August 12, and the outfielder strutted as he ditched the room key to his budget Marriott hotel on Montage Mountain. Back in spring training, Frazier had gestured toward Judge's locker and said that he couldn't wait for "the big guy" to get healthy so that they could patrol the outfield together; Frazier thought it would look cool to have his No. 77 in left field and Judge's No. 99 in right field. Instead, injury once again created an opportunity for Frazier, one he vowed not to waste.

Appearing in the lineup that night, Frazier homered in his first at-bat, going back-to-back with Gary Sánchez off the Braves' Huascar Ynoa. Frazier added a single and double, scoring a pair of runs in a 6–3 victory, all the while wearing his gaiter mask. Frazier said that it was "getting humid under there" in the late innings, but after weeks of at-bats that only his teammates could see, Frazier was thrilled to be back in the flow of an actual game—nine innings, nine men on the field. "I didn't start off in the big leagues as long as I would have liked, and there were a lot of unknowns," Frazier said. "Coming up and hitting a home run in my first at-bat was really special. It made me feel like I deserved to be there, even though I knew I should have been there. That was the ultimate thing I needed: to continue to go forward and feel confident."

On the original schedule, the Yankees were scheduled to participate in the *Field of Dreams* game on August 13 against the Chicago White Sox at a custom-built, 8,000-seat facility in Dyersville, Iowa. The ballpark would sit adjacent to the cornfield where Kevin Costner's character summoned the ghost of "Shoeless" Joe Jackson in the iconic 1988 film. Travel concerns initially prompted the league to substitute the St. Louis Cardinals for the Yankees, and the league scrapped the plan altogether weeks later, resetting their goal for a 2021 contest.

Instead, the Yankees hosted the Boston Red Sox that weekend. The Sox were already well below .500 and settling in for a rebuilding year under interim manager Ron Roenicke, who had taken the chair after Alex Cora's entanglement in the Astros scandal. If the Bleacher Creatures had inhabited their usual Section 203 haunt, they would have delighted in pouncing upon Boston's ineptitude. Instead, they watched from home as the Yankees feasted upon an inferior opponent, reeling off a four-game weekend sweep as the Bombers improved to 11–0 at Yankee Stadium. "It was difficult to watch, knowing we wanted to be there and couldn't," said Marc Chalpin, a veteran Bleacher Creature who frequently leads roll call. "It's such a part of our summers. It was so different not to be able to go to the stadium. It was a big hole; we really missed being out there."

Gerrit Cole fired seven sharp innings in the opener, allowing a run on four hits while striking out eight in his introduction to the storied rivalry. The righty was so locked in that he didn't realize that Judge was missing from the lineup until the second inning, when he saw Tauchman pounding his glove in right field. As Cole returned to the bench after the final out, he huddled with Sánchez and asked, "Hey, where's Judge?"

Recounting that scene after the game, Cole chuckled and said, "Some teammate I am." Cole fit into the group better than he let on, as evidenced by his teammates' razzing on the occasions that he claimed the most coveted accessory in the clubhouse. For years, the Yankees had been passing around an oversized wrestling-style championship belt, its blue leather emblazoned with a trio of golden plates that identify its owner as the "player of the game." Thus honored, Cole launched into a detailed soliloquy breaking down key at-bats, explaining to his teammates why he'd decided to throw a fastball or a slider in a specific situation. After a few sentences of that, someone would inevitably yelp, "Hey! This isn't a press conference!"

It was a tight group, and by 2020 standards, the Yankees were doing a decent job of adhering to the coronavirus protocols. All 30 teams seemed to feature on-field spitting and chin-strapped masks in the dugout, making enforcement virtually impossible—the equivalent of a car zipping at 70 mph through a 65 mph zone. The league focused on flagrant offenders, like Cleveland Indians pitchers Mike Clevinger and Zach Plesac, who broke protocol to leave their team hotel during an August trip to Chicago. Plesac was caught trying to sneak back to his room in the early morning. More damning, Clevinger was not forthcoming about his involvement, flying back to Cleveland on the same plane as pitcher Carlos Carrasco, who battled leukemia during the 2019 season.

Those actions prompted the demotions of both players, who comprised two-fifths of Cleveland's starting rotation. At least one Indians player threatened to opt out of the season if the hurlers remained on the active roster. By the end of the month, the Indians traded Clevinger to the San Diego Padres. Watching from afar, the episode spurred Yankees players to exhibit even greater compliance with the protocols. As Mark Kafalas, the team's director of security, repeatedly told them before each trip: if you couldn't do it for yourself, then do it for your teammates. "You can kind of divide it up from what part of the country and who the Republicans or Democrats were," Cashman said. "If you were coming from a certain state or a strong Republican foothold, then those were the ones that were less likely to mask up. We never had complete success in getting them all to adhere to it."

The second game brought another win, powered in part by a Frazier homer, and a reprise of the 2019 "Next Man Up" rallying cry. Blame the beat reporters, who had noticed DJ LeMahieu was leading the American League with a .411 batting average. With a beautiful inside-out swing that littered the right-field turf with hits and the season capped at 60 games, LeMahieu had a realistic chance of being baseball's first .400 hitter since Ted Williams in 1941. Tony Gwynn had mounted the last serious challenge, batting .394 after 110 games when baseball went on strike in summer 1994. LeMahieu's chase stalled as he winced after a fourth-inning swing, having experienced a left thumb sprain. The injury, which LeMahieu called a "weird freak thing," was similar to one that he had sustained in May 2018 as a member of the Colorado Rockies. The team's leadoff hitter was shelved for two weeks and expressed frustration that his injury had followed those sustained by Judge and Stanton, calling it "bad timing." "I pride myself on being out there every day, ready to go," LeMahieu said. "When you can't, it sucks. It's a bad feeling not to be able to be out there."

J.A. Happ could relate. In his 14th year wearing a big league uniform, the left-hander was none too happy to have his previous start skipped. He took it out on the Red Sox, pitching three-hit ball over five-and-two-thirds innings, backed by a three-RBI performance from Mike Ford. The game was televised by ESPN, and when the big-bodied, left-handed Ford launched a two-run homer off Chris Mazza in the third inning, Alex Rodriguez remarked that Ford looked a little like Babe Ruth. Informed of the comparison, Ford quipped, "We're both hefty guys."

Aroldis Chapman returned to the mound in the series' final game, a 6–3 victory that featured two Voit home runs. Chapman missed most of Summer Camp and the first three-and-a-half weeks of the regular season after testing positive for COVID-19. Chapman lost his senses of smell and taste during that time, but he could continue working out in a Manhattan apartment that featured stunning floor-to-ceiling views of Midtown. Chapman got creative in transforming his living space into a home gym, purchasing equipment and making extensive use of a training sock, which allowed him to throw without breaking a lamp or TV. "You've just got to find ways to get the work in and not lose too much of the rhythm," said Chapman, who pitched around a triple and a run-scoring double before ending the game on consecutive strike-outs—his first appearance since surrendering the season-ending homer to Jose Altuve in the American League Championship Series.

The victory was the Yankees' 10th straight over Boston, and the Red Sox were a staggering 1–15 at Yankee Stadium since they blasted Frank Sinatra's "Theme from New York, New York" in the visiting clubhouse after eliminating the Yanks in the 2018 American League Division Series. Reliever Zack Britton spoke the truth when he observed, "It's not the same Red Sox team over there."

Off to a scorching 16–6 start and having won all 10 games to that point at Yankee Stadium, everything was falling in the Yanks' favor. Voit thumped his chest, promising that the team was "locked in" would be "ready to go," no matter who the next opponent was. Their fortunes turned right around the time that the season went dark for Cashman—literally. The general manager was in his Yankee Stadium office when he lost vision in the bottom of his left eye. Puzzled, Cashman looked up his symptoms on WebMD on his office computer, and the site revealed the possibility that Cashman had suffered a detached retina. He was hurried to NewYork-Presbyterian Hospital, where emergency surgery was scheduled for that evening. "The blood was within a millimeter of my retina," Cashman said. "They said if the blood reached there, I was going to go blind permanently in my left eye."

The rehab was "horrific," in Cashman's words. For the first week, he had to lay face down on a massage table for 23 hours a day, rising only to eat and shower. An iPad rested on the floor, allowing Cashman to watch games and to keep in touch via text message. Unfortunately, his team didn't provide a lot of compelling viewing material. The bravado Voit had showed was dented over the next three nights, as the visiting Tampa Bay Rays continued to outplay the Yankees on both sides of the ball, outscoring the home team 20–10 in a series sweep.

Perhaps the outcomes would have been different if the Yankees had their full home-field advantage. Accustomed to the wild nature of a midseason crowd in the Bronx, Rays ace Blake Snell was unsettled by a lonely pregame walk to the left-field bullpen. Scanning the vacant bleachers, Snell simulated the authentic Yankee Stadium experience during his warm-ups, screaming to himself: "You suck, Snell!"

It worked—kind of. Voit and Sánchez went deep off Snell, who lasted five innings, but Masahiro Tanaka was hit hard over four innings as the Yanks were saddled with their first home loss of the year. Losing to Tampa Bay was getting old, and Cole went to the mound the next night, intent upon ending the slide. Cole was stellar through six-and-two-third innings, limiting the Rays to a pair of solo homers—one by personal nemesis Ji-Man Choi, who seemed to square the ace up better than anyone else in the league. But the Yankees only managed two runs off Tyler Glasnow. The tied score and Cole's building pitch count prompted the phone to ring in the bullpen, where Britton began tossing.

Cole's 109th offering sailed past Mike Zunino for a called third strike, at which point Boone pounced from the dugout, raising his left index finger to signal a pitching change. Cole was heated and made sure Boone knew it, carefully hiding his words from the television cameras as he screamed into his glove, stomping toward the first-base dugout. Cole continued fuming in the clubhouse, saying, "I think the body of work speaks for itself." Boone didn't love being on the receiving end, but he understood Cole's desire to keep the ball. Once upon a time, Boone's frustration had forced the Cincinnati Reds clubhouse kids to clean up a mess or two. "That's what we saw from Gerrit," Boone said. "He's as good a competitor as there is. He's an ace in this sport, and I love the fact that he wants the ball. When you're playing for a lot, sometimes that spills over with emotion. I always want my players to want the ball, wanting to be in there."

Britton ended that inning without incident, but the Rays broke through in the eighth. Britton dropped a throw at first base for an error, uncorked a wild pitch, then issued a walk before recording an out. Mike Brosseau came off the bench to single home the tie-breaking run, and Willy Adames added a run-scoring hit, handing the Yanks a 4–2 loss. Adding injury to insult, Britton felt his hamstring grab on the final pitch to Adames, a strain that would cost the reliever 10 days on the injured list.

The traffic in the trainers' room was building. Gleyber Torres was a few pounds too hefty for the Yankees' liking after the shutdown, which could have been a factor as the shortstop sustained strains of his left quadriceps and left hamstring while running out a ground ball. Almost simultaneously, James Paxton was diagnosed with a left flexor strain that would prove to be season-ending. Now the Yankees were the ones channeling Vincent LaGuardia Gambini: *What else could they pile on?*

The continued injuries were concerning but not completely unforeseen, according to Cashman. When Eric Cressey's groundbreaking programs were incorporated in January and throughout the abbreviated spring, Cashman spoke with Robby Sikka, the medical director of the NBA's Minnesota Timberwolves. Sikka told Cashman that he had crunched the numbers on similar programs over time, predicting that the Yankees would experience a rise in injuries during the first year before seeing improvement in subsequent seasons. Cashman had scoffed then, replying, "Yeah, that's not going to happen." But it had. Paxton thought that the abrupt halt in March and the accelerated ramp-up of July contributed to his injury and many others around the league. "We didn't get enough time going at a lower speed to build up," Paxton said. "A few weeks into the season, guys were not fresh anymore and the tiredness was building up. We didn't have that base we'd normally have."

Paxton had thrown his final pitch of the year, and the rest of the Yankees were about to have some more unexpected and unwelcome idle time. As they peeled their uniforms off in the Yankee Stadium clubhouse, news developed with the team across town. Two members of the New York Mets' traveling party tested positive for COVID-19 during the team's trip to (where else?) Miami, prompting the postponement of that weekend's scheduled Subway Series games at Citi Field.

Three weeks after their meeting in the 58th floor lounge high above the streets of Philadelphia, the Yankees were once again in the position of being game-ready with no games to play. They held a couple of socially-distanced workouts at Yankee Stadium, shifting back into Summer Camp mode, then boarded a flight to Atlanta to continue their season. "I was surprised we didn't have more hiccups, honestly," Britton said. "We knew it was going to be tricky going into this year. The way I tried to look at it was: let's all try to play 60 games if we can. I thought that was the best we could ask for."

• CHAPTER 11 •

PUNCHED IN THE MOUTH

The rumble usually started a minute or two after the bus rolled out of the hotel driveway, meaty forearms crashing into the plastic luggage racks that hovered over each seat. The decibel level rose when more joined the fun, the likes of Brett Gardner and Luke Voit contributing caveman-like grunts in anticipation of a show to come. Welcome aboard what the position players called the "Bang Bus."

Throughout the season, New York Yankees hitters would acknowledge hits by looking toward the dugout and flexing their biceps, rapping knuckles into forearm. The teammates returned the gesture, relishing the inside gag. It was an offshoot of the furious beating that Gardner inflicted upon the Yankee Stadium dugout during an August 2019 game, when his bat left many dents in the tin roof. That afternoon, Gardner was issued a dubious ejection by umpire Phil Cuzzi for making too much noise. There was no one to police such activities on the bus, where players rattled their ride and took turns ridiculing their teammates with the public-address microphone. There were several sharp wits and tongues on board, but none were better than Erik Kratz, the team's resident roastmaster general.

Everything was fair game for Kratz, who was Jeff Ross in shin guards. He would disregard pleas from his wife, Sarah, to be nice when he took turns on what he called "the hotline." If you did not care to have your hair, clothing, recent play, or any other low-hanging fruit mocked for the captive audience, you learned not to make eye contact with Kratz. That didn't happen often; most teammates loved it when Kratz doled out fresh material. "People off the street would not understand it," Kratz said. "If there was an HR department for the clubhouse, I would get complaints. You just don't take yourself too seriously in a baseball season. I've hurt people's feelings and apologized for it, but we're all going through the same things, whether it's Erik Kratz or Giancarlo Stanton. That's how you make it through a crazy season where you have to ride to the field and hold the spit in your mouth to see if you've got COVID."

That levity was welcome in an unpredictable circumstance where the pandemic and Mother Nature combined to play havoc with the schedule. With the entire Subway Series wiped, the Yankees had seen seven games postponed or rescheduled because of the virus. Toss in an August 25 rainout at Atlanta's Truist Park, and the Yankees were looking at three seven-inning doubleheaders over a five-day span. One-fifth of the Yankees' schedule wound up being played in six doubleheaders, which prompted Voit to remark that the season had been "a pain in the ass."

"Everything was so inconsistent," said Zack Britton. "Guys were frustrated. It almost felt like baseball was secondary to all the other crap that was going on."

The first four games did not go well for the heavy-legged Bombers, who were held hitless into the sixth inning by rookie Ian Anderson, the right-hander chalking up a victory to remember in his big league debut. Touched for three homers and charged with his first regular season loss in 15 months, having gone unbeaten in 28 starts, Gerrit Cole was on the losing side of a 5–1 decision.

Aaron Judge returned to the lineup in the second game of the twinbill, having promised the Yankees that they had been overly cautious in sending him to the injured list for a mild right calf injury. Dr. Chris Ahmad, the Yankees' team physician, warned Judge to be conservative in his play. Any recurrence of the calf injury, Ahmad said, would spell double the time on the shelf.

Playing his first game in 15 days, Judge didn't last long, feeling tightness while running the bases in the fourth inning. Aaron Boone noticed Judge appearing to favor the calf as he stood in the outfield two innings later and removed him after the sixth. A dismayed Judge said that he believed everything had been handled correctly by the team and blamed his own inexperience with calf injuries. "I didn't realize how much you use your calf in daily life and baseball, how explosive it is, and how weight-bearing it is," Judge said. "If anything, that's on me, trying to push it and get back as quick as I could."

Despite Masahiro Tanaka's sinker and slider dancing with aplomb for five innings, the Yanks dropped that game, too. With Tanaka cruising, Boone expected to send the right-hander back out for the sixth inning. He was stunned when Tanaka admitted his energy had been sapped by the 66-pitch effort, telling him that the soupy Georgia humidity had his "tank starting to empty a little bit." Tanaka's unvarnished honesty prompted activity in New York's bullpen, and Chad Green surrendered a two-run Freddie Freeman homer as the Yanks fell 2–1 to the Atlanta Braves. That made it five straight losses for the Bombers, freefalling into a 5–15 slide that negated their 16–6 start. It felt like they'd lost 30 in a row.

The trip to Atlanta couldn't end fast enough, but first they had to deal with unexpected cargo. Scheduled to work the next series against the New York Mets, the umpiring crew needed a lift to New York. Umpires typically pick up frequent-flyer miles by flying commercially, but given the pandemic, the league wanted to avoid potential exposure whenever possible. Mark Carlson, Mike Estabrook, Junior Valentine, and Chad Whitson found seats at the plane's front, having just called balls and strikes against the other passengers. The Yankees scrambled, trying to convince Delta to give them a bigger jet. As general manager Brian Cashman sighed then, "It feels like every day is 48 hours long."

Sports and the heaviness of real life collided again on August 23, when the shooting of Jacob Blake sparked a new round of protests, rallies, and marches throughout the United States. Blake, a 29-year-old Black man, was shot multiple times by Rusten Sheskey, a police officer in Kenosha, Wisconsin. Blake had attempted to enter his sport-utility vehicle following a scuffle with officers responding to a 911 call for a domestic incident. Blake's three sons were in the back seat when Sheskey fired seven shots at point-blank range, an incident captured on video. Blake's attorneys said that he was paralyzed from the waist down and that it would "take a miracle" for him to walk again.

Property damage, arson, and clashes with police followed. In Kenosha, two protesters were fatally shot in a confrontation with 17-year-old Kyle Rittenhouse, who was walking the streets with an AR-15-style rifle. Rittenhouse was charged with seven criminal counts, including first-degree intentional homicide. At the NBA's Disney World bubble, the Milwaukee Bucks refused to take the floor for Game 5 of their first-round playoff series against the Orlando Magic, prompting the league to postpone all three of the day's scheduled playoff games.

Following that lead, three games were nixed from baseball's schedule, including the Milwaukee Brewers' game against the Cincinnati Reds. At Citi Field, the Mets took their positions in full uniform as though they intended to play against the Miami Marlins and then left the playing field. Announced as the leadoff hitter, Miami outfielder Lewis Brinson draped a Black Lives Matter T-shirt over home plate. The teams doffed their caps toward each other, then returned to their clubhouses, leaving the shirt on the field. Dom Smith, a 25-year-old Mets outfielder from Los Angeles, shed tears that night. "The most difficult part," Smith said with red eyes, "is to see people still don't care. For this to just continually happen, it just shows just the hate in people's hearts. That just sucks. Being a Black man in America is not easy."

The Yankees saw the Mets the next day, preparing to host their cross-town rivals for five consecutive games to make up the contests lost to the previous week's coronavirus scare. The Yanks called an afternoon meeting on the suite level above right field, giving players an opportunity to confront the uncomfortable truths of racial inequality and injustice. It was described as a room in which many were hurting. As he had following the George Floyd killing, Stanton spoke passionately. He stressed to teammates that racial equality should not be a political issue and that they could help the cause, no matter their skin color. "It's not a time to just shut up and swing, shut up and dribble," Stanton said. "This is a time to take reality for what it is and start helping to make a damn change because this is unacceptable, what's been going on. It hurts, man. The conversations with my mom, with my grandma, hearing what they had to go through, and then seeing the similarities of what's going on now—it hurts, it's unacceptable, and it needs to be changed."

In that meeting, hitting coach Marcus Thames recounted a conversation with his 11-year-old son, Marcus Jr., who had watched the Blake shooting online. His tearful question to his father was: "Why does this keep happening?" The 43-year-old Thames, a Black man born in Mississippi, held his son and said that it had been happening all his life. "It's hard and it hurts," Thames said. "We're tired. The tears, the pain. We just want to be heard. We don't want money, we just want ears. Just listen to us. Me having to explain to my son again, what's going on out in the world. Seeing a man shot [four] times, knowing there were three kids in the car, boys that look like him, he shouldn't be terrified to be an African American."

Some players expressed reluctance to watch the Blake video. Stanton countered, saying that they should watch every second of it. The meeting ran long, bleeding into the allotted time for batting practice. No one seemed to be looking at the clock. The team did not discuss postponing the game, but emotions were fraught. Sporting a Black Lives Matter T-shirt, Boone excused himself from a pregame Zoom conference that meandered from injury updates to the concept of love. He sobbed after being asked how the events have affected his family, which includes two adopted Black sons. Returning to the microphone with tear-streaked cheeks, Boone composed himself and sighed. "It's been a hard and heavy year," he said, "a heartbreaking year in so many ways, and for my family, too. I think that's the case for a lot of people of all different backgrounds and races. My prayer is just that even though we're going through some dark times, that at the end of this, we're better for it."

It was hardly the festive atmosphere that usually accompanied the Subway Series. In previous years, rainouts between the Yankees and Mets had necessitated intracity doubleheaders. The most famous circumstance came in July 2000, when Dwight Gooden pitched the Yankees to victory on his old Shea Stadium stomping grounds in an afternoon contest. The NYPD ushered the teams across the Triboro Bridge for a night game in which Roger Clemens drilled Mike Piazza in the helmet with a fastball, setting the stage for the World Series theatrics to come. With no tickets sold and the ballparks almost empty, there was no urgency to relocate games between venues.

In the first game, Green spoiled Jordan Montgomery's solid effort by surrendering three homers, including a three-run shot to Pete Alonso and a go-ahead blast to Smith, hours removed from his tearful plea for equality. Back on the field a couple of hours later, all players wore uniform No. 42 as baseball belatedly celebrated Jackie Robinson. Since 1997, the barrier-breaking Dodgers great had been honored on April 15, the anniversary of his 1947 big league debut. With that opportunity lost, the league opted to circle August 28 for Robinson. It was an inspired choice; the date in 1945 was when Dodgers president and general manager Branch Rickey informed Robinson he would be the face of integration and also the date in 1963 when Rev. Martin Luther King Jr. delivered his "I Have a Dream" speech during the March on Washington. It would also be the date that actor Chadwick Boseman succumbed to colon cancer. Boseman's breakthrough performance came when playing Robinson in the 2013 film, *42*.

Though the Yankees wore their pinstripes, it was technically a Mets home game. Against a clear blue sky, the large video screen in center field played a Mets hype video, complete with sparklers draping the likes of Alonso and Robinson Cano. Prepared during their spring training in Port St. Lucie, Florida, it was what fans at Citi Field would have seen before the Mets took the field. The Yankees carried a one-run lead into the seventh inning, bringing Aroldis Chapman out of the bullpen for the final three outs of the shortened game.

There was trouble almost immediately. Chapman could not command his fastball, walking Jeff McNeil on eight pitches. When speedster Billy Hamilton trotted out of the third-base dugout to pinch run, everyone in the tri-state area suspected that Hamilton would be on the move. As Chapman raised his right leg, Hamilton broke. Chapman fired to first baseman Voit, who whipped a throw to second base—too late to nab Hamilton. Kratz tried to settle Chapman, who missed the strike zone with another pair of fastballs.

He tried a slider, which Amed Rosario parked into the left-field seats for a game-ending blast.

It was just about the 2020-iest development—the Yankees lost on a walk-off, seventh-inning homer in their own ballpark. The circumstances were so odd that Chapman had no idea the game was over. The reliever made eye contact with home-plate umpire David Rackley, raising his left hand to ask for a new baseball. None was forthcoming; Rackley's remaining responsibility was to make sure that Rosario stamped his foot on home plate before being enveloped by his teammates. Clint Frazier said that he personally watched the entire celebration, adding, "It's not fun."

The Yankees returned serve, finishing the weekend strong with wins in the next three games. Still upset by his inconsistent starting assignments, J.A. Happ made a terrific return to the rotation with seven-and-one-third scoreless innings. Happ had $17 million on the line because his contract included an option that would vest if he started 27 games or pitched 165 innings. Those numbers were unattainable in a 60-game season, and a technicality excluded Happ from having the numbers prorated. Happ was coming up on his age 38 season, and he suggested that the Yankees shuffled their pitching to keep him from the mound. "You guys are pretty smart," Happ told the beat reporters. "It doesn't take too much to figure out what could be going on."

The insinuation of dirty business irked Cashman. The GM stated that any objective observer would recognize that Happ belonged toward the back of the rotation based upon his 2019 season, when he pitched to a 4.91 ERA while serving up a career-high 34 home runs. If the Yankees could give the ball to Cole or Tanaka, they would do so. Any other external factors were out of the team's control. As Cashman remarked, "We didn't give the Mets COVID."

The game ended when former Yankees pitcher Dellin Betances, no stranger to experiencing command issues on that same mound, uncorked a walk-off wild pitch. The grueling gauntlet of doubleheaders concluded on a Sunday afternoon, and the Yanks won their most improbable game of the year. Win expectancy is a popular metric that can estimate an average team's probability of winning any game, given the inning, score, and base-out situation. When Gio Urshela lifted an easy fly for the second out of the seventh inning, FanGraphs' calculations said the Yankees had a 0.2 percent chance of surmounting their five-run deficit—500-to-1 odds. This time, the long shot came in.

Tyler Wade worked a walk, Thairo Estrada was hit by a pitch, and Voit stroked a two-run single to right field, chasing Mets reliever Jared Hughes. Grinding through a troublesome bout of plantar fasciitis that Boone simply described at the time as "foot stuff," Voit limped to second base when Edwin Díaz uncorked a run-scoring wild pitch. Aaron Hicks slugged a line drive over the right-field wall for a game-tying three-run homer. Cash those tickets. Urshela delivered the last lick one inning later, lacing a run-scoring single off Díaz that sealed the 8–7 victory. Hicks was moved to imagine what the atmosphere would have looked and felt like under normal circumstances, when the rafters would have been packed with Yankees die-hards and a splash of orange and blue. "Very different," Hicks said. "You love the fan atmosphere when we're playing in these kinds of series. You have Mets fans and Yankees fans talking crap to each other every single day. It's fun. It's electric to hear a whole bunch of different chants for whatever side they're rooting for."

Michael King had been on the mound to begin the first game, making his second big league start and fifth appearance. That made King a grizzled veteran compared to Deivi García, a 21-year-old top prospect who was summoned from the alternate site to make his debut in the nightcap. Boone thought the rookie would benefit from a few extra hours to go over the Mets' lineup, and for that, García had an ideal partner. He and Kratz had worked together numerous times the previous season in Triple A, where Kratz, impressed by the youngster's focus and warm heart, had proudly called García "my son." In turn, García referred to Kratz as *padre*, the Spanish word for father. Describing his relationship with young pitchers, especially those of Latin American descent, Kratz was moved to tears. "I love seeing what they can do, and I think sometimes some people forget where they come from," Kratz said. "There's people at home that want it just as badly for them and they're not around their family. Being older, hopefully I can be somebody that can step in and help that relationship. My Spanish isn't that great, but I try. I want it to be good. I've got kids, too, and I hope somebody would treat my kids that way."

In brighter spirits by game time, Kratz emerged from the first-base dugout, looking over his right shoulder to yell: "I'm so excited to play catch with my son!" Born during the Jimmy Carter administration, Kratz had 18 years, 11 months, and four days on García. To find a battery more separated, you'd have to go back to August 30, 1906, when the franchise was still called the Highlanders and 21-year-old Cy Barger lobbed pitches to 42-year-old Deacon McGuire. Kratz never intended for the "son" comment to be heard publicly, but he proudly gushes when asked about the hurler's bright future. "He is such an awesome kid," Kratz said. "His first start in Triple A, he was in the lunchroom before I got to the field, taking English classes. In a nutshell, that encapsulates who he is as a person. For me, that's way more than what he is as a pitcher. He wants to be great at baseball, but he's also a really good person."

The last time García set foot on the Yankee Stadium mound, he did not look ready for prime time. That was the final exhibition of Summer Camp, when García punched his ticket to the alternate site by permitting four hits with two walks, recording only five outs. The Mets didn't see that guy. The first Yankees pitcher ever to enjoy a debut of six or more innings without permitting an earned run or a walk, García carved through their lineup with a sneaky fastball and terrific curve. "I've always had the ability to dial in, concentrate, and not let anything bother me," García said. "It's an advantage to keep your emotions in check and not show any weakness."

García's 75th and final pitch induced a double-play grounder, after which Kratz found García in the dugout to offer a loving embrace, protocols be damned. It was an effort that garnered praise from many observers, including a prominent fellow Dominican. Early in the spring, García requested a belt with uniform No. 45 on it. The digits belonged to Cole, but García explained that he was paying homage to Pedro Martínez, whom he described as an idol.

Comparisons to the three-time Cy Young Award winner and first-ballot Hall of Famer were tricky business, but Martinez saw some similarities in the hurler's stature. Martinez was listed at 5'11" and 170 pounds during his playing days; García stood 5'9" and 163 pounds. An impressed Martinez reached out to congratulate García, promising that they would speak more in the future.

"That was great," García said. "I have so many different questions I would love to ask him, like, how do you plan executing? And how do you carry that plan over the game? There's so many different questions I would love to ask."

The score was tied at one through seven innings, sending the contest into extra innings. The Yanks were again the "road" team in their own ballpark, and with the bases loaded, Kratz was due to bat. Boone scanned the available names on his lineup card and pointed to Gary Sánchez, who was running out of time to reverse a miserable start to his season. Boone sensed that a matchup against right-hander Drew Smith could work in the Yanks' favor. As Sánchez reached for a bat, he carried a .123 batting average, having slugged five home runs while striking out 37 times in 81 at-bats. Less than 24 hours earlier, Cashman pledged support for the scuffling catcher, remarking that Sánchez remained "by far our best option on both sides of the ball." Sánchez was anxious to contribute, telling himself that he needed to drive a ball to the outfield for a sacrifice fly.

He worked the count to 2–2, fouling off a couple of fastballs and laying off a curveball and cutter before Smith tried a fastball up in the strike zone. Sánchez didn't miss it. The Statcast radars perched high above Yankee Stadium calculated the drive at 453 feet, and the clean thwack of ball meeting barrel told Sánchez all he needed to know. He flipped his bat toward the dugout and admired the first pinch-hit, extra-inning grand slam in franchise history.

The Yankees needed players like Sánchez to step up because no help was coming from outside. The trade deadline came and went on the afternoon of August 31 without a move. Operating vertically once again after his emergency eye surgery, Cashman tried to swap for Mike Clevinger, seeing the talented right-hander as a distressed asset after flouting COVID-19 protocols. The

Cleveland Indians didn't agree, insisting upon receiving García and Clarke Schmidt in a potential trade. Cashman balked, and Clevinger was traded instead to the San Diego Padres, with whom he would sustain a partial tear of his ulnar collateral ligament in September. The Yankees were also close to a deal for the San Francisco Giants' Kevin Gausman, but negotiations ended when the veteran righty voiced his preference to stay put.

Cashman pinned his hopes upon welcoming stars back from the injured list, stating that even if any of the deals were consummated, he wouldn't have been able to acquire talent at the level that a healthy Judge or Gleyber Torres could provide. The landscape was further complicated by severely limited financial flexibility, lacking the revenue of fans attending games. Other teams, including the Los Angeles Angels, Oakland A's, Arizona Diamondbacks, and Washington Nationals, furloughed scouts and employees early in the pandemic. In a precarious financial position that accelerated Fred and Jeff Wilpon's efforts to sell the franchise to billionaire Steve Cohen, the Mets instituted a sliding scale of pay cuts for all staffers. The Yankees held off for months before furloughing about 60 employees, including most of the coaches and support staff who would have been assigned to minor league affiliates. Several members of the sales department and two writers for the team's magazine were also let go. "It's the most awful decision a CEO could ever have to make," said Hal Steinbrenner. "I can't imagine a more awful decision. It was month after month of just agonizing—for me personally and for others as well. At some point, there are individuals in the organization that simply don't have anything to do. It's not their fault; it's the fault of the virus, but that's what happened."

On the field, the Yankees had another opportunity to close ground in the division race, welcoming the Tampa Bay Rays back to town. Those hopes were damaged when Ji-Man Choi victimized Cole again, mashing a two-run homer that continued Cole's issues with the long ball and prompted him to wonder if he was tipping pitches. Kevin Kiermaier added a solo shot in the second inning off Cole, who kicked the mound clay and tried to explain the disconnect between the feel of his pitches (good) and the results (bad).

As Boone watched Tyler Glasnow carry a no-hitter into the sixth inning, he resolved that a battery change was necessary. It would be the final time that Cole and Sánchez worked together in 2020.

The flourishing rivalry reached new heights the next evening. The Yankees had taken care of business through the first eight innings, as DJ LeMahieu homered twice and Urshela punctuated a daring dash around the bases with a terrific slide. Provided a two-run lead, Chapman entered, aiming to preserve Tanaka's first victory of the season. Chapman swiftly recorded the first two outs, and the Rays sent up pinch-hitter Mike Brosseau, a 26-year-old infielder/outfielder enjoying his second season in the majors.

Chapman's first pitch was a 100.5 mph fastball that buzzed over the right-handed Brosseau's head, forcing him to duck. Well aware of the tensions between the clubs, play halted as the umpires gathered on the grass between first and second bases, discussing if they could determine intent. Rays manager Kevin Cash complained that Tanaka had plunked Joey Wendle with a fastball in the first inning, after which Wendle had smirked and taken his base.

The umpires allowed play to continue. Chapman's next four pitches were closer to the strike zone, ending the game with a 100.1 mph heater that Brosseau swung through. The Yankees spilled onto the field to celebrate, Frank Sinatra's vocals echoing through the near-empty ballpark. The Rays weren't ready to leave. Several jawed from the third-base dugout, including Brosseau, still wearing his batting helmet and carrying a bat in his right hand. The Yankees moved toward them while Tyler Wade and Kratz attempted to calm the situation. The bullpens emptied as the umpires waved both teams toward their dugouts, reminding them that the protocols expressly forbid such displays. "That was just a bunch of nonsense," Wade said. "When you're in those moments, it's like tunnel vision. You don't really know what's going on around you. I didn't get shoved or anything like that. I was trying to play the middle guy, like, 'Hey guys, just chill out.' No one needs to get hurt. Let's relax. Everything will be okay."

The on-field fireworks lasted about two minutes, spilling into a war of words on Zoom. Cash was incensed, claiming that the situation was mishandled by the umpires and that, with one exception, no Rays pitcher had intentionally thrown at a Yankee over the past three years—an apparent reference to a May 2017 incident in which Matt Andriese was ejected after drilling Judge in the ribs. Cash accused the Yankees of "poor judgment, poor coaching, poor teaching."

"Somebody's got to be accountable," Cash said. "And the last thing I'll say on it is: I've got a whole damn stable full of guys that throw 98 miles an hour."

That was relayed to Boone, who called the comments "pretty scary," a reaction he expanded upon a day later by saying that Cash had been "reckless and inflammatory." Though Cash had a reputation for being candid and straightforward, *Tampa Bay Times* beat reporter Marc Topkin was surprised by how much Cash said that night, and how it was said. "What he said about Chapman, about Aaron Boone, and the Yankees organization—Kevin's not necessarily a guy that speaks in poetic terms," Topkin said. "He speaks what he thinks. If you go back and look back at what he said, he touched a lot of bases. You got a pretty good sense of how big of an issue that was to him and in that clubhouse."

Cash's not-so-veiled threats circulated rapidly throughout the Yankees' clubhouse, where the coaching staff had been counting up-and-in pitches on LeMahieu—seven in six games to that point, they reported. LeMahieu responded coolly: "It sounds like they're going to throw at us. We'll be ready."

MLB slapped both managers with one-game suspensions; though Chapman denied intent, he received a three-game ban, eventually reduced by a game. The next night, Boone entrusted the lineup card to bench coach Carlos Mendoza and ventured upstairs to a club suite. He watched the game alone, sipping from a plastic bottle of water without any peanuts or Cracker Jack in sight. The fan-free experience felt empty once removed from the dugout, though by the end of the first inning, it seemed better that there hadn't been paying customers to watch.

The Rays convened earlier that day for a rare team meeting, and some were hungry to exact revenge. Brosseau and Wendle spoke up in favor of just playing the games, which carried the day after about 15 tense minutes. Tampa Bay came out swinging against Montgomery, who surrendered first-inning homers to Brosseau and Randy Arozarena, a pair of names they'd see much more of later. The Yankees watched 10 batters come to bat, then had to wait longer when a pair of drones buzzed the field, prompting the umpires to halt play.

The Bombers bullpen had to soak up 25 outs, a task that became tougher because the umpiring crew—on high alert for drama—ejected right-hander Ben Heller for plunking Hunter Renfroe with a fifth-inning fastball. Heller and Mendoza shouted that the ejection made no sense, given the Yanks' dire need to squeeze length out of their lesser-used relievers. Their cries were disregarded. Jonathan Holder later allowed a second Brosseau homer in a 5–2 loss.

The Rays left town holding a four-and-a-half game lead in the American League East with 22 games remaining, and the Yankees privately acknowledged that their chances of capturing the division were dwindling. One more game remained to make up from the weekend that was lost to the Mets' coronavirus scare, sending the Yankees across town to a Citi Field that was in mourning.

Tom Seaver, the greatest pitcher in Mets history and a first-ballot Hall of Famer, died three days prior following years of deteriorating health. Black bunting hung from the main office entrance at 41 Tom Seaver Way, the address having changed earlier in the year to honor the legend. Boone recalled his favorite interaction with Seaver, a contemporary of his father's; when the players went on strike during the 1981 season, Seaver and his wife Nancy spent a few nights at Boone's home in the Philadelphia suburbs. Spotting Seaver messing around on a moped, Boone—then eight years old—dashed to the driveway, burning his calf on the muffler. Boone still has a scar from the incident.

In a poignant gesture, each Met rubbed dirt on his right pants leg to symbolize Seaver's iconic drop-and-drive delivery, doffing their caps to the retired No. 41 high above the left-field wall. They'd honor the 311-game winner in an even more appropriate fashion a few hours later, moving play-by-play announcer and longtime Seaver disciple Howie Rose to tears in the radio booth.

Chapman's alibi from the Brosseau dust-up was that he still didn't have pinpoint command of his fastball, following his delayed start to the season. He provided evidence to bolster that case. Three outs from protecting a one-run lead, Chapman issued a walk, prompting the Mets to insert Hamilton to pinch-run. Just as he had six days prior in the Bronx, Hamilton advanced to second base—this time on a Chapman balk. Chapman caught a break when Hamilton got greedy, committing a cardinal sin by attempting to steal third base with none out. The Yankees celebrated Kyle Higashioka's snap throw for a moment, then sighed when J.D. Davis cracked a game-tying homer that sent the game into extra innings.

In the next half inning, Wade committed a baserunning blunder of his own, getting doubled off second base when LeMahieu lined out to right field. Alonso ended the game with a 10th-inning blast off rookie Albert Abreu, handing the Yanks a 9–7 loss in a game they'd led by scores of 4–0 and 7–4. Chapman stated the obvious when he said that his team was "going through a tough, tough moment."

"There's going to be weeks where you get punched in the mouth," Boone said. "When you're going through a tough stretch, it sucks. It's heavy. I go home at night and hurt and don't sleep as well as I should. Those things eat at you."

• CHAPTER 12 •

SPRINT TO THE FINISH

The perfectly-placed slider broke low and outside, generating a feeble swing from the Baltimore Orioles' Hanser Alberto, who lost his batting helmet near home plate. Kyle Higashioka raised his glove to acknowledge Gerrit Cole, who reminded his catcher about their pregame huddle, when the pitcher had interrupted the breakdown of the nine batters in the Orioles' lineup. "We should keep that first ball and send it to David Keith," Cole said.

It spoke to Cole's field of vision that, hours before his ninth start of the season and his first with a new catcher, his thoughts had centered upon the West Coast scout who had tracked their respective high school careers. After a dozen years of twists and turns, Cole and Higashioka were finally paired together as a battery, intent upon getting the New York Yankees' season back on track.

Higashioka nodded, thinking that it was a great idea. They'd planned to save the first pitch, but Alberto fouled it off into the forest green seats of Camden Yards. A strikeout, the first of Cole's 10 that day, was better. The ball was rolled to the third-base dugout, its significance inscribed in large block letters—duties entrusted to Steve Donohue, the Yanks' trainer emeritus. When the padded FedEx envelope arrived on Keith's doorstep a few days later, he was floored.

"I was on a road trip in Utah, and Higgy texted me: 'Hey, did you get something in the mail?'" Keith said. "I got home around 11:00 a few nights later and opened the package. I immediately grabbed my phone and texted them both, saying, 'Man, you guys blew me away.'"

Cole had been a celebrated first-round pick, his decision to spurn the Yankees in favor of UCLA still prompting winces among scouts. Higashioka's rise toward the big leagues was more of a slow burn. Keith kept seeing the catcher on the fields at Edison High School and the San Gabriel Valley Arsenal youth academy, impressed by the 6'1" Higashioka's gap-to-gap power and his leadership qualities. "Kyle has a really quiet sense of humor. It takes a while to get to know him," Keith said. "He's not a Nick Swisher. He listens, he processes, and he replies. I was a catcher myself, and I noticed he barreled the ball up a lot. He wasn't a show-show, look-at-me guy, but I noticed that his teammates always gravitated toward him. You'd look up and four or five kids had formed a circle around Kyle. I liked it."

Keith recalled a sunny afternoon in 2008 alongside Damon Oppenheimer, the team's director of amateur scouting, watching a youth game at Angel Stadium of Anaheim. Oppenheimer asked who Keith liked for the draft and received a nod toward Higashioka, limbering in the on-deck circle. It was an exciting day for Higashioka, who once received a wave from All-Star outfielder Tim Salmon while walking that same warning track as a Little Leaguer. Higashioka scorched a line-drive double off the wall in left-center field, and Oppenheimer scribbled the 18-year-old's name into his notebook. After being selected in the seventh round that June, a $500,000 bonus would come Higashioka's way.

After plodding through Charleston, Tampa, Trenton, and Scranton/Wilkes-Barre, 22 straight hitless at-bats in the big leagues cemented Higashioka's defense-first reputation. A July 2018 home run off David Price of the Boston Red Sox snapped that string. Led by CC Sabathia, the Yankees gave Higashioka the silent treatment in the dugout, prompting the smiling catcher to exchange fist bumps and high-fives with imaginary teammates before he was embraced in a laughing celebration.

The Yankees believed that Higashioka would be a serviceable big league backup, influencing their decision to permit Austin Romine to leave as a free agent before the 2020 season. The Cole-Higashioka battery had indeed been a long time coming, and Keith gave the first strikeout ball a place of honor in his Dana Point, California, home, making sure to keep it out of sunlight. At a time when furloughs and layoffs trimmed the scouting ranks of many clubs, Keith considered himself fortunate to have his contributions remembered. "The thought that Gerrit and Kyle were sending it really meant a lot to me," Keith said. "I've known those guys for so long. You're with them so much in their high school years, and then as college goes, you text them back and forth to check in. Then to realize that, gosh dang, I guess it meant something to them. I thought that was pretty dang special."

It was indeed a nice moment, but the Yankees needed more than sentimental souvenirs to escape their skid. Visits to Baltimore had long served as their tonic for tough times, but that magic wasn't evident on this trip. Absent the throngs of New Yorkers who motored down Interstate 95 to take advantage of cheap tickets and plentiful crab cakes, the Inner Harbor jewel was no longer Yankee Stadium South. The Bombers split a doubleheader in the series opener. Summoned from the alternate site earlier in the day, Miguel Andújar drove home the deciding run of Game 1 with a ninth-inning single. Because the Yankees surrendered their designated hitter an inning earlier by moving Andújar to third base, reliever Jonathan Holder served as the automatic runner to start the ninth. Waved home by third-base coach Phil Nevin, Holder said he "felt like a real baseball player," scoring his first run since he was a high school senior in Gulfport, Mississippi.

New York dropped the nightcap, flushing a lead when Aaron Boone yanked Deivi García from a two-on, two-out situation in the fifth inning, calling upon Clarke Schmidt for his big league debut. The prior evening, Schmidt's late-night Xbox session was interrupted by a series of knocks on his hotel room door. Believing he was about to receive a noise complaint, Schmidt instead greeted coaches Sam Briend, Desi Druschel, and Mario Garza in the hall. The trio informed the 24-year-old pitcher that he needed to pack and travel to Baltimore, where the Yankees planned to add him to their taxi squad. "I didn't really think anything of it because the whole year I'd been getting my hopes up, and nothing really came of it," Schmidt said. "I just wanted to go into it with an open mind."

Five relievers worked in the first game of the doubleheader, and pitching coach Matt Blake told Schmidt that he had been activated. With first pitch only 25 minutes away, Schmidt didn't have time to call his parents, so he sent a text message and dashed to the bullpen. The debut was different than Schmidt would have imagined in all facets. Four runs came home as Ryan Mountcastle, Rio Ruiz, and Pat Valaika smacked RBI hits before Schmidt escaped with a strikeout. "I remember warming up in the bullpen and wasn't even thinking anything of it," Schmidt said later. "I was just like, 'Whatever, just another outing.' I was thinking of it like the same thing as throwing in spring training. In a normal year with fans, it's extremely loud, you're in Camden Yards, and you're going to be nervous. I was excited to reach a life-time goal, but at the end of the day, I didn't do my job."

Cole had the ball the next day, his sizzling heater helping to strike out eight of the first nine batters. Then Baltimore batted around for five runs in the sixth inning, a frame that opened when DJ Stewart's homer landed on Eutaw Street and was prolonged by a Thairo Estrada throwing error. The result was Cole's third consecutive loss. "It's a fickle game," Cole said. "And it can change really quickly."

It certainly had for Gary Sánchez. He'd served as the designated hitter while Cole and Higashioka revisited their high school years, then was stunned to learn that his name was not in the next day's lineup. Sánchez entered Boone's office, pleading his case to the manager and Brian Cashman, who had accompanied the club on the trip. The batting order did not change.

"He understood that it was the manager's decision to give him a timeout," Cashman said. "His message back essentially was: 'The only way I'm going to get through this is by playing.' He wanted to be all in and fight through it."

Sánchez's decline was a head-scratcher for Cashman and others. His tank should not have been empty; Sánchez was 27 and in the prime of his career, not a battered Jorge Posada on the way out the door. Yet like Posada late in his career, Sánchez was having trouble catching up to fastballs, especially ones high in the strike zone. The pinch-hit grand slam against the New York Mets had been an aberration, though his supporters still pointed to high exit velocity numbers and hard-hit percentages. If he made contact, it went a long way. Aware of the growing chorus of critics outside the organization, Sánchez pledged to keep a positive mind-set, asking the hitting coaches to crank the pitching machine into the 90s. The team still recognized Sánchez's potential as a front-line big league catcher, respected his achievement as the fastest player in American League history to crack 100 homers, but they couldn't wait much longer. "Gary got off to a rough start, and it felt like that monkey kept getting bigger and heavier on his back," said P.J. Pilittere, the assistant hitting coach. "You start looking up at the scoreboard to see what you're hitting, and the pressure mounts because you want to perform. He was trying to do too much."

Held to a hit over six innings by Baltimore rookie Dean Kremer, the Yankees continued to swing wet newspapers the next day, and the mood was foul—as poor as the air quality near the visiting clubhouse Zoom setup, which had been installed adjacent to the players' restroom. As Giancarlo Stanton fielded questions about the Bombers' lost weekend, toilet flushes could be heard over the microphone. Some reporters turned off their video cameras, not wanting their laughter to be seen during such a difficult time.

Boone said that his hitters were "pissed off" and challenged them to put forth a better performance the next night, when they'd play their first game at Sahlen Field in Buffalo, New York—the bizarre temporary home of the Toronto Blue Jays. The relocated ballclub underscored differences between how the coronavirus was handled by the United States and Canada. The Canadian government reluctantly granted the team an exemption to utilize Rogers Centre in Toronto for Summer Camp, mandating that players remain isolated at the ballpark.

That worked for intrasquad games, but with non-essential travel banned, Canada refused to permit other teams to enter the country. The Blue Jays scrambled, seeking the equivalent of a couch to crash on. A plan to utilize Pittsburgh's PNC Park fell through, spiked by Pennsylvania health officials. A subsequent effort to relocate the Blue Jays to Baltimore failed when Orioles medical staff expressed discomfort with having two teams share Camden

Yards. The fallback option was Sahlen Field, built in 1988, named for a Buffalo meatpacking company, and home to the Blue Jays' Triple A club.

Two global pandemics had come and gone since Buffalo hosted its most recent big league game in 1915, though the locals still couldn't buy a ticket. The Blue Jays rushed to upgrade the ballpark's lights, field surface, and player amenities. Batting cages were placed on the concourse, creating the visual of pinch-hitters marching down the stairs to take their at-bats, passing starting pitchers who sat in the seats behind each dugout.

A massive tent was erected in the right-field parking lot, its vinyl serving as the visiting clubhouse. The layout of prefabricated lockers, workout facilities, and offices were borrowed from a blueprint originally prepared for the *Field of Dreams* game in Iowa. It reminded the Yankees of their London trip with the Red Sox the previous summer, when a soccer stadium hosted the first big league games on European soil and featured high-scoring contests that played like arena baseball. "Buffalo was actually kind of cool," Zack Britton said. "If there's no fans, you'd rather play in a smaller stadium than a huge empty stadium. You've just got the stands that go baseline to baseline, bag to bag. It felt like the games were a little bit easier to deal with."

Cashman planned to accompany his team to Buffalo even before it lost three of four games in Baltimore, but the slide added concern to the GM's curiosity. During a similar skid in June 2009, Cashman booked a flight to address the players at Atlanta's Turner Field, a speech that was viewed as a turning point in helping the Yankees capture their 27th World Series title. Cashman toyed with speaking prior to the first game, but he was dissuaded by the whipping winds pelting the makeshift clubhouse, believing they would have drowned out his words.

Instead, Cashman watched from a club suite as the Yankees carried a 6–2 lead into the sixth inning, relaxing when Luke Voit and Aaron Hicks slammed first-inning homers. One wiseacre referred to Sahlen Field as "Coors Field with higher cholesterol," and like the mile-high home of the Colorado Rockies, the ballpark had proven conducive to offense. The Yanks learned that the hard way as Chad Green and Adam Ottavino combined to record only one out in a nightmarish 10-run sixth inning that saw 13 Blue Jays bat. The 43-minute barrage featured five hits, four walks, and an error. The Yanks' 12–7 loss was cemented when light-hitting catcher Danny Jansen launched a sinker toward the Interstate 90 on-ramp and rounded the bases for his first career grand slam. Of the 58 pitches that Green and Ottavino threw, only one generated a swing and miss. "I've never had an inning quite like that before," Ottavino said. "It's the worst feeling in the world. You let your team down. It hurts a lot."

The Yankees were in crisis, a favored juggernaut improbably on the precipice of missing the postseason altogether. Cashman prepared talking points in a room at the Westin Buffalo, leaning on the '09 playbook. His remarks then, delivered in a peppy monotone, centered on the belief that the CC Sabathia–A.J. Burnett–Mark Teixeira Yankees were better than they had shown. Cashman believed the same of his 2020 Aaron Judge–DJ LeMahieu–Gleyber Torres squad. He did not raise his voice or point fingers, but Cashman made it clear that the pitching, offense, and defense all had taken turns in the doghouse. "I don't do it often, but I do it when I feel it's necessary," Cashman said. "I usually run to the confrontation. I'm going to run to the fire to put it out and deal with it if I possibly can instead of hope that it goes away."

If nothing else, Cashman thought that the speech would be therapeutic for him, part of his mantra of leaving no stone unturned. He understood that some of the team's biggest stars were down with injuries, but there was no time to wait in a shortened season. In a nautical mind-set that week, Cashman said that his players needed to batten down the hatches and steer toward sunnier conditions. "The Coast Guard is not coming to save us," he said. "We've got to find a way to swim to shore."

The water remained choppy. J.A. Happ poured his heart out in a gutsy 113-pitch, 10-strikeout performance that night, but the bats remained mostly silent in a 2–1 loss. Though Boone said nice things about his team's energy and intensity, there was validity to Bill Parcells' quote about being what your record says you are. At 21–21, the Yankees were back at .500 for the first time since July 25, when they dropped the season's second game in Washington.

As Voit stomped to the interview setup, the slugging first baseman channeled Howard Beale's meltdown in *Network*: he was mad as hell and not going to take it anymore.

Voit thought that too many of his teammates were overthinking their at-bats, trying to create moments of glory by swinging for homers on 3–0 pitches rather than advancing runners and passing the baton to the next hitter in the lineup. Mostly, Voit was upset that the dugout seemed to be dead quiet, silence that was more evident because of the empty stadium. Saying that his team had been "playing like crap," Voit challenged them to "get back to what the New York Yankees are," adding that he felt "like teams aren't really scared of us right now." Voit would later remark that he was surprised that the interview remained PG-13. "We needed a kick in the ass, for sure," Voit said. "It was something that needed to be said. This locker room took it and ran with it. We just needed to play better, plain and simple, in every aspect of the game. It's almost not a bad thing that we went through it because good teams have to figure out ways to get through it."

The skid tempted Boone to try the tactic famously used by Billy Martin early in 1977, when he'd asked Reggie Jackson to pull the lineup out of a hat. That created a batting order in which catcher Thurman Munson hit second and first baseman Chris Chambliss hit eighth, but more importantly, it produced a victory. Ultimately, Boone kept his hat on his head. He'd seen encouraging signs in the defeat, and even more the next night, when Deivi García pitched beyond his years to snap a five-game skid. Backed by Torres' four RBIs, García fired seven innings of two-run ball. The laid-back righty celebrated his first victory in a deafening clubhouse that Boone described as "a discotheque," located at the intersection of joy and relief. Judge's J. Cole-heavy Spotify playlist blasted as the players shook hands on the field, walking briskly toward the parking lot to savor their party. "That was one of our biggest starts of the year," said pitching coach Matt Blake. "We're coming off that tough stretch, this guy's making his debut against a good lineup. You're not sure what's going to happen. He got us back on track, then had two or three starts in a row that were really solid. His maturity and feel for the game are advanced. He never let the moment get too big for him."

The streakiest Yankees roster in recent memory was about to get on another roll. Rain created a doubleheader on the 19th anniversary of the September 11 attacks, as the Yankees hosted the Orioles for a four-game weekend series. It was a breeze. The Yanks outscored Baltimore by a 16–1 margin. His locks tucked underneath a ballcap with the NYPD's yellow insignia, Cole fired a dominant two-hit shutout in the first game, then cheered from the dugout wearing a FDNY cap as Voit mashed a pair of three-run homers in the nightcap. Grimacing as he rounded the bases before exchanging spirited forearm bashes with his teammates, Voit and his trots served as a metaphor for the season—battered and bruised, sure, but still chugging toward the finish line.

The next afternoon presented a taut affair, carrying a 1–1 tie into the 10th inning. When the Orioles' Hunter Harvey uncorked a wild pitch, advancing the potential winning run to third base, Voit thought it seemed like a situation that would have generated a feeble pop-up or strikeout in their snakebitten dregs. But that was then. Voit squinted through encroaching shadows and lifted a fly ball that brought home LeMahieu with the deciding run, too deep for center fielder Cedric Mullins to attempt a throw. Because LeMahieu had made the last out of the previous inning and was on base as an automatic runner, Voit somehow notched a game-ending sacrifice fly while leading off an inning. Try explaining that to someone who drifted into a Rip Van Winkle nap somewhere in late 2019. Voit laughed, saying, "It's 2020, man."

The Yankees' pitching was fantastic, beginning with five-and-two-thirds sharp innings from Jordan Montgomery. Aroldis Chapman kept the game tied in the ninth despite a series of uncomfortable grimaces that drew Boone and Sánchez, concerned about a potential injury, to the mound. The response prompted Boone to spin on his heels, striding back to the dugout. Somewhere between the bullpen and the mound, Chapman felt his stomach rumble, setting off alarm bells that he *really* could use a bathroom break. Even in an empty ballpark, the umpires couldn't halt play, so Chapman had to get three outs as quickly as possible. He trotted gingerly toward first base on a fly ball to right field, then ended the inning with a pair of strikeouts. Chapman whirled toward center field with an uncharacteristically goofy grin after the last pitch, then dashed toward the clubhouse. "We ended up having a good laugh about it as he sprinted off the field," Boone said. "I'm usually not checking on those kinds of things. I don't think it's that common, where a guy is in the middle of the action, and it comes knocking on the door like that."

Torres' fashion statement helped complete the sweep. During the Buffalo series, Torres grabbed a pair of clear-tinted Nike glasses from his locker. He usually wears contact lenses during games, but peering through that non-prescription eyewear, Torres delivered a pinch-hit, two-run double that ran the win streak to five games. When his teammates insisted that he keep wearing them, Torres replied, "If I feel good and I hit good, what can I do?"

The Yankees' subpar showing in Buffalo had prompted some to declare the Blue Jays as New York's best team. A convincing 20–6 blowout reversed that narrative when the Jays arrived in the Bronx, highlighted by two Voit home runs that vaulted him past Jose Abreu of the Chicago White Sox for the league lead. Novice right fielder Derek Fisher misplayed a couple of balls before the Yanks slugged six homers and batted around in three consecutive innings. That provided a truckload of support for García, as LeMahieu and Voit each drove in five runs.

More carnage was on the menu the next evening, as the Yankees mashed seven homers in a 13–2 rout, highlighted by Higashioka's three-homer performance. LeMahieu went deep twice, Voit once, and Clint Frazier once, marking the first time in franchise history that at least six homers were hit in consecutive games. The seven homers were the team's most ever at the current Yankee Stadium despite its reputation as a short-porched launching pad. "It's crazy how baseball works sometimes," Higashioka said. "One minute you can't hit the ball to save your life, and then the next game you pop three over the fence."

The series finale featured an unforgettable fourth inning. Brett Gardner, LeMahieu, and Voit homered on consecutive *pitches* from right-hander Chase Anderson—*blam, blam, blam.* After an out, Stanton and Torres connected for back-to-back blasts—the first time that the celebrated franchise of Ruth, Gehrig, and Mantle had hit five homers in an inning. Voit's screams of delight could be heard from the press box after Stanton's homer. "You go down inside and you miss two home runs," Stanton said. "It was much needed."

The Yankees set a record with 19 homers over a three-game span. The combined blasts soared a combined 7,496 feet—approximately 28 New York City blocks. Those fireworks were fun, but as Boone departed the lit Yankee Stadium diamond that evening, he glanced skyward in a moment of melancholy. "This probably would have been a pretty raucous night, finishing off an important homestand," Boone said. "You miss walking off the field and sharing that with the fans."

Next up was a visit to Boston, the Yanks' only trip of the year to venerable Fenway Park. Opened the same week that the R.M.S. Titanic met its fate in the North Atlantic Ocean, Fenway's cramped red-brick corridors were a nightmare for social distancing, prompting the Red Sox to get creative in utilizing their limited space. While the Red Sox moved their lockers upstairs to the right-field suite area, buddying players as temporary roommates, the visitors wandered the runways and tunnels on the third-base side. Bullpen mounds, batting nets, and artificial turf were placed on the concourses, along with lockers. That meant the Yankees had to drop their drawers where fans would have normally waited for nachos and cold beer. "I was dressing in front of the funnel cake stand," said catcher Erik Kratz. "You got out of the shower and you felt like you were naked outside. If somebody had a drone on the field and they looked straight down the ramp, they would have seen my full moon."

Gardner said that he was shocked by the serenity of Fenway—no aroma of grilled sausage, organ music piped from the speakers above the center-field bleachers, nor vulgar shouts sloshing out of Section 164 as he patrolled in front of the Green Monster. That didn't stop Gardner from needling one of the newer members of the traveling party.

Jason Varitek, who won two World Series as the Red Sox's hard-nosed catcher, was back in uniform as a game planning coordinator. Varitek sent word that he wanted to meet catching Yankees coordinator Tanner Swanson, expressing interest in some of the coach's catching philosophies. Swanson and Varitek shared a conversation on the field, and when Swanson returned to the clubhouse, he found an autographed workout shirt at his locker: "*Tanner, best of luck, Jason Varitek.*" "I'm like, 'Man, that's pretty cool,'" Swanson said. "I kept it to myself, but more people kept asking me about it. 'Hey, we heard you got something from Tek.' Then the clubhouse guys are telling me they want to get it framed for me. Weeks go by, and Boonie pulls out a real Jason Varitek jersey. The whole thing was a prank. The original signatures were from Erik Kratz and Brett Gardner."

The winning streak reached nine games as Sánchez cleared the Green Monster with a ninth-inning laser, then Voit and LeMahieu delivered big hits in extra innings. With a chilly autumnal wind whipping the flags in center field, Voit's run-scoring knock in the 11th provided the Yankees with their first lead of the night. LeMahieu ripped a go-ahead double one inning later as the Yanks surged for a 6–5, 12-inning victory—their longest game of the year in terms of innings and time, clocking in at four hours and 55 minutes. "We're playing like we should be playing," LeMahieu said that night. "A couple of weeks ago, 4–0 felt like 20–0. Tonight felt very within reach."

Happ kept the good times rolling, firing eight scoreless innings in the next game as the Yanks breezed to an 8–0 blowout. With 12 straight wins dating to the previous season, it marked the Yankees' greatest run of dominance over the Red Sox since 1952–53, when their best player, Ted Williams, was busy flying combat missions in the Korean War.

It was an eventful night for Frazier, who lost his favorite undershirt, rescued an injured insect, then mashed a homer. The story started on the previous homestand, when Frazier spotted a picture of a young Derek Jeter in the office of Rob Cucuzza, the team's clubhouse manager. Jeter was wearing a turtleneck with the club's interlocking "NY" logo on the collar. Frazier knew style; by his own estimate, he'd spent more than $70,000 building a Nike sneaker collection over the past several years. That turtleneck was cool, and he wanted one.

Cucuzza checked in a storage room, reporting that two of the turtlenecks remained. Frazier asked for both and was handed one. He asked Gardner to get the second shirt, and Frazier beamed when Gardner came back a few minutes later, shirt in hand. Except Frazier left one of the shirts in his Yankee Stadium locker, bringing only one to Fenway. After batting practice, Frazier eyed Gardner wearing the turtleneck, knowing it had been plucked from his locker. "We're on a road trip to Boston and Buffalo with lows in the 40s, and he only brought one turtleneck," Gardner said. "I didn't know that when I took the turtleneck out of his locker. Since he only brought one, I felt like the one that I wore was mine. He left his at Yankee Stadium."

Even with his chilled forearms, Frazier performed a good deed. Returning to first base that night on a fourth-inning pickoff attempt, Frazier eyed a bug with a damaged wing struggling on the infield dirt. He reached into his back right pocket and used an outfield alignment card to ferry the critter to safety, gently placing it in foul territory. "I was trying not to step on the bug every time I went back to first base," Frazier said. "I just tried to get it out of the way. I didn't want to be the one to put it out of its misery. It looked like it was in pain."

Frazier instructed first-base coach Reggie Willits not to step on the bug, then dashed around the bases to score a run. One inning later, he was rewarded for the good deed, slugging a sinker over the right-field wall. Boone called Frazier's blast "a big boy home run," one that went out to the opposite field on a frigid evening.

The Yankees always believed that Frazier's bat would play, but 2020 represented an important step forward in his preparation. He showed more interest in scouting reports on how pitchers might attack him, data that Frazier minimally explored in previous years. Coaches were especially encouraged by his defensive improvement, which vaulted him into consideration for a Gold Glove that would have seemed improbable just one year prior. That was a running joke all year: when Frazier made a nice defensive play, he'd yank on a chain around his neck, a private message to his teammates as if to say, "That's gold." "Like I told him, that success didn't just happen. He put a lot of work in," Willits said. "He finally got to see the rewards this year. He got some confidence early on that helped him to relax, but he did so much work on his reads around the fence, correction routes, and angles. There were hours and hours so his body would react naturally."

It helped that Frazier was another year removed from the concussion that he sustained early in 2018. Frazier said that he quietly dealt with sensitivity throughout the 2019 season, when bright lights and loud noises triggered a sensation of fogginess. Frazier worked with a neurologist to overcome those issues and felt like a more prepared player when he arrived in camp the next spring. "I was having issues with my depth perception," Frazier said. "I was having issues with not wanting to run into the wall and have it happen again. I felt symptoms at times, but wanted to play and struggled with it. Now I feel like I'm back to what I was."

The weekend's last game was a 10–2 stinker with García serving up a pair of Michael Chavis homers in the first rough outing of his young career. It had been a dream for García to toss from the mound at Fenway, where his idol Pedro Martinez once starred. Wearing Martinez's uniform No. 45 on his belt, García could not get past the third inning, as Chavis drove in five of the six runs against him. "It was an important moment for me and my family," García said, "although the outing did not turn out the way I wanted it to."

The lopsided score presented Kratz with an opportunity to pitch—his sixth career pitching appearance and first as a Yankee. Kratz served up a J.D. Martinez homer in a 21-pitch inning frame that included eight knuckleballs clocked between 55 mph and 68 mph. He'd toyed with the knuckler all the way back to his days at Eastern Mennonite University in Harrisonburg, Virginia, and believed it was good—at least, until R.A. Dickey saw it. While they were teammates with the Blue Jays in 2014, Kratz showed his version of the knuckleball to Dickey. The former Cy Young Award winner's review was: "Ehhh." "I never let him see it again, but I love throwing it," Kratz said. "You can't usually throw it to the pitchers because if you hit them in the shin, they'll say, 'Oh, Kratz was messing around and threw me a knuckleball.' The team will just cut you for hurting a pitcher. But it's a fun moment of reprieve in an embarrassing game. I think every catcher has probably tried a knuckle-ball. Maybe it's the arm slot."

Kratz's floater wasn't the most notable junk tossed on the Fenway surface that day. While batting in the eighth inning, LeMahieu heard echoing shouts from the outfield. He peered through his orange sunglasses, attempting to locate the source. A middle-aged man wearing a Red Sox jersey and tan slacks—the first fan either team had seen all season—had scaled the back of the left-field wall. As two camera operators moved away, the man shouted gibberish about the Boston Marathon and 9/11, frisbeeing a light blue ballcap onto the warning track. Home-plate umpire Jansen Visconti screamed for time, and the intruder turned his attention to left fielder Chavis, wearing uniform No. 23: "Hey! You're not Michael Jordan!"

There were some bemused snickers in the Yankees' dugout while security officers pursued the man, who performed push-ups and briefly dangled off the edge of a catwalk, where he was in danger of falling into the seats some 25 feet below. He was not arrested, instead taken to a nearby hospital for psychiatric evaluation. Some in the press box expressed relief following the eight-minute delay, having feared that they were about to witness a suicide attempt. Boone said that he didn't want to make light of it because "it could have been a scary situation."

Naturally, this being 2020, the Yankees secured their entry into the post-season that night by virtue of the Seattle Mariners' loss to the San Diego Padres, confirming that they would be among the American League's eight playoff participants. That score was final by the time they traveled from Boston to Buffalo. The team gathered for a subdued celebration by the Westin's lobby bar, no goggles necessary. Players and coaches toasted their accomplishment by clinking champagne flutes, sneaking sips under their masks. "It's obviously not as fun as getting to spray champagne over everybody," Cole said. "Any time you can get the team together and acknowledge everybody in the room and the hard work that's put in—regardless if you're spraying champagne or just 'cheers' with masks on—it's nice."

Boone, the sixth big league skipper to reach the playoffs in each of his first three seasons at the helm, briefly addressed the team before the bubbly was poured. He said that he was proud of them for being back to "the dance" in what had been a challenging and crazy year for everyone involved, then reminded them of the speeches he'd given so many times prior. They knew what the goals and expectations were. "So let's go do it," he said.

There weren't many good times to be had at Sahlen Field, a place that the Yanks will not miss when the world returns to normal. They lost five of their seven games played at the Jays' temporary home, permitting 11 or more runs in three of the losses. Michael King was thumped for a loss in the series opener. But as the season shifted to autumn—a grim date on which the U.S. officially surpassed 200,000 deaths attributed to the coronavirus, more than any other country—Cole was dominant in a seven-inning playoff tuneup. The Yanks dropped the final two games by a combined score of 18–2. One was the year's sloppiest performance, in which they committed four errors and endured an eight-run inning, calling upon Kratz to flash his knuckleball for the second time in four games. The novelty had worn off. A dissatisfied Voit stomped in front of the Zoom camera once more, spitting that the display "was not Yankee baseball at all. Everything was bad. It's almost like we were the Bad News Bears."

"I didn't like what I saw in the inconsistency, especially in a short season," Hal Steinbrenner said. "I didn't like so many lows going with the highs. We lost 15 out of 20; I think a rash of injuries started that train. But again, we've got to get through that. The last week of the season, we had no excuses. We didn't play well. I didn't like the team not playing up to its potential as much as it did."

They had packed heavy for the year's final road trip, preparing to live out of their suitcases for an indeterminate period. The league instituted more stringent protocols in advance of the postseason, so even though the Yankees had three home games remaining, they would be isolated in a Lower Manhattan hotel for a series against the Miami Marlins. Players and staffers grumbled about the extra measure, wishing that they could return to the apartments and homes in which they'd lived for the previous 57 games. "I feel like we've already been doing this whole season," Judge said. "Now we're all getting taken away from our families to go do this. I'm not a fan."

Boone said that it was strange to know that his vehicle was gathering dust in Yankee Stadium's garage while he FaceTimed his wife and children, who were only a short drive away. He joked that he ensured there was "plenty of underwear" in his two large suitcases, hoping that he'd be on the road for the full month between the end of the regular season and the final game of the World Series. "It turned into a very long road trip," Boone said. "It was an extension of what we were going through all year long on the road. You felt like we could have handled it on our own, but you also understood this was the first time going through it for everyone. MLB was trying to put in measures to make sure we could absolutely pull it off."

The Yankees wrapped the regular season with a win and two losses against Don Mattingly and the Marlins, whose outbreak had nearly spiked the season before it could complete the first week of play. Across the street from where they celebrated the 2003 World Series title at the original Yankee Stadium, Miami secured a postseason berth, sporting "Respect Miami" T-shirts as they posed for a team photo on the mound.

There were tips of the cap offered to Mattingly and to Derek Jeter, who would always be considered part of the Yankee family. The organization also acknowledged someone who never came close to wearing the pinstripes— George King, who retired from the *New York Post* in November, when he turned 65. One of the last ink-stained, old-school scribes, King decided prior to spring training that it would be his last go-round with the club. He envisioned carrying his notebook and roller bag on a tour through his favorite American League cities. The pandemic nixed King's air travel, but he was sent off in style. Knowing that King's blue-collar drink of choice was a frosty can of Coors Light, the beat reporters chipped in to purchase 20 shares in the Molson Coors Beverage Company. Joe Torre, Joe Girardi, and Boone taped video messages lauding the writer's career, which were shown on the large screen in center field and also on the YES Network. King almost missed it, intercepted by a colleague just before a trip to the restroom. He looked down toward the dugout to see Boone, Cole, and Mattingly all waving their hats toward the press box. "It was easily the weirdest baseball season ever," King said. "I was in the top of Candlestick Park for the '89 earthquake. I was in L.A. with the Phillies for the Rodney King riots. That was scary. I was there when the '94 strike wiped out the postseason, so I've been involved in some events. But this was—I don't know—just weird. I hope that's the last of that."

Individual achievements highlighted the rest of that weekend for two lineup rocks. Voit completed the season with a career-high 22 home runs, becoming the eighth Yankee to lead the majors and the first since Alex Rodriguez in 2007. LeMahieu and Voit were the first teammates to lead the majors in average and homers since Hank Aaron (.355) and Eddie Mathews (46 homers) of the 1959 Milwaukee Braves, and both players would receive MVP consideration.

LeMahieu raked six hits in the last two games, including a 104 mph liner that fractured the right forearm of Miami starter José Ureña, ending with a .364 batting average. The 2016 National League batting champ (.348) while with the Rockies, LeMahieu became the first player to win undisputed batting titles in both the American and National Leagues. In his typical understated style, LeMahieu said it was "pretty cool." "I wish it was over 162 games and I wish there were fans in the stands, but it is what it is," LeMahieu said. "I'm definitely proud of it."

CHAPTER 13

PRESSURE IS A PRIVILEGE

The streets of downtown Cleveland were eerily silent on the afternoon of September 29, 2020, devoid of the frenzied activity that once accompanied each of LeBron James' game nights wearing the Cavaliers' wine and gold, or even any of the woeful Sundays that prompted die-hard Browns fans to drown their sorrows at Flannery's Pub or the Harry Buffalo on East 4th Street. Those establishments were nearly empty, most patrons having abandoned the bar stools months earlier.

There were few indications that a sports event was taking place inside Progressive Field, home of the Cleveland Indians. The distinctive tooth-brush-shaped lights beamed onto the playing field at the corner of Carnegie Avenue and Ontario Street, and a few souls stole glances into the ballpark from a parking garage high above left field. A lonely bass drum echoed from beyond the left-field gates—even John Adams, the team's best-known fan and a man whom Mariano Rivera once hugged to acknowledge his love of the game, couldn't come inside.

This was the playoffs, circa 2020. A few miles from where Donald Trump and Joe Biden knotted ties in their respective dressing rooms at Case Western Reserve University, preparing to square off in a chaotic presidential debate that would prompt much of America to clamor for a mute button, Gerrit Cole checked his reflection in a bathroom mirror. The gray uniform top with "NEW YORK" across the chest was buttoned and tucked in. It looked good. "This is why we got him," Aaron Judge said. "We didn't get him to throw in April. We didn't get him to throw in May. We got him to throw in postseason baseball for the Yankees."

Cole trusted that his routine would breed success. The day before a start, he liked to warm up and play catch across the outfield, each toss calculated with purpose. He'd then review video of the opposing team and crash into bed, sensing the best type of fatigue. It was science; Cole wasted no effort. He'd need to bring his A game against Shane Bieber, the American League's best pitcher to that point. A 25-year-old right-hander known for his California cool, Bieber came into the playoffs having won the pitching Triple Crown, leading the majors in wins (eight), ERA (1.63), and strikeouts (122). Bieber would receive unanimous selection as the AL's Cy Young Award while meriting MVP consideration, an honor that voters rarely bestowed upon a pitcher.

Those plaudits meant little as the American League wild-card series began with DJ LeMahieu digging his spikes into the batter's box. It was sweater weather, and the artificial crowd noise was cranked high. If you focused on the grass and not the thousands of empty seats, you could be fooled into sensing normalcy. "It really did feel like the playoffs," Aaron Boone said. "Other than when you looked in the stands and didn't see many people, the noise and stuff they had piped in, like the guy that beats the drum—it was loud in there. There were a couple of times in that game I said to a coach or a player, 'This is it. This is kind of cool.'"

LeMahieu stared at a couple of fastballs, one high and one low, then lashed a meaty offering into right field for a single. That brought up Judge, whose threat status seemed to be in name only. Since returning from his second stint on the injured list two weeks prior, Judge had struggled to lift the ball out of the infield. Limited to seven hits—only one for extra bases, a double—in 36 at-bats while striking out 13 times, some wondered if the New York Yankees should have Luke Voit hit second instead. Boone brushed away those criticisms, insisting that he liked the way Judge drove the ball in batting practice. He crossed his fingers that Judge would barrel one in a game, restoring his bruised confidence.

Bieber pumped a first-pitch fastball over the heart of home plate, and Judge's muscle memory responded. The swing produced an opposite-field drive that cleared the Cleveland bullpen in right-center field. Four pitches in, the Yankees had deposited a 2–0 lead into their ace's back pocket. It was a sequence that Cole described as "a left jab and a right hook," and as Judge rounded the bases for his first home run since August 11, the slugger flashed a gap-toothed grin. "Pressure is a privilege," Judge said. "For me, the regular season is kind of like spring training. The real season is the playoffs. If you want to see a team show up, it's the team that shows up in the postseason."

The Yankees were pumped; you could hear their bellows from the press box. The hits kept coming in a 12–3 rout, for which the Yankees credited their preparation. Cole was not the only one doing his homework. In the pre-series hitters' meeting, it was strange to discuss a pitcher against whom they had no recent body of work, relying instead upon video. Mostly, hitting coaches Marcus Thames and P.J. Pilittere stressed working long counts and hunting fat pitches.

Now Cole had to keep the throttle down. It would not be an issue. He came out firing pellets in a terrific performance, mixing a four-pitch arsenal. The Yankees had seen Cole's intensity before—no one could forget the anger in his eyes when he'd wanted to finish one of those regular-season games against the Tampa Bay Rays—but the playoffs seemed to raise it to a new level. Judge said that Cole looked like "an animal out there," and the Cleveland hitters could not disagree. He dissected them with precision, joining the great Tom Seaver as the only pitchers to strike out 13 or more without a walk in the postseason.

It was the type of performance that Kyle Higashioka planned upon, having spent the last few days in a deep dive on the tendencies of an Indians batting order that counted third baseman José Ramírez, shortstop Francisco Lindor, and second baseman Cesar Hernandez among its most prominent threats. According to catching coach Tanner Swanson, Higashioka was blocking and throwing the ball "better than he's maybe ever done" in that time period. The team had no interest in disrupting that, nor Higashioka's growing chemistry with Cole. "The postseason was a completely fluid situation," Boone said. "I made no decision to say, 'Gary is benched.' I was going home every night and sleeping on who I was going to start the next day. A big reason for that was how well Kyle was playing."

Though Gary Sánchez's place on the bench seemed to be a given, Higashioka said that he was on edge once the assignment was confirmed. "I was pretty nervous," Higashioka said. "Looking back to when I was the third-string guy, Gary caught pretty much every single playoff game. I didn't know if I was going to catch in the playoffs at all. Then I'm in there for Game 1 in a best-of-three series against a team we hadn't faced all year. If we don't win, we're really in the hole. This is where it really counts."

Cole remained in sync with his new personal catcher, scattering six hits over seven innings. Ramírez stroked a run-scoring double in the third inning, and left fielder Josh Naylor slugged a solo homer in the fourth, but otherwise Cole breezed. He retired 11 of the final 12 batters that he faced, each out drawing applause from a luxury suite high above right field. Yes, for the first time since March, the Yankees were hearing cheers that weren't pumped from an iPad. Among those voices were Cole's wife Amy and their three-month-old son Caden, who earned rave reviews as a rookie traveler. He slept for almost the entire flight from New York to Cleveland and only fussed a little during the game. "I spent some time with him in between naps," Cole said. "It was the first time we got to go to the ballpark together as a family, so it's something that I'll always remember. I never thought that his first game would be in Cleveland."

Voit added an RBI double in the third inning, Brett Gardner and LeMahieu contributed run-scoring hits in the fourth, and Gleyber Torres chased Bieber by reaching the left-field bleachers with a two-run homer in the fifth. It was part of a four-hit, three-RBI performance for the shortstop, who finally appeared healthy after a series of nagging injuries. The seven runs that Bieber allowed were four more than he had allowed to any other team during the season, and he did not retire the side in order during any of his four-and-two-thirds innings. Torres began lobbying for the championship belt after adding a run-scoring single in the seventh, prompting Judge to tell him, "Hey man, we've got a lot of ballgame left."

Gardner and Giancarlo Stanton added late homers to the 15-hit attack, and Luis Cessa recorded the final six outs. Though the audience dwindled by the end, the Yankees remained a winner in the ratings book, as 2.64 million viewers tuned in, bypassing the contentious showdown on other channels, where moderator Chris Wallace pleaded with Trump to respect the rules of the debate. The most repeated line from that night was Biden's retort to Trump: "Will you shut up, man?"

The Yankees thought they'd earned some silence themselves. Voit had bristled about criticism that they were a creation of their friendly confines in the Bronx, discarding their 11–18 record on the road as "a bunch of B.S." They'd marched into Cleveland and convincingly thumped an excellent Indians team. Boone said that it was a good start, then cautioned: "Now we've got to do it again."

They'd have to wait less than 24 hours for that opportunity. Back under the lights, Game 2 would test their mettle. A storm system approaching Lake Erie's southern shore prompted the start time to be pushed back 42 minutes, at which point league officials peered into the still-clear skies and shrugged, providing a green light to begin play. In the press box, Mandy Bell checked the radar on her cell phone. The Indians beat reporter for MLB.com, Bell had sat through enough rain delays in the ballpark to know that things were about to go badly. The Indians public relations staff saw what was coming, too, starting a whisper campaign to relay that starting the game was the league's decision during the playoffs—essentially saying, don't blame us for whatever happens. "It made zero sense," Bell said. "Everyone was looking around, like, 'Why are we about to do this?'"

As if cued by Ed Harris' all-seeing producer in *The Truman Show*, the rain began, and 21 mph gusts whipped from left field to right field. The Yankees went down in order against right-hander Carlos Carrasco, and Masahiro Tanaka's pants flapped ridiculously in the wind as he stood atop the mound for the home half of the first inning. Tanaka wiped his brow and peered toward home plate, attempting to focus. The ball was already soaking wet in his right hand. He retired the leadoff hitter Lindor on a ground-out, then left a fastball up that Hernandez lashed into left field for a double. Ramírez pounced on a splitter for a run-scoring double down the right-field line, providing Cleveland with an early lead. Judge chased the ball to the right-field wall, firing it back to the infield. Now buckets of rain were falling, and above Judge in the right field stands, some of the wives and girlfriends wanted to scamper for cover. Mai Satoda refused to leave her seat. Tanaka's wife squinted through her whipping chestnut brown hair and pressed her palms together in prayer. Nancy Arreola, Cessa's girlfriend, called to the group. "I told the girls, 'Hey, yesterday we were outside supporting Amy Cole,'" Arreola said. "Let's be outside, even if it's raining, even if it's super cold. We are a team. Let's be together."

Respite came as the umpires called for the tarpaulin. The Yankees trudged to their clubhouse down a run, wondering why the game had been started at all. That stance continued when play resumed with Tanaka back on the hill after a 33-minute cooldown. Naylor belted a two-run double to center field, and Roberto Perez picked up a run-scoring single, staking the Tribe to a 4–0 lead. "We were thinking, *I don't know if this makes a ton of sense, but it's not anything we can control*," said pitching coach Matt Blake. "Masa was going to persevere and handle it as well as anybody, but for the type of pitcher he is, feel is an important part of it. If his hands are numb, he can't throw a slider or a split the way he wants to."

The bats would have to pick Tanaka up, and they did. Stanton started the rally, launching a second-inning homer over the right-center field wall that trimmed the deficit to three runs. In the fourth, Aaron Hicks lifted a fly ball that center fielder Delino DeShields misplayed into a triple, slipping and falling. It almost certainly should have been caught, but after the first-inning rain debacle, the Yanks had no qualms about accepting a gift. Voit and Stanton followed by working walks against Carrasco, ending the righty's night. In came reliever James Karinchak, an eccentric fireballer who favored uniform No. 99 and sported a similar Veg-O-Matic haircut to Charlie Sheen's Rick Vaughn character from the *Major League* movies.

Urshela didn't flinch at the wannabe Wild Thing, barreling a full-count fastball into the left-field bleachers to give the Yanks their first lead of the night. Urshela flipped his bat and raised his right fist, admiring the first post-season grand slam ever hit by a Yankees third baseman. "I was trying to get a pitch to hit," Urshela said. "I tried to put the ball in play, trying to get a sacrifice fly. Thank God I got the homer."

Stanton lifted a sacrifice fly in the fifth that extended the lead, but that didn't hold. Cleveland placed two runners aboard in the bottom of the frame to chase Tanaka, and Ramírez greeted Chad Green with a two-run double. Batting ninth for the first time in his big league career, Sánchez restored the advantage in the sixth inning, clubbing a deep drive that carried over the wall for a go-ahead two-run homer. Off the bat, Sánchez was not sure if his drive off rookie righty Triston McKenzie had a chance. Right fielder Tyler Naquin played it as though he had a beat on the ball, then ran out of room on the warning track as the wind carried it to the front row. Considering the numbers of barreled balls off Sánchez's bat that found gloves during the season, it seemed like a fair swap. "The regular season is over," Sánchez said. "Whatever happened in the regular season, at this point, it doesn't matter. That's the thing about the playoffs—everybody starts from zero."

The game took an unexpected turn in the seventh inning. Sandy Alomar Jr. was acting as the Indians' manager, entrusted with the lineup card while Terry Francona retreated due to health concerns. With Zack Britton on the mound, Alomar made a curious decision, swapping the left-handed Naylor out in favor of the right-handed Jordan Luplow. Naylor had been Cleveland's hottest hitter over the previous two nights, mashing four hits in Game 1. Boone responded by summoning right-hander Jonathan Loaisiga, negating the platoon advantage. Loaisiga hung a curveball that Luplow belted to deep center field for a two-run double. The game was tied 8–8, and no one cheered louder than Naylor.

Cleveland reclaimed the lead in the eighth. Facing Aroldis Chapman, Hernandez lifted a soft flare into shallow left field. Gardner—wearing his trusty turtleneck—raised his glove to deke the runners, but no one was buying. DeShields scored the tying run. It almost went overlooked at the time, but Urshela ended the inning by starting a double play from the seat of his pants, scrambling to smother Carlos Santana's hard grounder and firing a strike to LeMahieu at second base. Urshela's stellar effort kept at least one additional run off the scoreboard.

"He is a great third baseman," Chapman said. "He saved the game there."

Now the Yankees needed a ninth-inning rally against closer Brad Hand, who'd converted all 16 of his save chances during the regular season, striking out 29 against four walks in 22 innings. Maybe it was the postseason pressure, but Hand didn't look quite that automatic. Stanton worked a five-pitch walk and was replaced by pinch-runner Mike Tauchman, who advanced to second base on an Urshela single. Torres followed with a high chopper that cleared the mound, tipping Hand's glove and falling safely to the infield grass to load the bases. One out later, Sánchez lifted a fly ball to center field that tied the game. LeMahieu followed with a tie-breaking hit up the middle, a seeing-eye single that bounced a half-dozen times and eluded two defenders before finding safety in the outfield grass. Standing at second base, LeMahieu cracked the slightest of grins while his teammates went nuts. Chapman nailed down the final outs of the longest nine-inning game ever played on a major league diamond. The Yankees secured a wild 10–9 victory that spanned four hours and 50 minutes—not including 76 minutes of weather delays. "That was one of the best games I ever played in my life," Urshela said.

Though social distancing prevented the Yankees from celebrating as in 2017, when they'd doused every corner of the Progressive Field visiting clubhouse with beer and champagne to celebrate their advance in the American League Division Series, they earned the opportunity to crack a few cold ones in private. Boone was absolutely drained, saying that he was thankful that the clubs didn't have to play again the next day. "I'm 47 years old. I've watched a lot of baseball," Boone said. "I don't know how you top that one."

Rest was on the agenda now. They would be permitted a leisurely trip to the West Coast (as leisurely as you could have in a COVID-19 environment, anyway) for the ALDS against the Rays, who had ended the Toronto Blue

Jays' season down at Tropicana Field. The Indians allowed the Yanks to hold an informal workout the next afternoon before boarding a jet to San Diego, a rare instance of a ballclub preparing for thier next series on the turf of a defeated opponent. The sweep sent a message to observers who discounted the club entering the playoffs, especially when they lost six of their last eight regular-season games. They'd led the American League in runs scored and plowed through the best pitching staff that the circuit had to offer, clobbering seven homers and scoring 22 runs in two games. Bring on the Rays. "What we did to the Indians, firing on all cylinders," Cashman said months later, "we could have beaten anybody."

• CHAPTER 14 •

Hotel California

There were gasps heard on the chartered bus as it maneuvered through dozens of orange traffic cones guarding a winding sun-splashed drive, decorated with palm trees and strips of manicured, infield-length grass. After leaving the gray skies of rust-belted Cleveland behind, the traveling party was catching its first glimpse of their new Southern California home away from home. Yeah, this was more like it.

With the American League Division Series set to begin at Petco Park in San Diego, the New York Yankees' players, coaches, and family members would unload their suitcases in the Park Hyatt Aviara Resort, a five-star resort in the coastal city of Carlsbad, California. They were mixing business with pleasure: if they weren't playing the most important games of the year, the luxurious accommodations could have doubled as a vacation destination.

Designed in Spanish Colonial architecture and set upon a plateau overlooking a lagoon and wildlife preserve, the resort featured an 18-hole golf course designed by Arnold Palmer and a 15,000-square-foot spa—not that the players got to practice putting or enjoy salt scrubs. The lodgings were closed to outside guests, but the Yankees had company; the Tampa Bay Rays were jetting across the country to check in, having also dispatched the Toronto Blue Jays in a wild-card series sweep. The Aviara would have housed the San Diego bubble regardless of which clubs participated, having been selected weeks prior by Major League Baseball and the Major League Baseball Players Association. That it wound up housing a pair of heated division rivals who would cross paths on the way to their morning saliva tests, having already exchanged on-field brushbacks, added another ridiculous wrinkle to the season's wild ride. "I did not like sharing the same hotel. I just thought that made zero sense," said Yankees reliever Zack Britton. "I was seeing the Rays players at the hotel every day, walking to get breakfast and stuff. If one guy on one team got sick, didn't that eliminate both teams with the contract tracing and everything?"

Fortunately, that question never needed an answer. It would have made a great story if Aroldis Chapman entered an elevator already occupied by Mike Brosseau, considering their fresh history, but nothing like that happened at the Aviara. In their first 24 hours under the same roof, Brett Gardner said that he encountered a few Tampa Bay players, but the teams were largely kept separate in different wings. "I just said 'Hey' and kept walking," Gardner said. "It's a big resort. We've got a lot of space. Say hello and keep moving along."

Gardner's example was wise: there wasn't much to talk about, even for the Yanks' resident smart aleck. The Rays owned the upper hand during the regular season, winning eight of 10 games, and the Yankees wanted to wipe Chapman's errant fastball from their collective memory banks. Kevin Kiermaier certainly wasn't in a chatty mood. The Rays' Gold Glove outfielder offered this: "I've said it many times: 'They don't like us; we don't like them. It's going to continue to stay that way.'"

Their animosity would be hashed out between the white lines in San Diego. Given its reliable weather, the location was one of the logical neutral sites since cancellations at that late stage would create scheduling nightmares. With the presidential election set for November 4 and a second wave of COVID-19 infections forecast with colder weather, MLB was adamant that they must complete the postseason by Halloween. As such, Dodger Stadium in Los Angeles remained in service, as did Minute Maid Park in Houston and Globe Life Park in Arlington, and both of the latter venues boasted retractable roofs.

It had been a memorable week, even for this strange year. The clubhouse televisions were reliably tuned to sports, but the players couldn't avoid the drama taking place in the nation's capital, their social media feeds cluttered with breaking news. They'd been in the air when president Donald Trump announced that he and first lady Melania Trump tested positive for the coronavirus, throwing the country's leadership into uncertainty. Marine One carried Trump to Walter Reed Medical Center, where he received experimental treatments, then instructed Secret Service officers to circle the block in a sport utility vehicle so he could wave at supporters. "Of course we talked about it," general manager Brian Cashman said. "How could you not? The whole country was talking about it."

The images raised eyebrows across the country, including the playoff bubbles, where protocols barred players from doing so much as collecting their usual Venti coffees from Starbucks. Aaron Boone's parents and brother Bret lived in the area, and he'd normally grab lunch or leave tickets at the will call window during a SoCal visit. There would be no hugs or chats on this visit. Instead, they texted. Some of the players thought the series had the vibe of travel ball tournaments they'd played in as teenagers.

Once the Yankees entered through the loading dock of 19 Tony Gwynn Drive in the gorgeous Marina District, Boone advised his players not to be sidetracked by whatever drama existed between them and the Rays. DJ LeMahieu kept his cards close to the vest even on his chattiest days, and he needed no such reminders as he dug into the batter's box, 60 feet and six inches from Rays ace Blake Snell.

"The Machine" showed up programmed to hit, lashing a full-count fastball into center field for a series-opening bullet single. LeMahieu advanced on a wild pitch and ground-out, then scored on an Aaron Hicks sacrifice fly. Easy breezy: the Yankees gave Gerrit Cole a lead, just as they'd done in the first game of the Cleveland Indians series. But the Rays weren't going to roll over, especially as Randy Arozarena announced his presence on the national stage. Soon to become a postseason darling whose life story would greenlight a quickie motion picture, Arozarena was still prompting Google searches that included the words "who is." Those filled the pipelines after the 25-year-old outfielder launched a Cole fastball toward a palm tree overlooking the center-field wall, clearing the 396-foot marker and tying the game.

Arozarena was having a moment, and Clint Frazier wanted to make the most of his. He'd had his phone on do not disturb prior to the first game of the Indians series, waking up to a couple of missed calls from Boone. The manager had not been delivering good news: Gardner started both games in Cleveland, and Frazier whiffed in his only at-bat of the series. Facing the lefty Snell offered a chance at redemption in this round, and Frazier lashed a high heater into the left-field seats, homering to begin his first postseason start. Few mortals could get around on a 95 mph fastball in that location—at least, not without legendary bat speed.

It was a sugar sweet moment for Frazier, who quipped that he "blacked out running the bases." He had finished an otherwise strong season on a 1-for-20 slide that dented his playing time. (Frazier later remarked that his luck soured as soon as Gardner borrowed that turtleneck in Boston.) He tried to shake things up, even playing without the mask that had garnered so much attention earlier in the year. He strutted around that night wearing an Elvis Presley T-shirt, a Kingly souvenir from a visit to Graceland, thank you very much.

Ji-Man Choi, Cole's personal nemesis, resurfaced in the fourth. In Cole's view, Choi's mystifying mastery stemmed from a batch of missed locations over the past few years. It happened again as Cole buzzed a 1–1 fastball that caught too much of the plate, bracing as Choi raked it for an opposite-field, two-run homer—the journeyman's fourth homer in 19 at-bats against Cole. "He handled a lot of their hitters really well," said catcher Kyle Higashioka. "They've got some good, scrappy hitters. I think if you can navigate the couple of danger men in the lineup, then you're in pretty good shape. But there were a few guys he struggled with—Ji-Man, especially."

Higashioka and Aaron Judge homered off a fatiguing Snell in the fifth, and Cole protected that lead. There was anxiety in the visiting dugout when Cole issued a two-out walk to Brandon Lowe, then surrendered a single to Arozarena, and fell behind Choi on a 2–0 count. Pitching coach Matt Blake visited the mound, recommending an intentional walk. Cole shooed him away.

It turned out to be the right call. Cole needed four pitches to retire Manuel Margot, including a mix-up in which Higashioka signaled for a fastball, then deftly gloved a curve that darted through the strike zone. Home-plate umpire David Rackley didn't give Cole the call, but Cole remarked that it was arguably the most important play of the game. If it had gone to the backstop, he said, "it could be a totally different game." Two more heaters followed, and Margot waved at one near his shoulders for strike three—Cole clocked at triple digits with a 100.1 mph heater, extinguishing a bases-loaded rally. He danced off the mound, unleashing a primal scream that could be heard from the press box, six stories above the playing field. "Big stage, big moment," Cole said. "I executed perfectly. I'm glad because I really got myself into a bit of a mess there."

In Tampa Bay's dugout, manager Kevin Cash observed that Cole got "nastier" later in the game, marveling to see him dial up his fastball when he needed it. Cole fanned another pair in a clean sixth, emptying the tank for his 97-pitch effort. When the cameras panned to the Yanks' dugout in the seventh, Cole had replaced his sweat-soaked uniform top with a hooded sweatshirt.

His work day was done, but Giancarlo Stanton was not. With his parents having made the drive from Los Angeles, Stanton turned the game into a blowout with a ninth-inning grand slam off John Curtiss, registering the Yankees' fourth homer of the night. The bench went nuts, especially Frazier, who said that it "was the first time I ever screamed for somebody else."

The bullpen polished off the last nine outs of a 9–3 victory, the Yanks' hitters agreeing to stick to "boys will be boys" when Curtiss buzzed Urshela with a fastball following Stanton's slam. Maybe the Yankees were looking too comfortable; Stanton had no complaints about swinging the bat in Petco Park, a building in which he'd won the 2016 Home Run Derby with a ridiculous 61-homer display. "It's SoCal," Stanton said. "I grew up about an hour and a half, two hours away. That was the first game that my parents were able to come to, so that helps."

The Yankees were mashing like the juggernaut that everyone envisioned in the first spring training. In one week, they crushed the AL Cy Young winner in Shane Bieber, beat one of the best relievers in James Karinchak, and saddled Brad Hand with his first blown save. Now they'd tagged Snell for three homers, pulling away against the Rays' stable. Boone offered a reminder that it was one win; they needed three.

Back at the Aviara, the mood was jubilant—especially among the wives and girlfriends, who were beginning to feel like they were part of a larger family. They even had a uniform. Luke Voit's wife Tori produced navy blue sweatshirts for each woman, sporting the Yankees' top hat logo on the left shoulder and their player's surname stitched in white near the neckline, punctuated with a heart. "We had more fun than the players," said Nancy Arreola, the girlfriend of pitcher Luis Cessa. "They were going to the stadium and coming back. We had spinning classes, a painting class that we'd all do together. Sometimes we'd use the swimming pool; we'd have breakfast together. It felt like a mini-vacation."

Some of the players looked longingly from their balconies, wanting to hit balls from the adjacent golf driving range. They were told that absolutely no one was to leave the property. The league officials were serious, as Brett McCabe learned early. The Yankees' strength and conditioning coach, McCabe laced up his sneakers, placed his earbuds in, and cranked up the music for a jog. He made it perhaps a quarter-mile before being stopped by an angry security officer. McCabe slunk back to his room, and the players thought it was hilarious.

Even though they couldn't leave the hotel complex, they could leave their rooms. Some of the alternate site players discovered that they could watch the action from poolside cabanas. Each team brought injury replacements on the trip, providing two-hour windows each morning for their on-field workouts. The logistics worked better in Cleveland, where the hotel was only a mile from Progressive Field. In California, the players had to bus the 32 miles from the resort to Petco Park, then return around 1:00 PM—just as the active players were leaving for San Diego. "We ended up watching most of the games at the hotel, overlooking the ocean," said pitcher Clarke Schmidt. "At first, we weren't allowed to have room service, but then MLB said they would comp all of it. We were like, 'All right, we're going to destroy this.' Poke bowls, salmon steaks, hamburgers, cheeseburgers, wings. We might have ordered a few beers here and there."

As the Bombers snuck in a little R&R, packing on a pound or two, the brain trust was cooking up a covert plan to stretch their admittedly thin pitching staff. Boone bypassed Masahiro Tanaka to announce Deivi García as the starting pitcher for the second game, making him the franchise's youngest starting pitcher ever in a postseason contest. There was a measure of trickery afoot as he walked to the mound, as the 21 year old's outing was intended only to be a cameo.

The team had discussed making a similar move at times during the regular season, but the opportunity never lined up, according to Blake. They wanted to try it against the Rays, hoping to exploit a platoon advantage against a lineup that boasted left-handed strength. As García tossed his seventh pitch, left-hander J.A. Happ was warming, part of a bait and switch. "One of the logistical challenges was J.A. hadn't come out of the bullpen that year," Blake said. "He had come out of the bullpen in the past, so we weighed that. We had talked about it with J.A. two or three times. It's a riskier move because of the postseason and the guys that are involved in it, but we felt like the matchups made sense."

García permitted a homer to Arozarena in a 27-pitch first inning, then yielded to Happ. Facing hitters for the first time in 11 days, Happ had few answers for the Rays. Mike Zunino slugged a two-run homer in the second inning, and Margot lifted a two-run shot in the third inning, by which time the Yankees sensed that their plan had backfired. Boone said that the first kernels of the García-Happ switch came after the sweep of the Indians. Members of the coaching staff, the front office, and the analytics department ruminated over a two-day period. Boone once described the majors as a "copycat league," and they were cribbing from a move executed by the Blue Jays in Game 1 of their wild-card series, when right-hander Matt Shoemaker and left-hander Robbie Ray combined for six innings of one-run ball. "I'm sure there will be people that [say], if we just started a guy and went with him, we win the game," Boone said. "That's kind of ridiculous. All over the league, things like this are done—and done really effectively."

That was true, but Happ seemed to be a curious choice, given that he had been irked by his unpredictable schedule earlier in the season. Even prior to the ALDS, Happ made it clear to Boone and the coaches that he did not like entering as a bulk reliever, voicing a preference to start. Boone replied that the Yankees believed that the decision would give them their best chance to win. Happ promised to do his best. "They know how I felt about it," Happ said. "Ultimately, I pitch when I pitch. You've got me. There was no hesitation and no dwelling on what was going on. I was focused and trying to perform. I wish I would have done a better job."

Boone said that one factor was that left-handed batters produced a .577 OPS against Happ over the previous three seasons, spanning 388⅓ innings with the Blue Jays and Yankees. It was a much smaller sample size, but García held lefties to a remarkably similar .579 OPS through his first six big league starts. What's more, Happ and García posted similar numbers against lefties through the 2020 regular season. Lefties were 14-for-62 (.227) against García with a homer and 11 strikeouts, while they were 10-for-49 (.204) with two homers and 11 strikeouts against Happ. The upgrade, if there was one, seemed to be negligible.

Back on August 9, when left-hander James Paxton started against Tampa Bay, Cash loaded his lineup with seven right-handed bats. Had the Yankees announced Happ as their Game 2 starter, they would have expected a similar batting order, a poor matchup for Happ. By tabbing García, they reduced that number from seven to five, as Cash selected a batting order of five lefties and four righties. Reflecting later, Cashman recited dates and statistics to defend the strategy, citing Happ's two scoreless innings behind Chad Green in Game 6 of the 2019 American League Championship Series against the Houston Astros, as well as five sharp innings behind Jonathan Loaisiga on September 25, 2019 against the Rays. It should be mentioned, though, that the Yankees lost both games. "We didn't ask J.A. Happ to do something he wasn't used to doing," Cashman said. "I know he's a starter, but he's had 15 postseason appearances in his career. He's had four starts in the postseason, so his whole postseason career is coming out of the 'pen. He was given advance notice. Of course, he would have liked to have started."

The decision was panned by experts, including two former Yankees. On his podcast, CC Sabathia excoriated the decision to lift García after three outs, believing a neutral-site, empty-ballpark game was a perfect place to trust a rookie. Alex Rodriguez said that the front office had tried to be too "gimmicky," proving that they could think along with the Rays. "Game 2 was a mistake, and it was a mistake for about 20 different reasons," Rodriguez said. "The players start saying, 'What are we doing?' You start spending so much time to figure out how to outsmart the Ivy Leaguers over there. That's not your game. Don't play *Jeopardy!* Play baseball. Players win championships."

At the ownership level, Hal Steinbrenner believed the logic had been sound. Steinbrenner focused his attention instead on Happ's inability to navigate the Tampa Bay lineup, seemingly stamping the end of the lefty's time in pinstripes: "The bottom line is: in order for a plan to be successful, the different components of the plan have to be well-executed. And that didn't happen here."

Despite the early deficit, Stanton tried to keep his team in the game, homering in his first two at-bats against right-hander Tyler Glasnow. Boone was wowed, remarking that he may have never seen a ball hit like Stanton's second-inning drive, a letter-high curveball that flew over the right-field fence on a laundry line. Stanton's second blast, a three-run shot in the fourth, was a video game shot that appeared to travel farther than its announced distance of 458 feet, rattling into a vacant terrace area underneath the left-field video screen. Glasnow didn't bother to look as Stanton touched rarified air, joining Lou Gehrig and Reggie Jackson as the only Yankees to clear the fences in four consecutive postseason games. "That's pretty cool," Stanton said, "but that's stuff you look at after the year is done."

Individual achievements and long homers were indeed fun, but the goal was to win a ring. To do that, the Yankees would need to rely upon some of their lower-leverage arms. Given the scarcity of postseason off days (something that came as a surprise to the baseball operations department when the schedule was finalized on September 15), Boone said it would be impossible to ride two starting pitchers and four high-impact relievers in a series. He considered it essential that the Yankees squeeze production from the 12th or 13th men on their staff.

Happ exited with two outs in the fourth inning, and Adam Ottavino faced a few batters in the fifth before Kiermaier greeted Loaisiga with a run-scoring single. Again showcasing electric stuff and less-than-stellar results in the same outing, Loaisiga served up a solo homer to Austin Meadows in the sixth. "We walked the left-handers and gave up home runs to the right-handers," Blake said, disappointment still in his voice months later.

Beyond their sputtering pitching, the Yankees barely made contact in Game 2. Tampa Bay hurlers notched 18 strikeouts, a record for a nine-inning postseason game. Even so, they mounted a ninth-inning rally, bringing the potential go-ahead run to bat. Gio Urshela and Gleyber Torres worked walks against right-hander Pete Fairbanks. Two outs later, LeMahieu made contact for a run-scoring single. That brought up Judge, who chopped a slider to third base for the last out in Tampa's 7–5 victory.

Now it was a best-of-three series. The Yankees liked their chances with Masahiro Tanaka, arguably their coolest customer, on the mound. Six years before Cole held up his faded childhood memento in Yankee Stadium's Legends Club, Tanaka took a turn as the toast of the town, leaning into a microphone in that same room and announcing in practiced English: "Hello, my name is Masahiro Tanaka. I am very happy to be a Yankee."

Tanaka beamed that morning in February 2014, proud to have aced his first test on United States soil. Mastering that line was easy; he was no stranger to a challenge. Tanaka had become a household name as a high schooler in his native Japan, collecting strikeouts in the Koshien tournament, an event comparable to the United States' level of interest in March Madness.

As a professional, Tanaka enjoyed seven dominant seasons with the Tohoku Rakuten Golden Eagles, including a 24–0 record with a 1.27 ERA in 2013. Highlighted by a lethal splitter that fell off the table, Tanaka's talent deserved to be tested against the world's best.

After a posting process, Tanaka agreed to a seven-year, $155 million contract with the Yankees, citing their winning pedigree. He was, as he announced to a room of more than 300 reporters that day, coming with the expectation of delivering a championship. Tanaka was a must-see attraction through the first 17 starts of his rookie season, compiling a 12–3 record with a 2.27 ERA while striking out better than a batter per inning.

That changed when Tanaka walked to the mound for a July start against the Indians, which saw him surrender five earned runs over six-and-two-thirds innings. Receiving treatment after the game, Tanaka casually mentioned that he was feeling discomfort near his right forearm. Doctors confirmed a small tear of Tanaka's ulnar collateral ligament, and three specialists advised the team to try rehab instead of immediate Tommy John surgery. That set the course for the years to follow; he missed two-and-a-half months, then compiled five full seasons without issue. By 2020, Tanaka said he no longer thought about his elbow, and most stopped waiting for it to blow mid-game. "He was a tremendous import from Japan," Cashman said. "He had a seamless transition and impacted us in such a positive way. He's someone that every time you gave him the ball on the mound, I know we were going to get his best effort, and typically we got great results, too. Everything we thought he could be, he was as advertised."

Wearing his pinstripes as the Yankees assumed the role of "home" team under the postcard-perfect conditions, Tanaka worked a scoreless first inning—helped by a stellar over-the-shoulder Judge grab against the right-field wall, battling the setting sun—before giving up a soft run on three second-inning singles. LeMahieu needed about three more inches on his vertical leap to snare one, a Michael Perez liner that fell for an RBI single.

Judge evened the game with a sac fly, but Kiermaier golfed a first-pitch Tanaka curveball for a three-run homer in the fourth inning, clearing the right-field wall. Tanaka returned to the mound in the fifth, but Arozarena made it a brief stay. Tanaka spun a slider against the sizzling "Cuban Rocket," who ambushed a drive toward the Western Metal Supply Co. warehouse in left field. The Yankees could only shake their heads, marveling at Arozarena's emergence. He had become "the best player on Earth," in the words of his teammate Glasnow, months after being quarantined alone in a Florida apartment. Arozarena's fitness routine featured chicken and rice for most meals, one of the few dishes he knew how to prepare, and 300 push-ups each day. The result was 15 pounds of extra muscle, which Arozarena kept on despite a positive COVID-19 diagnosis. He didn't even appear in a big league game until August 30. "I was glad that he continued to do what he was doing for the rest of the postseason," Higashioka said. "Then I knew that it wasn't just us. He was on the kind of hot streak the likes of which I haven't seen very often. Every single mistake got punished."

Boone ambled from the dugout to claim the ball from Tanaka, who wondered if the meaty offering that produced Arozarena's third homer of the ALDS had also marked his final pitch as a Yankee. Higashioka thought the Rays sat on certain pitches and made a mental note to be more unpredictable next time he caught Tanaka—if there was a next time. They carried other what-ifs to the clubhouse four innings later; perhaps their predicament would have been different if not for a pair of questionable strikes in the third inning.

They were banging on the door against right-hander Charlie Morton, who seemed to be struggling to throw strikes from the stretch position. Hicks followed Judge's sacrifice fly with a walk that loaded the bases, and Voit looked at three pitches out of the strike zone to begin his at-bat. The fourth pitch appeared outside, so Voit reached down to unbuckle his shin guard. Mark Carlson—coincidentally, one of the umpires who rode that plane from Atlanta to New York back in August—called a strike. The next pitch also went Morton's way, preceding Voit's sharp inning-ending ground-out. Boone said it was "a big opportunity" lost, and it indeed felt that way. If either of Morton's pitches on 3–0 and 3–1 had been called balls, a run would have been walked in, giving the Yankees the lead and sending Stanton up with the bases still loaded. Instead, nada.

The Yanks also took issue in the fourth inning when Willy Adames walked on a close pitch that nixed a strikeout, throw-out double play. Higashioka sent a rope to second base that would have cut down Joey Wendle, running on the full-count pitch, but Carlson tipped the at-bat in Adames' favor by ruling Tanaka's slider had missed the zone for ball four. Describing his mind-set as "very frustrated," Tanaka said that he thought it was a strike, and Kiermaier sent the next pitch over the wall. "It definitely was a turning point in the game," Higashioka said. "That really could have swung the momentum our way big time. Earlier in the at-bat, he did call a pitch around that height for a strike. So it definitely could have gone our way."

And, of course, the predicament was ripe for second-guessing the decision to use García as a surprise opener. Boone said that he wouldn't participate in that coulda-shoulda. Meanwhile, Blake said that Tanaka's bumpy outing provided no guarantee he would have pitched better if given the nod for Game 2. "Masa threw against seven left-handers and gave up five runs in five innings," Blake said. "It's hard to say if we had just gone straight with one or the other that we would have seen a better outcome. It didn't work out the way that we were hoping, but I think our process to get there was pretty sound."

Stanton's sensational postseason was being wasted, as the slugger launched a late two-run blast—his sixth homer in five playoff games. Already more vocal in the hitters' meetings, offering his opinions on how the team should attack opposing hurlers, Stanton was strapping the team across his broad shoulders at a most crucial time. The Yankees were counting spots in the lineup until he would bat again. "That should eliminate anybody's questions about whether he can play in New York or not," Cashman said. "Bottom line is: when he's healthy, he's a beast. It felt like he was going to hit a home run every game in the postseason against elite pitching."

As he sat in front of the Zoom camera that evening, sporting a cutoff Nike shirt that showcased his bulging biceps, Stanton understood the simple math. They'd need to win the next two games, or they were going home. "We've got to come out swinging," he said. "It's now or never. So let's go."

• CHAPTER 15 •

GIVE ME THE BALL

The monstrous drive soared toward Luke Voit's unsmiling headshot on the National League's largest scoreboard, a blast that prompted the slugger to drop his bat and enjoy a moment of admiration. The frustration of the previous two evenings dissipated into the Southern California haze, and the New York Yankees truly believed in that moment that they were destined to write a comeback story.

Voit was staring skyward to track that disappearing sphere in the second inning of Game 4 between the Yankees and Tampa Bay Rays, the brash 29-year-old having obliterated a slider thrown by right-hander Ryan Thompson. As he limped around the bases for the first postseason homer of his career, gamely performing on one good foot, Voit couldn't help but think: *we're going to win it.* "I wanted to be there for the boys when we needed it," Voit said, months later. "Sometimes the boys needed a jump start. I think there's a lot of leaders in our clubhouse and I think there was a time and place for each one of us to say something. Sometimes you've got to face up to get the guys where you want them to be."

And where the Yankees wanted to be on that October evening was San Diego, unwilling to check out of their rooms at the Park Hyatt Aviara. As Gerrit Cole entered the visiting clubhouse a few hours before Game 4, he locked eyes with Aaron Boone, who was in his office. The manager offered a generic query about how Cole was feeling, and his ace provided a movie hero response. "Give me the ball," Cole replied.

Boone nodded. That was the plan. As he stalked the dugout in the moments before first pitch, the manager said that he sensed a different "edge" from his players, dressed in their home pinstripes. They had better have an edge; they were nine bad innings from going home. They had not come all this way to go out with a whimper, which Voit made clear with a drive that came to rest 453 feet from home plate in the Estrella Jalisco Landing, a second-deck seating area under the massive high-definition scoreboard. It had so much arc that they probably had a good view at the Altitude Sky Lounge across the street at the Marriott Gaslamp Quarter, a rooftop deck bar that offered one of the few legal ways to watch part of the ballgame in person. DJ LeMahieu added a sacrifice fly that pushed the Yankees' lead to 2–0, and Jordan Montgomery returned to the mound, having already retired the first six Tampa Bay batters in order.

It was already a career highlight for the 27-year-old lefty, who carried the nickname "Gumby," a reference to his gangly 6'6" build, since his days at the University of South Carolina. He had been a contributor during the Yankees' surprising 2017 season, an underappreciated addition to the Baby Bombers of Aaron Judge, Gary Sánchez, and Luis Severino. Montgomery pitched to a 9–7 record and a 3.88 ERA in 29 starts that year, but watched each playoff game from the bullpen, as the phone never rang for him. He underwent Tommy John surgery early the next year, beginning a long road back to full health.

On the mound for the first time in two weeks, Montgomery scattered three hits over four innings, generating swings and misses on pitches out of the zone when he needed to. Stuck with runners at second and third bases with none out following a leadoff walk and a Kevin Kiermaier double, Montgomery's biggest test came in the third inning. Montgomery found his touch, releasing a full-count change-up that struck out Mike Zunino, then issued a walk to load the bases before inducing Brandon Lowe and Randy Arozarena ground-outs, limiting the damage to one run.

Montgomery struck out four before yielding to the bullpen, an effort that would earn the presentation of the clubhouse championship belt. As Chad Green, Zack Britton, and Aroldis Chapman combined for five innings of scoreless, hitless relief, Gleyber Torres provided breathing room by banging a two-run homer into the Western Metal Supply Co. warehouse. His teammates roared as the ball reached the rarely-visited fourth deck of the turn-of-the-century structure, around which the structure was built.

As Chapman faced (who else?) Mike Brosseau with two outs in the ninth inning, finishing off the 5–1 win, Boone saw Cole standing nearby in the dugout. Cole liked to sidle up to the coaching staff late in games, absorbing chatter as they first-guessed strategy. Boone offered confirmation of an assignment that had long been assumed: "You're pitching tomorrow." Cole nodded. Tampa Bay countered with Tyler Glasnow on two days' rest. It was a rematch of the previous season's American League Division Series Game 5, when Cole's Houston Astros had advanced. Houston awaited again, and one of these two clubs would see them in the American League Championship Series.

The mood seemed celebratory. As the beat reporters filed their final dispatches from the Petco Park press box, cheers were heard beyond the outfield walls. Curiosity prompted a walk one block north toward Bub's at the Ballpark, a rollicking sports bar with pub grub. San Diego had not become a Yankee town overnight. The noise came from Padres fans seated at outdoor tables, watching on television as their team played a "home" playoff game against the Los Angeles Dodgers in Texas. The scribes shook their heads and said, "2020."

In what had already been a heavy year, the Yankees were about to take another hit. A coast away in Lake Success, New York, Whitey Ford watched the first pitches of Game 4 on television. Surrounded by family members, the greatest pitcher in franchise history did not see the final out, passing away peacefully at age 91. Nicknamed the "Chairman of the Board," Ford was a key piece of the team's mid-century dynasty, a first-ballot Hall of Famer who brought six World Series championships and 11 pennants to New York.

Ford's name appeared in the club's press notes during the ALDS; García's surprise opening assignment in Game 2 moved him alongside Ford as the only 21 year olds to start a postseason game for the Yankees. Ford's outing went much better than García's. Casey Stengel tabbed the rookie for Game 4 of the 1950 World Series against the "Whiz Kid" Philadelphia Phillies, and Ford delivered on that sunny Saturday at Yankee Stadium, firing eight scoreless innings before left fielder Gene Woodling dropped a fly ball in the ninth inning, plating two unearned Philadelphia runs. Woodling expressed dismay at ruining Ford's shutout, but it was the first of many World Series wins for the lefty, who finished one out shy of a complete game as Allie Reynolds sealed the championship with a strikeout.

As the players arrived for Game 5, each of their road gray uniform jerseys bore Ford's uniform No. 16 on the left sleeve. The digits rested above an oval patch with the initials "HGS" for Henry G. "Hank" Steinbrenner, who passed away in April. Boone said that he prayed for Ford's family, remarking that he hoped there was comfort in that Ford had been watching the Yankees when he passed. The club's all-time wins leader with 236, Ford's final game was another victory. The hashtag #WinItForWhitey circulated on social media, and Britton spent time familiarizing himself with Ford's career achievements, mentioning Ford's military service. Ford spent the 1951 and '52 seasons in the Army, remaining stateside at Fort Monmouth in New Jersey, where he pitched for their baseball team. They'd play about four days a week, drawing crowds in the thousands, and the fort commander wanted Ford to pitch every game to boost attendance.

Given that experience, Ford could have offered sage advice to Cole, who was preparing to take the ball on short rest for the first time in his professional career. In 216 starts with the Pittsburgh Pirates, Astros, and Yankees, Cole's employers had never seen fit to rush him back to the mound with fewer than four full days between starts, though Cole had seen many of his peers compete successfully under those circumstances. Earlier in the week, Cole scrolled through his phone and crowdsourced for advice, mentioning CC Sabathia, Justin Verlander, Zack Greinke, and Dallas Keuchel among those who had offered pointers.

In 2008, Sabathia hoisted the Milwaukee Brewers upon his beefy shoulders, carrying them to a National League wild-card berth by insisting that they give him the ball as frequently as possible. Sabathia made his final three starts of the regular season on short rest, to the chagrin of his agents, who were terrified by the possibility of an injury spoiling what promised to be a lucrative free-agent contract in a few months. After Sabathia got that big money from the Yankees, manager Joe Girardi sent the lefty to the mound on short rest twice during the 2009 postseason, pitching well against the Los Angeles Angels and Phillies while helping the team avoid giving the ball to less-appealing options in Joba Chamberlain and Chad Gaudin.

Cole said that he did not believe pitching on three days' rest was sustainable over an entire season, though it had once been the norm. The No. 16 on Cole's left sleeve showed that; 156 of Ford's 438 starts were on three days' rest, during which Ford had pitched to a 2.97 ERA. He'd just have to go old school. Cole found no challenge in getting his juices flowing. "Any time you're in the lineup in a do-or-die game, obviously your teammates have faith in you, your manager has faith in you," Cole said. "As a player, it's always a good feeling. You always want to be out there in the big moment."

Game 5 got off to a shaky start for Cole, who struck out leadoff hitter Austin Meadows on three pitches before walking Lowe and hitting Arozarena with a pitch. Cole induced a ground-out, then walked Yandy Díaz to load the bases, bringing pitching coach Matt Blake to the mound for a chat. When Cole threw three consecutive balls to Joey Wendle, Boone fingered his lineup card, mentally scanning how he'd fill the next eight innings if his best pitcher faltered.

The coaches exhaled when Cole escaped, receiving the benefit of low strike calls from home-plate umpire Marvin Hudson to punch out Wendle looking. The 25-pitch inning produced anxiety, but no Tampa Bay runs. Cole found his groove from there, retiring eight consecutive batters, picking up support when Judge parked a fourth-inning homer into the right-field seats. Judge's blast came off Nick Anderson and cleared the 322-foot marker. On the bench, Gio Urshela bashed the dugout railing with his bat, screaming, "Let's go!" It was only the first home run that Anderson, one of the league's most dominant relievers, had permitted to a right-handed hitter all year. "Judge never got quite locked in timing-wise and still hit three homers in the postseason," Boone said. "That was a big homer to give us the lead in Game 5. With Aaron, it's always getting to the point where you really get locked in, then he's the best player on the field. He grinded through those last couple of weeks and never got that timing exactly where it needed to be."

Judge's swing gave Cole some razor-thin margin for error. Though Cole and catcher Kyle Higashioka had performed their due diligence by going over the Rays' scouting report, this was the fifth time that Cole was seeing the lineup in the span of a few months. He could have recited their strengths and weaknesses in his sleep, whirling his index finger in frustration, saying that it was "just like on a tape recorder with these guys."

Showcasing a fastball that crackled as hot as 100 mph, Cole emptied his tank before Meadows launched a deep fifth-inning drive toward right field. Judge moved back, feeling as though he had a beat on it. He was under it at the wall, raised his glove, jumped, and—nothing. Judge's skull banged into a padded overhanging lip of the right-field scoreboard, sending the 6'7" outfielder sprawling to the warning track as the game-tying home run rattled into the seats.

Judge had never played at Petco Park before the ALDS. The Yankees' most recent visit was in July 2016, six weeks ahead of Judge's big league debut. Though he spent the workout days inspecting the unforgiving chain-link fence and each angle of the right-field wall, the protruding lip caught Judge by surprise in that moment. Bringing back homers is difficult enough without overhead obstacles. "I was right there," Judge said. "I think I've got a shot at any ball that gets hit to right field. That's a tough one, especially with Cole out there competing his butt off. I've got to get up there and rob that one."

Watching the play develop from the back of the mound, Cole thought that Judge had a chance. Meadows had not reacted as though it would be a homer, but it kept carrying. From the dugout, outfield coach Reggie Willits also expected that Judge would glove the ball. "That San Diego outfield is a really difficult outfield to play," Willits said. "There's so many nooks and crannies out there—weird angles where if it goes six inches one way or the other, you've got to be aggressive or hold back. There's so many things in a play that have to go perfect for it all to line up, but as a defender, I'll never put anything past Judge making a play."

If there was any flaw with Cole's performance over his first season in a Yankees uniform, it was susceptibility to the home run; 23 of the 29 runs he permitted in 2020 came via the long ball. Cole bowed out after Brett Gardner saved his bacon with a leaping catch against the left-field wall in the sixth inning, stealing what would have been Arozarena's fourth home run of the ALDS.

The Yankees searched for a big swing to break the game open, but they came up empty. The lineup produced only three hits, the last of which came on Aaron Hicks' sixth-inning single. Voit struck out against Pete Fairbanks in that frame, leaving two men on—part of a parade of missed opportunities, as they went hitless in eight at-bats with runners aboard. Voit's at-bat was their only chance with a runner in scoring position, and only one more Yankee would touch base before the lights dimmed on their season. "I knew he was going to attack me," Voit said. "I've had success off him, too. It was kind of like that the whole series. I didn't do a lot with runners in scoring position. We just didn't hit when we had guys on and we had plenty of opportunities. They had some studs coming out of their bullpen."

Boone scrambled, hoping to create magic. He sent up Mike Ford to pinch hit for Higashioka in the eighth, favoring a left-on-right matchup with Diego Castillo. Ford hadn't registered a hit since August 31, but Boone was dreaming big, having witnessed the then-rookie first baseman belt a pair of pinch-hit homers the previous September. Facing Castillo, a reverse split anomaly whose fastball-slider mix was tougher on right-handed hitters, the gamble resulted in a Ford strikeout.

It was on to the ninth inning, which culminated in a poetic showdown—perhaps the inevitable conclusion in a clash of American League East titans who made no secret of their mutual dislike. The audience watching at home got to see Chapman on the mound and Brosseau at the plate, reprising their respective roles from an incident that cleared benches a coast away five weeks prior. No one had forgotten the 101 mph fastball that buzzed over Brosseau's batting helmet back in the Bronx, nor Kevin Cash's warning about the Rays' "stable" of hard-throwing relievers. In fact, the comment had generated some new apparel in their traveling party, as the team sported "Tampa Bay 98ers" gear. Giancarlo Stanton had deftly dismissed that in one of the Zoom sessions, observing that "shirts and hats don't mean anything."

Yet Chapman's high-octane arsenal seemed best suited in short spurts, and the Yankees frequently hemmed and hawed over asking four outs from their closer during the regular reason. That made it surprising when Boone came to the mound in the seventh inning, relieving Britton with two outs and a runner at first base. Their season on the line in a tied game, the Yankees were going to sink or swim with Chapman. One night after he'd expended 23 pitches to lock down Game 4, they were asking him to get seven more outs and send them on to the next round. It didn't get that far. Chapman struck out Lowe to end the seventh inning, then opened the eighth by getting Arozarena to ground out sharply on two pitches.

Up came Brosseau, who had overcome long odds to become a central figure in the budding rivalry. Forty rounds passed in the 2016 draft without mention of Brosseau, then a senior shortstop at Oakland University in Rochester, Minnesota. Brosseau had pop and plate discipline, but his stocky 5'10" build didn't inspire scouts to put their names on the line. Short an infielder for their Gulf Coast League club, the Rays offered Brosseau $1,000 to pack his bags and report to Port Charlotte, Florida. It was there that Brosseau learned to play every infield position and left field, trying to boost his lottery ticket chances of a big league future. "Luckily, I was picked up by a team like the Rays, who use versatility and use everybody," Brosseau said. "Coming out of college, I did what I could to get on some radars. It was a blessing in disguise."

Four years later, after stops in Bowling Green, Kentucky; Charlotte, North Carolina; Montgomery, Alabama; and Durham, North Carolina, Brosseau tossed a bat weight aside and acknowledged catcher Gary Sánchez, then locked his stare once more upon Chapman. The flamethrower got ahead quickly with a pair of fastballs—one called on the inside part of the plate, one a high heater that Brosseau swung through. Chapman tried a splitter that narrowly missed, pitcher and catcher hesitating for a strike call that never came.

The next pitch missed high, and Brosseau waggled his bat, intent upon battling. He flicked a nasty slider foul toward the third-base dugout, then tipped a heater foul into the seats. Chapman touched 101 mph on the radar gun with his next pitch, close but missing low and in. Sánchez raised his glove as to say, "You've got this," and Chapman showed a wan smile as he received the toss back to the mound.

Now the count was full. The eighth pitch was a slider that Brosseau golfed high down the left-field line into the upper deck but clearly foul. Pitch No. 9 was a fastball that Brosseau tipped to the backstop, pelting an advertisement for Hankook tires. On the TBS broadcast, analyst Ron Darling observed: "The swings against the fastball get better and better for Brosseau."

Chapman had thrown the kitchen sink in this at-bat and was running out of fresh options. He'd increased his slider usage in previous seasons, combating a velocity dip by giving opponents something else to ponder besides triple-digit heat. But the slider had yielded Jose Altuve's pennant-winning homer one year prior, prompting hand-wringing about the supposed cardinal sin of getting beat with your second-best pitch. Try the fastball again, Sánchez suggested. Chapman nodded.

Pitch No. 10 came in hard—clocked at 100.2 mph. It went out harder. Brosseau barreled it toward left-center field, where Gardner raced backward, looking over his right shoulder, his cleats transitioning from the soft grass to the crunch of the warning track. Gardner spun to his left, then heard the ball plunk into the second row of seats. Grinding his fist into his glove, Chapman grimaced, again experiencing a turn of events that had grown too familiar for his tastes. "I'm a closer," Chapman said. "I'm the one that finishes the game. And almost always when these things happen, it's going to happen to me because I'm the one that either wins or loses the game."

Chapman was hardly the first star closer to surrender a momentous home run. Dennis Eckersley gave up Kirk Gibson's memorable blast in the 1988 World Series, ending an eight-pitch at-bat, and another to Roberto Alomar in the 1992 ALCS. Mariano Rivera still aches over the homer that Cleveland Indians catcher Sandy Alomar Jr. hit in the 1997 ALCS, and the all-time saves leader watched helplessly as Luis Gonzalez's bloop single decided the 2001 World Series in Arizona.

But for Chapman, this was going to be back-to-back years in which he'd thrown pitches that effectively ended the Yankees' season. And in 2016, if not for a well-timed rain delay and Jason Heyward's motivational speech,

Chapman's gopher ball to the Indians' Rajai Davis might have continued the Chicago Cubs' championship drought. Chapman composed himself, retiring the next two batters to send the game to the ninth inning. Three outs separated the Yankees from winter.

Castillo struck out Stanton and Voit, bringing up Urshela as the last hope. The big-bodied Castillo rolled the ball in his glove, went into his windup, and tried a sinker that Urshela lashed toward left field. *Crack.* Freeze that moment, and it's easy to conjure an alternate outcome. Maybe that ball scoots past the third baseman Wendle and rattles into the left-field corner, allowing Urshela to hustle into second base with a double. Torres would have been the next to bat, already with one of the Yanks' few hits that night. Castillo's pitch count would have risen to 30—territory he only touched once during the regular season. Who knows what might have happened? Reggie Jackson had a great line from his father that he loved to pass along to younger players: "As long as you have a bat in your hands, you have a chance to change the story." Brian Cashman, the Yankees' general manager, liked it so much that he had it engraved into a plaque he displays in his Yankee Stadium office.

But there were no more at-bats left in the Yankees' season. Wendle jolted left, reaching across his body with his glove hand, snow-coning the ball before it struck the infield dirt. It was a catch. Urshela was out. Wendle pumped his fist, Castillo embraced catcher Michael Perez, and the Rays spilled over the first-base dugout railing, leaving the stone-faced Urshela to plod through the party. Boone repeatedly called the ending "cruel," and he was correct.

When the Astros eliminated the Yankees in 2019, the visiting clubhouse at Minute Maid Park remained closed for a few extra minutes. The reporters were granted access to a room that was pin-drop silent, save for the cracks of open palms against bare shoulders. Players hugged deeply, their cheeks stained by tears. There was a similar vibe in the moments following the loss in San Diego with no dry eyes in the room. Players, coaches, and front-office members alike unloaded within those walls, releasing the pent-up emotions of a trying season and its abrupt conclusion. "Unfortunately, we've been there now a few times, where we've lost to the team that has gone to the World Series," Boone said. "One of the things that I said to the team, right away, was 'Thank you.' From the trainers to the clubhouse staff, coaches, and all the players, I know how hard this was on everyone. I know what so many people had to sacrifice to pull this off. My first comment to them was one of gratitude and appreciation for the commitment we got in such a difficult season."

A few others spoke. Gardner was emotional in the face of his uncertain future in the Bronx, holding no desire to wear another uniform but also lacking a contract for the next season. He did not want his last game as a Yankee to be in an empty stadium. Gardner told his teammates that he was proud to have played alongside them, stressing that they should not be complacent with having reached the ALDS. Whether he came back or not, Gardner said the team was capable of so much more. "I started looking around and I was like, 'Oh man, there's a lot of guys that don't know what their future holds,'" said infielder Tyler Wade. "That was super emotional. I didn't want to leave."

In the seats upstairs, Masahiro Tanaka's wife Mai Satoda was sobbing. Tanaka's seven years in New York were effectively over, his rich contract falling short of producing the championship that the right-hander had intended to deliver. They were so used to the certainty of the season—Tokyo to New York, then back. Tanaka would test free agency for the first time as a major leaguer, ultimately deciding to return to his original team in Japan. "Maybe no more Yankees?" she said, wiping away tears as the other wives and girlfriends consoled her.

Erik Kratz also wished to address the group. Kratz was not on the active roster for the ALDS, but Urshela's lineout stamped the end of his career as an active player—unless, as he frequently joked, Cashman made a qualifying offer (one year at $18.9 million). Kratz had played his last year with hopes of representing Team USA, but the pandemic spoiled that. Instead, after a journeyman career that included nine big league uniforms and a bunch more in the minors, Kratz told the team that he was proud to go out as a Yankee. "Being on that team, it's an opportunity that a guy like me probably should never get. But I did," Kratz said. "And it wasn't missed. That opportunity was something that I'll remember forever."

Down on the field, the Rays were smoking cigars and laughing. Someone rolled out a large portable speaker, the type that would be used in a bumping nightclub. Their playlist needled their vanquished opponents, swaying to Frank Sinatra's "Theme from New York, New York." It had been close, but they'd earned the right to troll. The Yankees had scored more runs than Tampa Bay across the five games, 24 to 21, posting a better batting average with runners in scoring position (.241 to .190). Their pitchers compiled a lower ERA, 4.40 to 4.50, yet the only statistic that mattered was in the win column—three to two. "I can't think of a guy that wasn't pissed off," Britton said. "The Rays are a good team and they had a lot of things going for them, but we had opportunities. We were plenty capable. It felt like we were in every single one of those games, and we did something to ourselves to give the lead back. Everyone was just deeply frustrated that we went through all this protocol stuff, everyone was away from their families, and we couldn't get out of our own way."

"We ran into a really hot Tampa team," LeMahieu said. "We were better than they were. I think they just made a couple plays that we didn't. Moving forward, we've got to make those plays. They had our number, and it was disappointing, but I really think we're going to get over the hump here."

The dancing grew more aggressive when the Jay-Z/Alicia Keys collaboration "Empire State of Mind" was cued. The track served as the accompaniment for the Bombers' most recent World Series championship in 2009, coinciding with the opening of the new stadium. Its beats served both as a time capsule of a thrilling time in the South Bronx and a reminder that the search for the next championship title had now extended to an 11th season. "Those scars are going to continue to make this team stronger, continue to make this team better," Judge said, his words soaked in anger and disappointment. "It's just going to make that World Series title so much sweeter in the end."

• CHAPTER 16 •

HINDSIGHT IS 2020

The Delta Air Lines jet clocked 537 miles per hour as it passed over the battle-ground state of Pennsylvania, 35,000 feet above the city streets and country roads where volunteers for the Joe Biden and Donald Trump campaigns hustled for support in a presidential election billed as the most important of a lifetime. It was three weeks from Halloween, 25 days until Election Day, and 28 days until the race would be called in Biden's favor. The peak foliage of crisp reds and yellows announced that it was autumn, but it felt like winter for the New York Yankees, who had run out of innings to play. Hal Steinbrenner picked up the telephone in his Tampa, Florida, office, express-ing his disappointment. "We invested a lot of time, energy, and money into the team," Steinbrenner said. "We all felt that we had a team that could win a championship, and we failed to do that. We didn't even come close. All I can do is apologize to our fans; they deserved a better outcome than they got."

Steinbrenner's public apology, beamed across the tri-state area from the transmitter atop the Empire State Building that amplifies Michael Kay's radio show, recalled his father's actions after the team lost to Tommy Lasorda's Los Angeles Dodgers in Game 6 of the 1981 World Series. While the Dodgers celebrated on the field below, three security officers guarded the glass doors to the executive offices, allowing The Boss privacy to draft a missive. That night, George Steinbrenner wanted the newspapers to print that he would "sincerely apologize to the people of New York and to fans everywhere for the performance of the Yankee team in the World Series."

Falling two wins shy of a championship was tough. Not reaching the play-offs was worse. The Yankees did not return to the postseason until 1995, and

227

Joe Torre guided the club to a title the next autumn. Though Hal Steinbrenner felt that an apology was justified when the winter of 2020 arrived too early, he expected that there would be no parallel drought to follow.

"We absolutely were good enough to win," Steinbrenner said later. "It's a second season once you get into that arena, and I just felt that parts of our team were inconsistent in playing up to their potential, particularly the offense. All year long, there were tremendous highs and equally extreme lows. I felt that we were better than Tampa, but we needed to bring our consistent A game. And I just think we didn't entirely succeed in that."

With tray tables down and seat backs reclined upon approach to New York, it was a jet less populated than it had been for the flight to San Diego, when the players' wives and girlfriends savored the novelty of traveling with the team. Many skipped the trip back to New York. Jordan Montgomery and James Paxton wandered past the Hudson News shop at San Diego International Airport, catching commercial flights to their homes in South Carolina and Wisconsin, respectively. Zack Britton boarded a plane bound for Texas, eager to hug his wife and children for the first time since he reported for Summer Camp. "I would say it was the most unfun season I've ever had," Britton said. "Being gone from your family for a long period of time, the testing, the travel, and just showing up at the park later—I think it got a lot of people out of their comfort zone. We were fortunate that we could play. At least we weren't cooped up at home like the majority of the nation and the world. Because of that, I think everyone felt like we were really lucky."

Gio Urshela returned to his native Colombia, where he contracted COVID-19, experiencing a mild case that included three days of chills. The episode prompted Urshela to make the rounds there and in New York, distributing hand sanitizer to the less fortunate. Luis Cessa summoned a car service, avoiding the formerly-friendly skies in favor of a five-hour ride to Arizona. Luke Voit went back to Missouri, then relocated full time to the Tampa area. By December, he was already taking batting practice in the cages at Steinbrenner Field. "Being at the facility was kind of a gloomy feeling," Voit said. "I felt like I let the team down, but that's fuel for the fire. I'm looking forward to getting out there and playing again. It was such a weird year, and I feel like it's still in the back of my mind. We couldn't go out to dinner, grab a drink, or whatever. We were just stuck at those hotels. You had to find ways to get your mind off of COVID."

Some did not have that luxury. YES Network analyst Jack Curry was absent from the pre- and postgame shows throughout the postseason, later revealing that he had been sidelined by the coronavirus. A dapper dresser in his mid-50s who looks about 10 years younger thanks to a consistent running program, Curry said that he was "absolutely floored" for about a week by COVID-19. "I took all of the appropriate and necessary measures," Curry said. "At the YES Network, everyone was very vigilant about masks and washing your hands. We got everything delivered; my wife Pamela worked for Lysol for 27 years, so she's a germ expert. It just proves how random and vicious this can be. There were days when I felt like I ran a marathon and I'd done nothing more than wake up and have a cup of tea."

Gary Sánchez prepared to play in the Dominican Winter League, seeking more at-bats to heal his miserable stat line. Miguel Andújar, Deivi García, and Domingo Germán were also among the players in action, preparing for a spring training that seemed as though it would begin on time. Closing the book on his playing career, Erik Kratz purchased a puppy, surprising his eight-year-old daughter Avery with a mini goldendoodle that they named Bella. "It's time to spend more time with the family," Kratz said. "I'm excited to be home and figure out what my next stage is. I know God will let me figure that out."

At least the guys could finally swap out their clothing, having lived out of a suitcase for weeks. After weeks of enduring strict protocols on a journey that took the team from Boston to Buffalo to New York to Cleveland to San Diego, bench coach Carlos Mendoza described a different universe once his plane touched down at Tampa International Airport, hugging his wife at the baggage claim. "I'm like, 'Man, I feel like I just got out of prison,'" Mendoza said. "I was actually seeing people. When you were at the hotel, no one was allowed to leave, and you see the same people you see at the ballpark. The very next day, we went grocery shopping and not everyone was wearing masks. Everyone was pretty much living a normal life in Florida. It was pretty frustrating."

While the Tampa Rays proceeded past the Houston Astros in a seven-game American League Championship Series, Brian Cashman marched through the darkened hallways leading to his Yankee Stadium office. He was one of the few people in the building; many of the cubicles showed calendars frozen in March, their inhabitants working remotely. There would be questions to field once again, the uncomfortable mea culpa that accompanied the end of each baseball season. "Every now and then, I daydream about if it was a longer than a 60-game season," Cashman said. "Say it was a 100-game season. You'd have Paxton back. Domingo Germán might have been back in play because the suspension would have passed. It didn't work out that way, but that gives you great hope moving forward. We had a good team, I thought."

Cashman's office overlooked a grassy patch of Jerome Avenue, strewn with discarded masks and uncollected garbage in front of shuttered storefronts. The neighborhood had grown rougher in the past year, evidence of the financial strain that the pandemic inflicted upon New York City's boroughs. That was especially true underneath the elevated tracks of the 4 train, where winter never ended for familiar gameday haunts like The Dugout and Stan's Sports Bar.

Those venerable establishments made their nut counting upon foot traffic from 81 home games, which would fatten their savings to survive the winter. The rent was still due, and they were hanging for dear life. The New York baseball community lost its favorite hangout in Foley's NY, a midtown bar on West 33rd Street in the shadows of the Empire State Building. It couldn't recover from keeping kegs untapped on St. Patrick's Day, an unplayed March Madness tournament, and what would have been baseball's originally-scheduled Opening Day.

Yet there was optimism in the production of viable COVID-19 vaccines, the first of which were administered in the United States by December. Baseball received its dose of optimism two months earlier at Globe Life Park in Arlington, Texas, where games were attended by the first fans of the 2020 season not made of cardboard: first the National League Championship Series between the Atlanta Braves and Los Angeles Dodgers, then the World Series matchup of the Dodgers and Rays.

Attendance was limited to 11,500, the roof was kept open, and more than 30,000-seat bottoms were pinned shut with zip ties. Yet there were living, breathing humans watching, cheering, and spending money. The paid crowd of 11,388 that witnessed Game 1 of the World Series was the smallest Fall Classic tally since 1909, when Ty Cobb's Detroit Tigers and Honus Wagner's Pittsburgh Pirates battled at Detroit's Bennett Park. After a year of zero fans, 11,000 felt like 111,000. Social distancing measures like mask wearing and hand washing were in place, along with digital tickets, a no-bag policy, pre-packed concessions, personal protective equipment for stadium staff, and a ban on parking lot tailgate parties.

Was it a headache? Sure. But it provided an argument that limited attendance could safely work as a short-term fix. Against seemingly insurmountable challenges, baseball had triumphed. It completed a 60-game regular season that included travel between cities, snapping into a stricter environment that ensured completion of the largest postseason ever played. It had been said that the 2020 World Series champion would somehow be illegitimate, a why-bother response to the labor battles and inherent difficulty in pulling off a season. By October, even the skeptics changed their tune, recognizing that the players, training staffs, and front offices made sacrifices that would never would have been required in a 162-game season. "I'm amazed that it mostly turned out okay," said Lindsey Adler, the Yankees beat writer for The Athletic. "I hope that there aren't situations where people got very sick that we didn't know about. There were moments where the baseball really did feel fun and consumed my attention, even though the stands were empty and everyone was wearing masks in the dugout. It was just nice that baseball made me feel the way it always has."

It had been 58 days since the league's last positive COVID-19 test when third baseman Justin Turner was sent to the clubhouse, his Dodgers protecting a 3–1 lead in the eighth inning of World Series Game 6. Led to a medical office deep inside Globe Life Park, Turner was informed that he had the coronavirus. The season was concluding with an echo of its beginning, when the Washington Nationals delayed handing their lineup card to the Yankees before the July 23 opener, putting out fires after star infielder Juan Soto tested positive.

Six outs separated the Dodgers from their first championship since 1988, and Turner's actions over that time would be heavily scrutinized. The 35 year old posted a tweet shortly after the final out, saying that he had no symptoms while adding: "Can't believe I couldn't be out there with my guys!" Minutes later, Turner was indeed back on the field, sharing a kiss with his wife Kourtney before holding the trophy and mingling with Dodgers personnel. Turner wore a mask at times, though it was removed for a team photo, capturing Turner between manager Dave Roberts and Andrew Friedman, the team's president of baseball operations.

Rob Manfred, baseball's commissioner, appeared on the field after the final out to present the Dodgers' Corey Seager with the World Series MVP award. Manfred said that the evening was "bittersweet" for the league. With the pandemic headed into what Dr. Anthony Fauci warned would be the darkest winter in modern American history, Manfred thought that baseball set an example for sports and businesses to return to a more normal operation level. "We're glad," Manfred said that night, "to be done."

Back in the Bronx, Aaron Boone and Cashman could sympathize. On some level, there was satisfaction that they had navigated the pandemic season—even if it ended earlier than they would have liked. Walking the carpet of the home clubhouse at George M. Steinbrenner Field in February, they had set the bar high, setting goals of a division title and then a championship. Suffice it to say that the season had not gone as anyone in that room would have anticipated.

"Even though they're physically gifted to the point where they can put on a uniform that says New York Yankees on it, it doesn't take away that they're still human beings," Cashman said. "They're getting paid a lot of money, but they have political opinions, they have opinions on the social justice movements, they have difficulties being removed from their families. There were a lot of different things that were very polarizing to navigate, and they did their best to compete for a championship. Even though we failed, I was really proud of our group."

At times, the Yankees had looked like world-beaters. They'd won 16 of their first 22 games, averaging 5.7 runs per night while mashing 40 homers. Then came the tailspin in which they lost 15 of the next 20, their runs per game trimmed to 3.5 with 21 homers. That seemed too much to overcome in a shortened season, but they snapped back with a 10-game winning streak, during which they averaged 8.5 runs per game and belted 29 homers. Then they limped to the finish with six losses in eight games, a span in which they averaged 4.4 runs and connected for only four homers. The biggest disappointment came in the playoffs, especially Game 5 of the American League Division Series against the Rays, when two runs would have changed their fate. "I think a lot about the eighth inning of Game 5," Boone said, referring to the frame in which Aroldis Chapman surrendered Mike Brosseau's deciding home run. "There was the heartbreak of that on the backside of what's been such a difficult season. There was a little bit of an emotional, physical, mental exhaustion to it all. When you add all that we went through socially, and the virus, and the protocols, and the different things we had to do every day just to post—that was added weight. I got home and just kind of collapsed a little bit."

Like the school districts that grappled with the risk of conducting in-person classes, the Yankees were the lone big league team not to host their minor leaguers for Instructional League games, opting instead for online coaching. They were stung by the problems that the positive COVID-19 tests created back in the spring, necessitating the quarantine of more than 150 minor leaguers and staff members. No one involved wanted to go through that again. Cashman preferred to use the funds to remove coaches from furlough, freeing them to instruct players by Zoom, telephone, or voluntarily for one-on-one instruction. "We did not think it would be a productive venture, putting our employees at risk and the players at risk in the process of testing," Cashman said. "We thought it was more likely a waste of money. In this environment, that's bad to waste money."

The Yankees promised that they would again field one of the league's biggest payrolls in 2021, but they were watching their bottom line. They claimed to have lost more revenue than any of their peers playing before empty houses—approximately $250 million, by one estimate. While 29 of MLB's clubs remained hesitant to reveal their inner workings, the Atlanta Braves had to. Publicly traded under the Liberty Media umbrella, the Braves reported a 48 percent revenue drop from July to September 2020, bringing in $110 million over that period. They'd raked in $218 million over that same period in 2019 with fans in the stands. "Listen, it's no secret—every business is being financially injured," said Lonn Trost, the Yankees' chief operating officer. "Look at a restaurant, which can't have 25 percent of its patrons. The business is not normal, and the effect is the same."

To hear Manfred tell it, MLB had become a mega-sized version of the family down the street, juggling maxed-out credit cards and driving on bald tires. According to Manfred, the 30 clubs amassed $8.3 billion in debt, posting approximately $2.6 billion in combined operational losses. Others noted that the league cashed its full postseason media package by completing the dangling carrot of a made-for-TV playoff schedule. "The great thing about baseball is that you learn we are a big blue ocean, and not to get caught up in the waves," said agent Scott Boras. "We've got an ever-growing economic giant. These games are part of our lives. With Hollywood shut down and production companies gone, there is such a demand for fresh content. They don't have sitcoms, dramas, movies. They have baseball."

Boras said that the straits could not be all that dire if Steven Cohen saw the Mets as a worthy investment vehicle, forking over a record-shattering $2.4 billion to set up what should be epic crosstown battles for New York's attention. Full recovery will come after the fans are able to return, and Steinbrenner pinned his optimism for a return to normalcy on the vaccines. "Like many clubs, we took a good, hard look at the way we do things," Steinbrenner said. "We made reductions in our overall budget going forward as far as the number of people, but primarily as far as processes. The vast majority of jobs will come back. I made that clear to everybody in a staff meeting with all of our department heads, and they conveyed it back to their employees."

Five days after Election Day, Biden was projected as the winner of the election and many of New York City's neighborhoods erupted into celebration. CNN correspondent Polo Sandoval stood at the east corner of West 44th Street in the heart of Times Square, his jet-black hair coiffed while sporting a blue blazer and a white medical-grade mask. The strains of Jay-Z and Alicia Keys' "Empire State of Mind" could be heard as the network cued Sandoval live. "You would think that the Yankees just won the World Series based on the massive crowds that are coming together on the streets of New York City," Sandoval told host Anderson Cooper, gesturing at the jubilant throngs filling Seventh Avenue, many snapping selfies and most wearing masks.

The unrestrained joy seemed to be a foreign emotion in a scarred city. New Yorkers had not forgotten the incessant wails of ambulances echoing through canyons of empty avenues in March and April, when refrigerated trucks served as makeshift morgues and the rest of the country prayed that the pandemic would be walled off by the Hudson River.

That, of course, had not happened. It was everywhere, and everyone's problem. The United States saw daily death tallies that exceeded the 9/11 attacks, the autumn months bringing accelerated spread into Thanksgiving and Christmas—just as Major League Baseball had predicted when they insisted that the World Series be completed by Halloween. Trump eventually ceded the White House but not before his supporters participated in a deadly January 6, 2021 riot at the Capitol that resulted in the president's second impeachment and the permanent deactivation of his Twitter account. Biden's inauguration took place in a city with tanks and barbed wire filling its streets, having seen 15,000 National Guard troops deployed there to keep the peace.

Inside MLB's offices on Avenue of the Americas, the league plodded with uncertainty toward 2021. The teams produced full-season schedules as though everything would return to its state of normalcy. The Yankees might be on the field in Tampa on February 27, playing their first spring game against the Detroit Tigers. But they might not. Opening Day would be played at Yankee Stadium on April 1, hosting the Toronto Blue Jays. Or maybe not. "I have no clue, any more than you do," Steinbrenner said. "Are people going to be comfortable taking the vaccine? Are people going to be comfortable coming back and sitting even six feet away from someone in a stadium? There are just so many unknowns, but we've got to stay positive. As far as I'm concerned, we're going to go on time. That's the way I've got to be thinking."

Even the rules were in flux: the expanded postseason, a universal designated hitter, runners on base to begin extra innings, seven-inning doubleheaders. Those were instituted as temporary safety measures, but collective bargaining would be required to enact permanent change. Considering the teeth-grinding nature of the summer clashes between the league and the players' association, the safe bet was on another series of contentious battles. And no one knew when reporters would be allowed to ask questions again face-to-face. "If given the choice, I would veto any Zooms for the future," said Meredith Marakovits of the YES Network. "I never want to be on Zoom again."

As the Yankees conducted their professional scouting meetings remotely, crowdsourcing opinions on potential free agents and trade acquisitions, it was much easier to come to a consensus on a player's outlook—yes, infielder DJ LeMahieu should be their top target in free agency—than to plan for another season that could be just as unpredictable as 2020. They also had to wonder if the window was closing on a dynasty that had not hit full stride. The core that was supposed to celebrate championship No. 28 couldn't be called Baby Bombers anymore; Aaron Judge and Sánchez would be free agents in a couple of years; Gleyber Torres would be after the 2024 season. All the group desired was another chance to power up the machine and take aim on October, preferably without the wild curveballs that 2020 tossed. "The whole world got flipped upside down," Judge said. "Families got impacted, the game got impacted. There were a lot of little things that changed—no family, no friends. We still played our games, but there was no one there to experience it with us. I'm never going to take that for granted again. I think that's going to help me later in life, too; just don't take the little things for granted."

Acknowledgments

The most bizarre year of our lives began with a road trip. My wife Connie and I loaded the trunk of our sport utility vehicle to the brim with suitcases and toys in early February, using Instagram to document the journey down Interstate 95 for spring training in Tampa. We could never have imagined that each check-in from a gasoline station mini-mart, McDonald's drive-through, or South of the Border captured a slice of American life that was about to be altered—perhaps permanently.

Travel is one of the great perks of covering a Major League Baseball team. We have made the most out of that incredible opportunity, turning the American League into our backyard. Our daughters Penny (age four) and Maddie (age two) were seasoned veterans before they could walk, accompanying the Yankees to Baltimore, Boston, Chicago, Los Angeles, San Diego, San Francisco, Seattle, Tampa, Toronto, and more. They even attended the first game in London, though they were more interested in their souvenir ice cream helmets than the score.

Over the years, Tampa felt like a second home, and we occasionally daydreamed about spending more time there. Be careful what you wish for. We had a great routine: I'd spend the afternoon with the team at Steinbrenner Field while Connie and the girls met new friends at the beach, playground, or pool, then reunite for a bite on Bay Street or Armature Works at the end of the work day. When the Yankees left town for that trip to Florida's East Coast on March 10, my "home team" spent the evening dining with Cinderella at the Happiest Place on Earth.

Years from now, we'll probably swap stories about the days when the world stopped. When the pandemic sent the Yankees scattering across the country, we were reluctant to return to the New York area. One additional week in a rented corporate apartment became two, then a month. We projected normalcy in an insane time by cooking dinners, playing games, and going on long walks. The girls made hundreds of FaceTime calls to their beloved Puddin' and Pops back in Pennsylvania, who brightened those days by performing generous "magic" that appeared in brown Amazon boxes.

The prevailing thought was that when baseball resumed—if it resumed—it would be in Florida. The Sunshine State's rising case numbers moved Summer Camp to the Bronx, throwing us a curve. We packed up and motored 1,200 miles north on I-95 through the new abnormal, wearing masks and gloves to pump our three tanks of gas, not lingering for a moment more than necessary.

Covering baseball in a pandemic presented new challenges. As the Yankees took the field for their first workouts, I tearfully hugged my wife and children, not knowing when we would be together again. Out of an abundance of caution, we lived separately throughout the season. My hosts were Brian and Joanna, my incredibly gracious brother- and sister-in-law, who did not flinch in welcoming a 38-year-old boarder into their beautiful new home for weeks on end. I apologize for repeatedly setting off the security system at 3:00 AM after night games.

The fear and uncertainty of COVID-19 also brought a greater appreciation for the importance of family. We could not have gotten through the year without our amazing roster of All-Stars. To Mom, Dad, Ray, Eileen, Joan, Allison, Brian, Danna, Emma, Griffin, Jaclyn, Jacob, Joanna, Joe, Linda, Raymond, Samantha, and Shawn: your laughter and love in our weekly Zoom parties all meant more than you know. When we can all be in the same room again, I promise that the first drinks will be on me. Thanks again to Joe, who provided valuable feedback as the first fan to read this book, and to Dad, who is still teaching me about baseball 30 years later.

My MVP, as always, was Connie. Life as a "baseball WAG" is a challenge under normal circumstances, and I am continually amazed by her warm heart and ability to effortlessly dote on two active toddlers. A social media whiz, she was the brains behind our Penny's 2 Cents videos, providing the world with much-needed sunshine during a very dark time. Penny even appeared on her own T-shirt, thanks to our friends at Rotowear! You are our glue. Thank you for your inspiration, knowledge, and motivation. I love you more than anything. You have earned a break until the next book!

To Penny and Maddie, our sugar and spice girls. Penny, you endlessly entertain us with your theatrics, singing and dancing at every opportunity. Maddie, you have your mother's looks (thank goodness!), but I fear that you may be an accident-prone athlete like your old man. Not a day goes by that you do not make your Mommy and Daddy marvel with wonder. We are so proud of the beautiful and smart stars that you are. Whether it is on Broadway or a ballfield (or anywhere in between), you will go on to greatness. Everything we do is for you. We love you.

Thank you to Gerrit Cole for the foreword and the New York Yankees players, coaches, and front-office personnel who were interviewed, spanning many hours in person, on the telephone, and Zoom. Your assistance was greatly appreciated, and I hope that your stories were told well. Thank you to the broadcasters, reporters, and writers who continued to cover the sport with aplomb, especially my teammates at MLB.com. You are the best in the business.

I would like to acknowledge my terrific colleagues in the Yankee Stadium press box, who have challenged me to become a better reporter since my first day on the job. Your attention to detail is second to none. Though the majority of this book was captured in real time or subsequent interviews, resources included: The Athletic, Axios, CNN, ESPN, FOX News, MLB.com, MLB Network, MSNBC, *New York Daily News*, *New York Post*, *The New York Times*, *Newsday*, North Jersey Media Group, NJ Advance Media, SNY, *The Washington Post*, WFAN, YES Network, and CC Sabathia's *R2C2* podcast. Even though the beat was socially distanced, we still managed to have fun.

Happy retirement to George King, who showed us the right way to cover this game we love.

Thank you to Stacey Glick and the team at Dystel, Goderich, and Bourret, and to Jeff Fedotin at Triumph Books, who also did a terrific job editing *Mission 27*, my previous book with Mark Feinsand. Thank you to the fans; we missed you greatly and cannot wait to welcome you back. Most importantly, thank you to the front-line responders and essential workers who toiled tirelessly throughout the pandemic, allowing us the glimpses of normalcy that baseball provides.

It was a heck of a year, everyone. Let's never do it again.